The Economics of Regulating Industry

M. A. UTTON

Basil Blackwell

First published 1986

Basil Blackwell Ltd
108 Cowley Road, Oxford OX4 1JF, UK

Basil Blackwell Inc.
432 Park Avenue South, Suite 1503,
New York, NY 10016, USA

British Library Cataloguing in Publication Data

Utton, M.A.
The economics of regulating industry.
1. Trade regulation – Great Britain
2. Industry and state – Great Britain
I. Title
338.941   HD3616.G73

ISBN 9-631-14424-2

Library of Congress Cataloging in Publication Data

Utton, M.A. (Michael A.), 1939–
The economics of regulating industry.
Bibliography: p.
Includes index.
1. Industry and state.   2. Trade regulation.
3. Economic policy.   4. Industrial laws and legislation—
Economic aspects.   I. Title.
HD3612.U88 1986   338.9   86-11785
ISBN 0-631-14424-2

Typeset in 10/12pt Ehrhardt by Columns of Reading
Printed in Great Britain by T.J. Press Ltd, Padstow, Cornwall

The Economics of
Regulating Industry

For my parents
Lucy and Arthur Utton

Contents

Preface

The economic 'regulation' of markets is a term that has been much more closely associated in the past with the US economy than with those of Britain and others in Western Europe. At first glance it may seem paradoxical that the country ostensibly most committed to the operation of the market mechanism should also be most ready to intervene. However, a closer examination reveals that it is precisely this commitment that explains much of the attitude to regulation. Under certain conditions markets may allocate resources efficiently, but where some or all of those conditions are absent they may fail dramatically. An original and continuing reason for regulation, therefore, is to correct such market failure. Thus much of the regulation of the markets for consumer products can be seen as a response to the failure of those markets to provide sufficient, objective information. Most competition policies are an attempt to maintain or restore competitive conditions, and thus improve economic efficiency. Where technology appears to make competition impossible, the resulting natural monopoly may be regulated in a way that, in principle, simulates competition. In these and many other ways the initial move for regulation may thus be to promote 'the public interest'.

However, the enormous growth in regulation that many observers are agreed has taken place over the past thirty to forty years cannot all be explained in these optimistic terms. American writers in particular have questioned whether even a majority of their complex regulatory system has sprung from this 'public interest' motive rather than from the partial or sectional interests of a particular group.

In Britain discussions of the economics of regulation have tended until recently to be highly fragmented. Thus issues concerning information in consumer markets may be discussed in courses in micro-economic theory, while related issues of consumer protection may make an appearance in applied economics. Competition policies are usually discussed as an adjunct to courses in industrial or business economics while natural monopoly and the policies of nationalized industries are more likely to find a place in public sector economics. The main purpose of the book, therefore, is to bring these issues together under the common theme of the economics of regulating industry, in the belief that the same analytical framework can be applied to all of them and indeed to others that have not been included. Furthermore the recent industrial policy in Britain of privatizing large public sector enterprises is likely to make the issues of regulation much more prominent in policy discussions in the future than hitherto.

Parts of the discussion in the book have been tried out on colleagues and students at the University of Reading over the past two years and I am grateful to them all for their insights and forbearance. I would also like to thank Margaret Lewis for her customary skill in typing most of the penultimate draft.

List of Figures and Tables

PART I

The Economics of Regulation

1

Market Failure and the Case for Regulation

I INTRODUCTION

One of the main themes of the Wealth of Nations is that markets freed from artificial constraints, especially those imposed by the state, will under many circumstances promote the public interest. The famous invisible hand theorem was used against the prevailing Mercantilist philosophy of the mid-eighteenth century and was influential in creating the atmosphere of reform that accompanied the Industrial Revolution. Since Smith's day theorists have refined his analysis to a point where it is scarcely recognizable or at least, in Stigler's words, 'to a degree of purity similar to Pears soap'. In addition in popular presentations of his ideas by some of his modern followers it is argued not only that free markets promote an efficient resource allocation which accords most closely with individual preferences but also that the presence of economic freedom of this kind is a necessary condition for continued political freedom.

In many of those economies, however, which still rely heavily on markets for the coordination of economic activity, the amount of regulation of one kind or another is now at a very high level, and many would argue that it is still growing. In some cases the regulations go back many years and have near universal approval, such as laws governing the employment of children. Other cases are of much more recent origin and have aroused considerable controversy, such as the laws concerning the employment of different racial and sexual groups. These examples relate to the terms and conditions on which different groups may be employed. However, a moment's reflection suggests a wide variety of cases of market regulation with different objectives and taking different forms. Thus the terms on which firms can trade with final consumers are regulated in a great many ways. For many products much information has to be provided by law to the consumer at the time of purchase. In other cases suppliers cannot provide advertising 'messages' about their products through certain media (e.g. cigarette advertising on television) or do not provide advertising messages about their services at all (e.g. some professions). The law lays down the times at which some traders may sell their goods to the public (the Sunday trading laws) or restricts the number of traders in a particular district (the licensing of alcohol sales).

Similarly the production activities of firms are widely regulated. The regulation may range from the kinds of equipment or materials that producers may use (e.g. the size and condition of commercial vehicles, ingredients in food products) to the method of price fixing (cartels have to be registered) or the kinds of technical information used (without a licence firms cannot use patented information). In many cases the way producers handle waste products may be subject to close regulation.

It should be clear from these preliminary examples that the initial stimulus to regulate may arise from a variety of motives. In some cases the objective may be the protection of employment conditions of vulnerable groups or the health and safety of consumers. Other regulations may be largely concerned to re-establish competitive conditions or prevent the abuse of a position of dominance, or again to protect the natural or man-made environment. The prohibition of the sale of certain products on Sundays or the advertisement of contraceptives on television may originally have been concerned to preserve spiritual or moral values.

The examples also illustrate the point that while much regulation of markets may stem from the law, other pieces of regulation may derive from administrative action where a voluntary agreement is arranged with producers. In some important cases the regulation may be entirely based on the rules of a professional association. Thus although professional status may derive from a statute, the rules of practice may be drawn up and administered by the governing body.

In all cases it is safe to conclude that the final outcome of the market process is different once the regulations are in force from what would have happened had no regulation been adopted, but equally the degree of difference may vary considerably depending on the kind of regulation that is applied. One of the main purposes of this book is to attempt to analyse the impact of various kinds of regulation, whether they are having the effect that was originally intended and whether the kind of regulation in force is efficient in the sense of achieving the desired end with the minimum cost. Although in general discussions of particular pieces of regulation it may not always be articulated in this way, the well-known and unifying concept used in economic analysis to explain the possible need for regulation is that of 'market failure': the notion that in a number of contexts completely free markets do not yield the best performance in terms of economic welfare, with the implied corollary that the performance can be improved by some form of regulation. In this introductory chapter we examine a number of ways in which markets may 'fail' and indicate some of the regulatory corrections that can be adopted and that are discussed in later sections of the book.

II ATTRIBUTES OF A WELL-FUNCTIONING COMPETITIVE SYSTEM

In order to throw our subsequent discussion into sharper relief it is useful to summarize briefly the advantages of a smoothly functioning system of competitive markets. We will understand a competitive market to consist of an inter-related group of buyers and sellers all of whom have full information about products and prices, where there is free entry to the market for sellers and buyers, and where no individual buyer or seller is large enough to influence the terms of trading. Three characteristics of such a system stand out. First, economic waste is kept to a minimum because the system allows for the continuous adjustment by consumers and producers to changes in their individual circumstances and to changes in their view about the future. Individuals make constant assessments of the balance of costs and benefits to them of a particular action. While neither producers nor consumers are free from mistakes, corrections can be made with the minimum of disturbance. Some consumers may have misjudged the properties of certain goods and subsequently adjust their spending patterns. Some producers may over-estimate future demand and be left with unsold stocks which they have to dispose of at a reduced price. The corrections made at the level of the individual consumer or enterprise, however, help to keep the response flexible compared with a system dependent on more centralized control. The speed of adjustment may therefore be faster and more efficient.

Secondly, the carrot-and-stick form of the incentives in competitive markets also makes for a high level of productive efficiency. On the positive side the lure of profits for producers tends to ensure that they make available goods and services at the lowest possible cost. The fewer the resources used in the production of one good or service, the more resources there are for producing others. On the other hand those who are less successful in keeping their costs to a minimum are likely to suffer a loss of their market and eventual bankruptcy. In this case some of the resources may be maintained in their current use, administered by others, while the remainder are used more productively elsewhere.

Thirdly, the same set of incentives will tend to stimulate innovations and their use in the most socially desired directions. Indeed one group of writers place this innovating process, and the role of the entrepreneur in it, at the centre of their analysis of the market process.[1] Rather than focusing on the efficient allocation of a given set of resources that a competitive market system may provide, their emphasis is on the growth of resources that flows from the innovative energies of entrepreneurs, released by the expectation of profit.

Furthermore these desirable achievements – minimum waste, efficiency and innovation – may be attained in ways that are themselves desirable. The production and allocation of goods and services through competitive markets greatly reduces the need for the central collection and analysis of information about resource flows and consumer demands. Information about changes that are taking place will be reflected in price signals to which producers and consumers can respond according to their own judgement and preferences. The decentralized and impersonal nature of competitive markets helps to produce a sense of 'fairness' in the outcome and minimizes obstruction to change from those who are likely to be harmed, because, for example, the demands for their products, services or skills has diminished. In general, to the extent that freely functioning markets are regarded as a 'unanimous consent arrangement'[2] they help to minimize the need for coercion in the organization of society.

The above sketch of a freely operating market system is, of course, highly informal. Much effort and ingenuity has been put by economic theorists over a very long period into deriving the formal properties of a competitive system.[3] It is when we look more closely at the formal model, and especially at the assumptions on which it rests, that the various sources of market failure can be distinguished. Essentially 'market failure' occurs when one or more of those assumptions cannot be met, even imperfectly, or where they may hold 'eventually' but where the lapse of time is unacceptably long. It is convenient to consider first those sources of failure that come from production and then those deriving from consumption.

III SOURCES OF MARKET FAILURE

The 'classical' cases for regulation by the state concerned natural monopolies which D. H. Robertson characterized more colourfully many years ago as the 'octopoid industries'. Industries that were subject to very great internal economies of scale so that unit costs of a firm first in the field fell over the entire range of relevant output would not sustain enough firms to ensure anything like a competitive performance. Instead of many firms charging competitive prices, the technology of the industry would rapidly lead to the monopoly by one firm that had been alert to the cost-reducing opportunities and that, unregulated, could charge a monopoly price. These industries, usually designated public utilities – water supply, sewage disposal, gas and electricity supply, rail transport and telecommunications – usually have two other characteristics, which until recently have tended to make them candidates for regulation. Generally they require very large capital investments much of which consists of very costly installations running under roads, lands and into individual dwellings. They are also fundamental to the whole economy in a sense that most other industries are not. Their products or services are used by nearly every individual or organisation in the economy, instead of by a relatively narrow group. The term 'octopoid' for such industries is thus singularly appropriate: it conveys the idea of the industries' 'tentacles' literally stretching into each dwelling or firm. The case for regulating such industries has probably the widest acceptance although the practical methods of regulating to achieve the best results is still the subject of great controversy.[4] Much recent theoretical work has attempted to specify more precisely the conditions under which apparent natural monopolies can be sustained in the long-run.[5]

In Europe, and particularly the UK, industries traditionally regarded as 'natural monopolies' have tended to be nationalized and thus prone to direct control by the central government (whereas in the US such industries have remained in private hands but are usually subject to the supervision of a regulatory commission). Although the British nationalized industries are in principle run by a public corporation that operates at arms length from the government, there have been frequent complaints that, in practice, governments have found it convenient to use them as additional instruments for achieving their macro-economic objectives.[6]

The issue has been complicated in the UK by the nationalization of some industries or firms where the traditional natural monopoly arguments did not hold, for example, coal-mining, shipbuilding, aerospace (now de-nationalized) steel (nationalized, de-nationalized, re-nationalized) and cars (in the form of BL). In some cases the central reason may have been political (as in the case of coal-mining and steel) while in others almost fortuitous (cars). However, it is very difficult to find any coherent economic rationale for the miscellaneous collection of industries that have found themselves recently in the 'public' rather than the 'private' sector of industry.

On the other hand for those industries that fall some way short of being 'natural monopolies' but where, nevertheless, economies of scale and size are substantial enough to support comparatively few firms efficiently, the traditional case for some kind of antitrust regulation can be made. The second aspect of market failure on the production side is thus related to monopoly but in this case the achievement of monopoly returns will often require collaboration between existing firms. In a number of countries joint attempts by a group of firms to behave like a unified monopoly are either illegal (as in the US) or closely circumscribed (as in the UK). Similarly where the internal or external (i.e. by merger) growth of one firm has left it practically in sole possession of the domestic market orthodox economic analysis gives a number of grounds for regulation by antitrust policy. In particular where existing firms attempt to prevent the entry of new competition, the case for intervention may be especially strong.

Broadly speaking whereas antitrust regulation may attempt to achieve or maintain the conditions necessary for competition (by prohibiting cartels and some mergers, for example) natural monopoly regulation may attempt to replicate the results of competition (by pursuing marginal cost pricing or keeping returns to a 'normal' level).[7]

Thirdly, an aspect of market failure that has received much public attention recently is where private and social costs diverge.[8] The competitive model of market transactions usually proceeds on the assumption that all costs (representing alternatives foregone) are taken into account in a firm's production decisions and are therefore reflected in market prices. It has long been recognized, however, that this is an over-simplification which in an increasing number of cases does not hold. Many production decisions may thus impose costs on third parties that are unaccounted for in the price system and in the absence of some form of corrective intervention will lead to resource misallocation. While there may be a large measure of agreement on the basic analysis of external effects there is considerable controversy on how regulation should proceed and which methods are both practically feasible and relatively efficient. Part of the problem is that external diseconomies in production can be so diverse in their effects and consequently extremely difficult to monitor and hence control. For every well-publicized case of water or air pollution, an unknown side-effect of a new drug or the destruction of a natural wilderness, there are probably hundreds of seemingly minor externalities whose aggregate effect is a considerable reduction in economic welfare.

We should mention, fourthly, an important source of market failure on the production side, certain aspects of which are relevant to our discussion, although a full treatment lies outside the scope of the book. Public goods can be distinguished as having one or two special characteristics (and sometimes both). First they may be non-exclusive in the sense that their provision for one person, or one group, automatically ensures their provision for others: my neighbour's Cruise missile also protects me;[9] a high level of public health benefits me, even if I am rather careless about my own health. A second aspect may be the non-divisible nature of some public goods. My use of, say, a park or a motorway does not deny its services to other users[10] whereas my consumption of a nut cutlet (a private good) does deny it to others. Another example of a public good is much closer to our main purpose and will be discussed in some detail later. Information, especially *new* information about products, production or organization methods, is non-divisible in very much the same way as that just mentioned. Once the information is known one group's use of it does not diminish it in any way as *information*. It can be used over and over again without deteriorating or becoming damaged. What does change if it becomes widely available is its value to the original inventor or discoverer. If everyone is given free access to it, as they are to many other public goods, then the future source of new information is likely to be reduced. One partial and rather paradoxical solution to this problem has been the regulation of the use of new information by granting inventors a monopoly of its use in the form of a patent. In the case of the 'octopoid' industries, therefore, regulation is thought necessary because of the natural evolution of monopoly, while in the case of new information, regulation takes the form of a grant of monopoly.

Most aspects of market failure on the production side have been recognized for some time and have produced a variety of regulatory responses. On the other hand, full recognition of sources of failure stemming essentially from the consumer's side of the market is of more recent origin. A great deal of recent theoretical work has been concerned with the full implications of the fact that in many markets for final consumer's goods the buyer may possess very imperfect and incomplete information about the product. A key assumption of the model of competitive markets is that buyers possess full information not only about product prices but also about the characteristics, qualities, and effects of the products they may purchase. Under these circumstances (together with the other assumptions about production conditions) competitive markets will, as we have seen, lead to the maximization of consumer welfare. Where the consumer has very little knowledge of products and where full information is either impossible or extremely costly to acquire, markets that appear 'competitive' in other respects will fail to produce an efficient result. In some cases, for example, full information about a product may be unknown by anyone, including producers, at the time of purchase or consumption. Recent tragic cases with certain drugs are the most immediate examples. In many more mundane examples while information about the characteristics of products may be known to producers, the cost of acquiring that information for an individual consumer may be out of all proportion to the value he or she attaches to the good concerned. For *all* potential consumers taken together the value of the information might outweigh the total cost of acquiring it, yet because of the difficulty and cost of organizing to act jointly, consumers may continue to act separately and suffer the consequences, i.e. they will make decisions that turn out to be sub-optimal because of their imperfect information.

In both cases, therefore, the lack of information and the market failure that it implies may be grounds for regulation. In the first example regulation may take the form of controls over the sale of products where serious risks to health are possible and in the second case regulation may simply amount to a requirement for producers to supply specified pieces of information about the product.

In connection with the second case, we can note another source of market failure, related to the idea of a public good. It might be argued, for example, that if consumers require more information about products and services before making a choice, then they could buy such information from specialized firms and that if there was a genuine untapped demand for information on the part of consumers, the firms would be likely to make large profits. The reason they do not, and indeed the reason for which such profit-making firms do not exist, is because of the 'public good' nature of unbiased information about consumer products. Any consumer purchasing such information can get the full benefit of it by making a more informed choice without in any way detracting from its use by other consumers who will not have paid to acquire it. It will thus be very difficult for any firm to recoup the full value of the information that it provides. As a result the market will under-provide such information and in the absence of regulation inefficient choices may be made. It is frequently difficult to determine how much information sellers should be required to provide so as to make consumers' decisions more efficient. If they have to give 'too much' information one source of inefficiency may merely be exchanged for another, i.e. the cost of supplying the additional information may be greater than the additional benefit derived from it by consumers. In practice, as we see below, both the form and extent of consumer protection may be very hard to determine.

Consumers frequently complain that the quantity and quality of one type of information from sellers may serve to mislead and thus cause non-optimal choices to be made. The claim is, therefore, that unless properly regulated, certain markets will fail to lead to an efficient result because consumers make their decisions, at least in part, on faulty, incomplete or biased information in the form of advertising. Since the starting point for many market models has been to assume complete information on the part of participants it is then exceedingly difficult to accommodate the notion that in most, if not all, markets consumers are largely ignorant about the variety of products and product qualities (broadly interpreted) that may fill their particular needs. Whereas manufacturers of consumer goods have always known this and therefore argue that advertising must be used to inform potential customers – thus making the market more nearly 'perfect' – opponents have tended to argue that advertising by interested parties cannot improve the quality of consumer choices, precisely because it is partial and open to abuse.

As far as consumers are concerned, therefore, much of the argument has revolved around the extent to which advertising improves the market by adding to the 'genuine' information available to consumers, and the extent to which it merely attempts to persuade consumers to choose one brand of a product rather than another, even though both are technically indentical. While analytically the distinction may be clear, it is evident that in practice the precise division between information and mere blandishment is impossible: one person's information may be another's propaganda. It is largely for this reason that regulation of advertising *per se* has tended, in the UK, to be left to the industry itself through a code of practice policed by an independent committee.

Self-policing of another sort ensures that consumers receive no advertising messages at all about certain services. Thus certain of the professions such as medicine, law, accountancy and architecture have strict rules (laid down by their governing bodies) against advertising – apart from the bare minimum necessary to inform the public of their existence. The ground usually given for such prohibitions (infringement of which may lead the person concerned being struck off the professional list and therefore unable to practise) is that it is a necessary additional safeguard to protect the public from the unscrupulous who might otherwise tout for custom. Such practices are also, it is claimed, likely to bring the professions into disrepute and undermine the confidence that the public has at present in the quality of the professional services offered. The preservation of the quality and standards of service are also given as the main reason for strict control, through stringent examinations, of the numbers being admitted to the professional bodies. If this were the real and only reason for limiting entry, then we would normally expect that existing members would have to demonstrate regularly, say at periods of five to ten years, that they were still technically competent. As far as we are aware no professional body has introduced re-examinations for this purpose. They lay themselves open to the criticism, therefore, that a major objective of the restrictions on entry are to maintain the income of existing members, just as entry restrictions on the supply of less august goods and services can usually be traced back to such a purpose. The line between protecting the public as opposed to 'conspiring' against them is thus a controversial one. It is an especially sensitive issue when a regulation ostensibly introduced (by statute) for one purpose, protection of the public, is then apparently converted by a professional organisation into a means not only of closely monitoring competition between existing firms but even more dubiously of preventing the entry of firms that may wish to provide a lower-priced service or product.

IV CONCLUSION

The concept of 'market failure' is a useful starting point for an analysis of the regulation of industry. By focusing on natural and artificial monopoly, external effects and incomplete or defective information we can begin to isolate those problems that the various forms of regulation have attempted to tackle. We have so far used the term 'regulation' in a very broad sense to cover any direct intervention in the operation of a market and this involves a wide variety of objectives (protection of employees, consumers, the environment; maintenance of professional incomes) and takes a number of different forms (legal restrictions on production and selling methods; administrative restraints; rules self-imposed by professional associations). In chapter 3 we delineate clearly the criteria we have used in selecting the topics covered in later sections of the book and this will involve narrowing the definition of regulation.

Although the concept of market failure provides a useful focal point for structuring the preliminary analysis, it has to be treated with some caution. The fact that welfare economists have located certain ways in which freely functioning markets may fail to produce an optimal result invites the conclusion that in such cases the government should use its authority to correct and improve market performance. Natural monopolies may thus be 'regulated' to use marginal cost pricing, production externalities may be 'internalized' by skilful use of taxation, inventors allowed to hold a monopoly over the rights to their invention, and so on. The implicit assumption made in this approach is that the government regulation will definitely move the economy towards the optimum rather than away from it. Recent research, however, has suggested that while in some instances this may well be true, in others, regulation may work against improved performance and either be to the advantage of a particular group or have unanticipated secondary costs which may outweigh any primary benefits. In chapter 2, therefore, we review a number of different hypotheses concerning the impact and incidence of economic regulation.

2

Developments in the Economic Theory of Regulation

I INTRODUCTION

Growing directly out of the analysis of market failure sketched in the previous chapter is the public interest theory of regulation. On this view, if free markets cannot produce an acceptable performance in terms of efficient resource allocation and the satisfaction of consumer demands, then the government should regulate those markets so as to correct the situation. The implication is that the government, as guardian of the public, rather than a purely sectional, interest should regulate wherever market failure appears. The instruments of regulation may differ but the government must be prepared to operate in whatever market is necessary. If the public interest theory is broadly correct, therefore, we should expect to find regulatory policies in a wide range of industries: where natural or artificial monopoly is present; where external effects dominate; where public good attributes are significant. In discussing this explanation of regulation below, however, we need to be aware that it depends on a rather narrow view of the 'public interest'. Governments frequently have many other micro-economic objectives apart from correcting for market failures, so at any one time we should anticipate interventions in many markets that have only a very tenuous connection with market failure as usually understood.

Indeed, observation of how regulation had developed in the US led some academic observers more recently to formulate a quite different explanation of how it arises and what are likely to be its effects. Rather than the government simply responding to market failures, in the newer theories it is seen as subject to the demand for regulation by particular interest groups which for a number of reasons expect a greater joint gain from government action (in the form perhaps of controls on entry, standards or a tariff) than they can organize for themselves. On this view there should be certain key structural characteristics that make some industries especially likely to seek out regulation for their advantage. Although conceptually distinct this hypothesis, which is due to Stigler (1975), is clearly related to the notion that while a regulatory body may *initially* have been established to correct a market failure, over time, for a number of distinctive reasons, the regulators are effectively 'captured' by the regulated. They end up, therefore, serving the interests of the industry members, just as in the Stigler case. We suggest below that although these explanations can be applied fairly persuasively to some industries in the UK and especially the US, they do not provide the general explanation for regulatory policies that was originally claimed. We have to recognize that regulation in all its forms covers such a wide range of markets, and varies so much in form and scope at different time periods, that no simple hypothesis could be expected to explain even a majority of cases.

An important outcome of discussions of the more recent theories of economic regulation has been a growing awareness that just as market failures can be identified using conventional economic analysis, so also can bureaucratic or regulatory failures. For a long time after the main sources of market failure were analysed and the corrective policies proposed, it was implicitly assumed firstly that, on the whole, policy, once implemented, would achieve the desired result, and secondly that the process itself was relatively costless. The public interest was therefore served by a series of efficient regulatory policies. What the newer theories highlighted, however, was that policies may satisfy instead narrow sectional interests, which may in fact impose greater burdens than the original 'failure' they may ostensibly have been designed to cure. Furthermore related developments in the economic theory of bureaucracy suggested that regulatory policies may also impose considerable costs (in the form of dead-weight losses) on society. One conclusion, therefore, has been that at the very least regulations that are thought to be in the 'public interest' should themselves be subject to detailed cost–benefit analysis in order to determine whether they really do produce an efficient result.

In the course of this chapter, therefore, we not only set out in more detail the various hypotheses that have been offered to explain the widespread resort to market regulation but also mention some of the alleged costs and benefits that derive from it. The discussion thus provides a general introduction to the more detailed treatment in subsequent sections of the book.

II THEORIES OF REGULATION

In principle the public interest theory of economic regulation amounts simply to the normative response to the positive analysis of market failure.

Positive analysis can show that, for example, natural or artificial monopoly can lead to a misallocation of resources. According to the public interest theory the government reacts to this by intervening with policies designed to correct the faults. Thus in the case of natural monopoly, to prevent the public being exploited by having to pay a monopoly price which implies that output is being restricted to below the socially desirable level, government regulation of prices is introduced. In particular, since under certain circumstances optimal resource allocation occurs where price is equal to marginal cost, the regulators can use this as their guiding principle. Similarly, firms enjoying an artificial monopoly, sustained perhaps through collusion and attempts to control new entry to the industry, can be forced to mend their ways by a vigorous antitrust policy which makes collusion illegal and opens up the market to fresh competition (possibly from abroad). Again, where one group is suffering the costs imposed upon them by the external effects of the production of others, government taxation of the offending output can ensure that the externality is internalized and the output reduced to the socially optimal level.

In short, wherever market failure can be discovered the public interest theory of regulation implies an appropriate government response in order to get the market to operate as closely as possible to what would be the competitive solution. Since market failures occur whenever the rather long list of conditions necessary for competitive markets are not even approximately met, the potential scope for regulatory policies appears to be almost limitless. Although it was acknowledged that where the costs of administering the regulation were greater than the potential benefits of correcting the failure, intervention was not justified, this does not seriously affect the case for widespread regulation of industry.

While there are undoubtedly costs of administering any regulatory policy, the costs involved in a settlement *negotiated* between the parties are usually reckoned to be very much greater. Firstly, in most instances there will be many more customers (or sufferers) than producers. Mobilizing support amongst many people for a negotiated solution is likely to be extremely difficult and therefore costly. It is likely to be made even more difficult, secondly, by the problem of free riders who expect to gain from any settlement but deliberately suppress their true estimate of their anticipated gain in order to minimize their financial contribution to the campaign and negotiations for a settlement. The transactions costs (broadly interpreted) of such a remedy are thus likely to be prohibitively high. It follows also that the argument that inaction signifies compliance and acknowledgement that the costs (of the monopoly or an externality) are smaller than the benefits to be derived from their modification does not hold. Benefits to individuals may be small but when aggregated may far exceed their costs – including transaction costs – that the market failure is imposing. The case for government intervention in many instances is thus usually conceded, even by keen admirers of the efficiency of market forces; see, for example, Posner (1974). The analysis has, however, performed a useful function. In the case of externalities, for example, it has highlighted the symmetrical nature of the problem: third parties may have costs imposed on them by producers but, equally, curtailment of production to reduce external effects imposes costs on the producers in the form of revenue foregone. It also draws attention to the importance of transaction and enforcement costs. Clearly the net benefits expected from the regulation must at least equal these costs for any improvement to take place. Thirdly, it provides a means of distinguishing those cases where, given some degree of market failure, government action may be necessary, because of the high transactions costs and the severity of the free rider problem, from other cases where private action between the parties concerned may be sufficient.[1]

A more fundamental criticism of the public interest theory of regulation comes from the theory of second best. The criticism is not of the public interest theory as an explanation of why regulation may be introduced but of the inference that attempts to get markets to perform 'as if' they are competitive will actually lead to an improvement. Although the formal proof of the theory is somewhat involved[2] its central conclusion is well known and in the present context can be expressed as follows: If an otherwise competitive economy is subject to some constraint on competition in an important sector (because, for example, of natural monopoly or the need to supply certain public goods) then piecemeal (regulatory) policies that attempt to ensure a competitive performance in other sectors may not

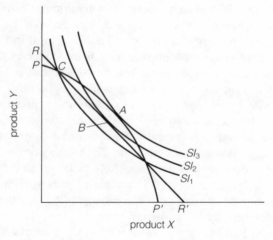

Figure 2.1 Constrained optimum and piecemeal policies

necessarily lead to the best resource allocation attainable. Such policies may actually move the economy away from, rather than towards, the constrained optimum. The problem can be represented schematically as in figure 2.1. The curve PP' shows the production possibilities for the economy in question. The curves labelled SI_1 SI_2 SI_3, are social indifference curves expressing the preferences of the society as a whole. The Pareto optimal position for the economy would be at point A where the social indifference curve SI_3 is tangential to the production possibility curve. If, however, the economy is constrained in the way indicated above and represented in the diagram by the line RR' the point A is unattainable. Under these circumstances if government policies nevertheless proceed as if the unconstrained optimum were still attainable, the economy may end up at a point like C. Now C is certainly on the production possibility curve but it is also intersected by the social indifference curve SI_1, which represents a lower level of social welfare than that attainable (even given the constraint) at point B. Although the output configuration implied by the point B is off the production possibility curve, it is preferable to the point C. In general, therefore, once an economy is constrained in a way that makes the achievement of the best allocation unattainable (i.e. point A in the example) it may not be the second-best to try to ensure that all remaining (marginal) conditions for an optimal resource allocation are met. In the present context, this may mean that regulation to enforce marginal cost pricing in natural monopolies or antitrust policy to ensure approximately the same result in other industries may not achieve the best result and may not therefore be in the public interest.

The reason the conclusion has been put in terms of 'may' rather than 'will' is because without a great deal of detailed information about the interactions and interdependencies of markets in an economy it is not possible to say whether a particular regulatory policy in one market will improve or worsen the performance of the economy overall. Taken literally this rather devastating conclusion is a recipe for policy paralysis, for all market economies are shot through with constraints that are irremovable. In practice it has not meant the abandonment of piecemeal policies on the grounds that full information about all their possible ramifications cannot be traced through, but it has had the salutary effect on economists asked for policy advice of making them more cautious and circumspect before recommending a particular move. There are very few, if any, for example, who would suggest that policies should attempt to create conditions of perfect competition in as many markets as possible, regardless of technology and the level of demand.

It has also been pointed out that as a theory of economic regulation the 'public interest' theory is incomplete. There is nothing in the theory to explain the mechanism through which market failures, once discovered, are made the subject of a corrective policy. As we have seen, market failure can take a wide variety of forms and occur in very many different activities. A complete theory with predictive power should be able to explain the incidence of regulation in the economy. Yet the public interest theory does not stand up very well when confronted with even casual observations from the UK. If the public interest theory is correct we should, for example, be able to explain intervention in the following industries in terms of market failure: air transport, bus services, milk-marketing, optical services, coal-mining and car production. The list is obviously intended to be illustrative rather than exhaustive and other examples are mentioned below. However, it is very difficult to fit even these cases into the explanation offered by the public interest theory. Clearly some regulation is required to allocate scarce air space between rival airlines, but for most of the postwar period air transport routes have been usually operated to the advantage of national airlines with little or no prospect of entry for other firms. The need for some form of regulation has thus, for the most part, been used to erect entry barriers against competition which in other industries would be seen as a form of market failure. Very similar points can be made about the provision of bus services where strict licensing of both long- and short-distance carriers was for a long while used to inhibit competition, even though no one would claim that the industry showed strong elements of natural monopoly. The regulation of milk-marketing through a monopoly agency seems mainly designed to assist milk producers rather than milk consumers. In all of these cases it is no longer seriously disputed that safety standards can be effectively maintained without preventing new entrants to the market. This argument can also be forcefully applied to the provision of optical services where an understandable concern to maintain the standards of eye care has been turned almost by accident into a very effective regulatory barrier to entry and a price structure quite out of line with costs (Office of Fair Trading, 1982).

In all of these illustrative examples, therefore, it is very difficult to link a market failure to a regulatory policy to a resulting industry performance that is 'in the public interest'. A sectional interest has benefited at the expense in most instances of consumers. The pricing policy of the firms or organizations concerned have borne little or no relation to those principles – particularly marginal cost – that a market failure analysis endorses. If anything, this criticism is even stronger in the case of coal-mining and motor car manufacture. Whereas the nationalization of some power industries (gas and electricity) could at least in part be explained in terms of the natural monopoly elements of important sections of their operations, that rationale cannot be applied to coal-mining which requires neither a national grid for distribution nor underground supply connections to each consumer. At the time of nationalization there were strong sociopolitical reasons for which the Labour government was committed to public ownership and repeated policy decisions since (not least the requirement that the electricity industry should take a large proportion of coal output) have re-inforced rather than diminished the conclusion that regulation in the industry was to the advantage of employees and their dependants rather than to ensure an efficient resource allocation. 'Regulation' in the motor industry has mainly taken the form of subsidy to the only remaining UK-owned mass producer of cars, BL. By 1984 the firm, which was also effectively nationalized in 1974, had received more than £2.5 billions in subsidies. There was no question in this case of regulating the whole industry in the public interest because of market failure. With one exception[3] the other UK motor manufacturers (all part of foreign-owned multi-nationals) received no similar support, and yet continued (along with Japanese and other importers) to erode BL's market share.

Clearly we are not arguing that such support, or regulation in the previous examples, should not necessarily have taken place, but simply that the 'public interest' theory, derived from conventional notions of market failure, does not predict them. A theory of regulation based simply on welfare economics and market failure has too narrow a base. It necessarily assumes that the sole objective of regulation is the maximization of welfare through the optimal allocation of resources, regardless of equity, the aspirations of the regulators themselves, or the political debts that the party elected to power has to repay. Writing in 1974 Posner summed up this part of the debate as follows: 'Some fifteen years of theoretical and empirical research, conducted mainly by economists, have demonstrated that regulation is not positively correlated with the presence of external economies or diseconomies or with monopolistic market structure' (p. 336). Recent developments in the theory of regulation, as we shall shortly show, have attempted to take account of at least some of these factors. However, one important area of policy that *can* be satisfactorily explained in terms of the public interest hypothesis is antitrust and competition policy. Artificial (as opposed to natural) monopoly can, as we have seen, lead to market failure in a number of ways whether it involves one firm or a series of firms acting together. Antitrust measures designed to regulate the behaviour and performance of private monopolies have been almost exclusively concerned to improve efficiency and resource allocation.[4] They have not systematically favoured one interest group at the expense of another (except, of course, that the enforced abandonment of a cartel may favour consumers at the expense of producers) and they have operated across a wide range of industries wherever artificial monopoly was thought to be significant. In fact both the original Monopolies and Restrictive Practices Act (1948) establishing the Monopolies and Restrictive Practices Commission (MC) and the subsequent Restrictive Practices Act (1956) made extensive use of the phrase 'the public interest': the MC was to enquire into monopolies and restrictive practices and decide whether or not they operated 'against the public interest'. Although the guidance in the legislation as to what constituted the 'public interest' has been widely criticized,[5] it is significant for the present context that its main emphasis was on the achievement of the most efficient production and distribution of goods and services. Even in the Restrictive Practices Act where there appear to be concessions to sectional interests,[6] the final decision rests on whether the Court could be satisfied that the advantage of allowing the cartel to continue were not balanced by any detriment to the public interest, and in some decisions a sectional interest group convinced the Court in the first part of the procedure, only to fail when the general consideration of the public interest was considered.

Thus antitrust policy probably comes closest in principle to the original public interest theory of regulation. However, it was the increasing recognition, especially in the US, that the incidence and performance of regulatory agencies did not match the predictions of the theory that led to the development of an alternative approach.

A key paper was that of Stigler (1975) but similar ideas and extensions were discussed by Peltzman (1976) and Posner (1974). Stigler's central thesis was that 'as a rule, regulation is acquired by the industry and is designed and operated primarily for its benefit' (p.114). Stigler uses standard economic analysis of demand and supply to explain the presence of regulation and then draws on the theory of cartels to try to pinpoint those industries where it is most likely to arise. Having observed that US experience with regulation did not, for the most part, conform with the public interest theory, he argued that certain industries will attempt to have the coercive powers of the state used to their own advantage. Although he lists four such powers, he places particular emphasis on the first two: the power of the state to use its taxation to give grants or subsidies to particular groups and the power to control entry to an occupation or industry. In some cases the two are clearly linked. Subsidy to an industry will be dissipated among too many firms if entry is relatively free. Control of entry may take a variety of forms including compulsory licensure with a regulatory body that strictly controls numbers, and tariffs or quotas which effectively cut down the volume of supplies available to a market. Demand for such regulation is likely to come from groups that have the most to gain but also where the effectiveness of private cooperation may be the most difficult to attain. Even in the absence of antitrust policy industries with a large number of firms will find it difficult to maintain an agreement on prices. Not only are such cartels likely to be hampered by attempts at secret price cutting by members and free riders who remained aloof from the original agreement, but also, to the extent that the cartel is able to keep prices above competitive levels, its subsequent cohesion will be threatened by new entrants. On the other hand, in industries with few firms the internal problems are likely to be much less severe, and while entry may remain a problem, the very structure of the industry may make it relatively difficult.[7] The demand for regulation may be strong, therefore, in multi-firm industries with easy entry. Examples cited by Stigler were agriculture, road haulage and occupational licensure (e.g. lawyers, architects, pharmacists, dentists, registered nurses and beauticians).

Furthermore, the attempt to attain the industry's objectives by regulation rather than simply through the market, may to a large extent overcome the free rider problem which usually hampers any private arrangements. Since the *form* that regulation can take (direct subsidy, control of entry, tariff or quota, price fixing) is varied, firms will have an interest in trying to ensure that the type of regulation they themselves most desire is the one that is pressed upon the government. They will therefore wish to be present or be represented at the preliminary meetings to put their case. If they remain apart they may still be able to take advantage of any regulation that is won for the industry, but it may not be the kind they favour.

While the type of industry just described may provide a number of telling examples to support the hypotheses which the public interest theory does not really explain, Stigler clearly envisaged it having a wider applicability. Indeed he argues that 'most industries will have a positive demand price (schedule) for the services of government.' However, since these services do not come free and since some industries may be able to make their own (low-cost) private arrangements, prominent and powerful oligopolists may *not* be in the vanguard of the demand for regulation.

The political theory of interest groups also has a bearing on the economic theory of regulation. The effectiveness of a campaign is likely to depend closely on the relative dispersion of any costs and benefits involved. For example, if the benefits of a piece of regulation (say entry prevention) are highly concentrated amongst a small group (existing members of the industry) while the costs (higher long-run prices) are widely dispersed amongst a very large group (of customers) then not only is the regulation more likely to be implemented but the regulators will behave in the way Stigler predicts, in the interests of the regulated. In such cases, the industry and its agency will strive to remain as invisible as possible, to prevent the mobilization of a counter-group to oppose the regulation. However, if it becomes contentious it will be defended by attempts to show that the public benefits by higher safety standards, lower incidence of fraud and protection from 'cowboy' operators (Wilson, 1974). Similarly where the proposed policy move is to repeal a piece of onerous regulation to the advantage of consumers but to the detriment of a small group of producers such a change is likely to meet fierce resistance. We need to look no

further for an example of this than the delays involved in trying to de-
regulate air transport in the US and the similar problems encountered in
the UK and Western Europe.

The opposite case is where regulation imposes costs on a small well-
defined group but where the benefits are diffused amongst a great number
of individuals. According to Wilson, for many political scientists the
likelihood of any regulation having this kind of impact actually coming into
effect seemed so remote that it could be safely ignored. However, he
argues that there are sufficient examples, especially from recent US
experience, to support the case and thus weaken the general applicability of
Stigler's theory (a point that we take up below). He cites in particular the
general provisions made in the 1960s and 1970s for consumer and
environmental protection that impose additional costs on relatively small
groups of producers while for the most part conferring only modest
benefits on a very large number of consumers.

If Stigler's view of regulators providing aid and comfort to the regulated
is essentially correct, it is hardly surprising that regulatory measures
sometimes seem to bear little relation to market failure. A number of
writers have also observed that although Stigler's theory is logically distinct
from and has a sharper focus than the earlier 'capture' hypothesis, in
practice it may be very difficult to distinguish them. The 'capture' hyothesis
is simply that although regulatory agencies may start out as guardians of the
public interest, they very soon succumb to the power and influence of the
industry they are supposed to regulate and finish up protecting it rather
than the public. It is not usually suggested that regulatory officials are
corrupted[8] but simply that they come more and more to identify with the
problems of the industry which also controls the information on which the
regulators have to rely for assessing its performance. In the 'mature'
regulated industry, therefore, regulation will be seen to work in favour of
the members rather than to correct a market failure and improve resource
allocation. At this stage, therefore, the outcome of both hyotheses will be
the same. Regulated industries where the controls work to the advantage of
existing firms can be used to support either or both theories, even though in
the Stigler case it is plain that the prime movers in the process were the
firms themselves.

Joskow and Noll (in Fromm, 1981) have also pointed out that empirical
tests of the theories run the risk of becoming tautological because of the
way the data have inevitably to be selected. Although the population of
regulated industries may be large and growing, the *form* in which the
necessary observations have to be made severely circumscribes the number
of industries or groups that can be used in the tests. The information used
in the test is also the information used to determine which are the
successful interest groups. For example, the Stigler theory suggests that

occupational groups with many members may organize to press for control of entry along the lines mentioned above. In principle the theory could be tested by drawing a random sample of properly identified occupational groups and then measuring whether a significant proportion of them had organized in the way predicted and, equally important, obtained as a result substantial financial benefits. In practice the data for proceding in this way are not available and it may be necessary simply to identify those groups that have been successful in their attempt to gain occupational licensure. It may thus be impossible at present to frame a test of the theory that could be rejected and its scientific basis may for this reason be weakened.

We referred above to another criticism of the sectional interest theories. A number of observers have noted that while they help to explain the way regulation has developed in several narrow and well-defined industries (air transport, parts of agriculture, some professions, road haulage in the US) there have been many other developments in regulation, especially over the last two decades, that they cannot explain. General measures to protect consumers from unsafe products and unscrupulous finance companies or to improve the environment have not been enacted as the result of pressure from well-organized groups that stand to gain most of the benefits from the regulation. Some of these measures, which are discussed in subsequent sections of the book, not only impose costs on existing manufacturers or practitioners but the benefits are widely dispersed among a great many members of the public who can have had only a very tenuous connection with the move to introduce the regulation. Neither version of the sectional interest theory could have predicted in advance, for example, the introduction of the Consumer Credit Protection Act in the US or the Consumer Protection Act in the UK both of which establish requirements for publishing details of actual rates of interest to be charged in hire purchase contracts; or measures to control the use of lead additives in petrol; or the required increases in safety devices in motor cars.

It is also extremely difficult to explain such policies in terms of the market failure theory discussed previously. Regulation of consumer credit terms seems largely designed to protect consumers, especially the poor, from themselves, although it is doubtful whether, at least in the US, the regulation has actually achieved its objective of protecting the poor from 'exorbitant' interest rates. Similarly additional safety measures in cars and their enforced use by drivers and their passengers, despite fierce opposition from libertarian groups, has the essentially paternalistic aim of saving consumers from their own 'irrational' behaviour.

Both kinds of theory, therefore, give a partial explanation of what has become an increasingly complex issue. However, Stigler's approach has also served to draw attention to the importance of analysing the *process* of regulation itself. In fact his theory of regulation can be seen as an important aspect of the much broader issue of *rent-seeking*, where rent refers to the amount that factors can earn over and above their supply price. To the extent that members of an industry or occupational group can successfully band together and achieve regulation that works to their advantage they will clearly be able to earn economic rents. An obvious example, as we saw above, is where the regulation effectively controls new entry to the industry or group. It is important to distinguish clearly between rent *creation* and rent-seeking. As Buchanan (1980) shows rent creation flows directly from the pursuit of profits by entrepreneurs attempting to exploit hitherto unsatisfied demands, usually through a process of change in production and distribution methods. In the absence of artificial constraints these rents will eventually be competed away, having performed the useful economic function of signalling where resources are more highly valued. In contrast, rent-seeking is an attempt to exploit a particular form of institutional arrangement (in the present context, government regulation) which has the effect of preventing entry and thus preventing the erosion of the economic rent by new competition.

A rather special example of this took place in the UK during 1984 and concerned British Airways. It involved an attempt to maintain a profitable piece of regulation rather than to create a new one. At the time of the proposal to de-nationalize British Airways by floating it on the Stock Exchange, there was considerable pressure both from smaller competing companies like British Caledonian and official bodies like the Civil Aviation Authority (1984) that a sizable proportion of British Airways' authorized routes should be hived off to the other companies. If they were not, there were fears that a public monopoly[9] would merely be replaced by a private monopoly which would then be able to demolish existing competition. To counter this pressure British Airways ran a nationwide advertising campaign to explain why it should be allowed to keep all of the routes that had been allocated to it over the years while it was in the public sector. Clearly the company would be much more likely to remain highly profitable if it passed into the private sector with its route structure intact.[10] The campaign was obviously aimed, therefore, at maintaining whatever economic rents were available by preventing or minimizing new entry.

Not only does successful rent-seeking allocate to the privileged industry or group returns that are unnecessary for the continued supply of the good or service, but the *process* of attempting to acquire the necessary regulation and subsequently ensuring that it is maintained also uses resources (of consultants, public relations firms, lawyers, advertising agents, etc.), which have a positive opportunity cost and therefore impose welfare losses on the rest of society. In other words if the good fairy, scourge of lobby consultants and advertising agents waved her wand at midnight and made all rent-seeking pointless, the resources previously devoted to the rent-seeking industry would (eventually) be re-allocated to their next most highly valued uses, examples of which we leave the reader's imagination to provide.

In the past economists have devoted a great deal of attention to the resource misallocations that result from monopoly pricing. Empirical studies that attempted to measure the welfare losses from monopoly initially concluded that they were extremely modest. Although subsequent research has suggested that the original estimates may have been too low, the emphasis has also shifted away from the direct effects of monopoly pricing to what is believeed to be the much more significant impact of resource misallocation resulting from rent-seeking activities.[11] Whereas monopoly pricing may be confined to those industries dominated by a single supplier (or a small group able to coordinate their pricing policy) rent-seeking may be undertaken by a much wider range of industries but especially by those industries that on usual measures have a 'competitive' structure. Conventional analysis suggests that such industries will, on average, earn only normal returns. Observations that they are earning 'average' or 'low' returns might appear to confirm the analysis. If, however, they are engaged in an attempt to win protective regulation an unidentified amount of their profits may be used for this purpose. In future, therefore, we may expect much more attention to be paid to the resource costs of rent-seeking and rather less to the direct costs of monopoly pricing.

In the analysis of economic regulation two further points serve to underline the importance of this change of emphasis. Firstly, a number of writers have noted the tendency for regulation to take on a momentum of its own and almost inevitably become more and more deeply involved in the affairs of the industry it is supposed to regulate. For example, in the case of a regulated monopoly the agency may initially attempt to ensure that only 'normal' profits are earnt. The response of the firm may be to allow its costs to rise through increased internal slackness both on the shop floor and in the executive suite, where, in addition, management may find it appropriate to pay themselves larger salaries. The regulatory agency may then find it necessary to audit the firm's costs and prices structure, in an attempt to achieve the original purpose of regulating profits. If the monopoly has been using discriminatory pricing for different segments of its market, according to relative demand elasticities, the agency may conclude that this is unjustified and insist on uniform pricing. The firm may, in its turn, respond by withdrawing some services altogether or imperceptibly reducing the quality of the good or service on the ground that it can no longer 'afford' to provide the range of products previously sustained by price discrimination. Again this may provoke the agency to a further response. The point, however, should be clear: the scope of regulation may through time continually increase. The process has been aptly termed the 'Tar-baby' effect by KcKie (1970), after the famous children's story.

Unless the terms of reference of the regulatory agencies are very tightly drawn up it is also likely that the fact that they are public bodies, generally seen as responsible for the efficient running of an important industry, that will make them the repository of complaints that they are in some way failing to provide a proper good or service to the public. In the case of American regulatory agencies Wilson has argued that this inevitably means that they feel they should do something to correct or improve the situation and this again pulls them further into the day-to-day affairs of industry (Wilson, 1974).

The last point is clearly related, secondly, to some recent developments in the economic theory of bureaucracy. According to the public interest theory of regulation, market failures can in principle be corrected by the low-cost intervention of officials who will administer policies designed to improve resource allocation and economic welfare. The analysis of public bureaucracies suggests that in practice the administration of policies is likely to be different. It recognizes the point that while economists have been content, until recently, to assume that individuals operating in input and product markets will pursue their own self-interest, when they form part of a civil service or regulatory agency, they have been assumed to behave in a completely selfless way pursuing what they perceive to be the public interest. The contrast cannot really be justified. If it is assumed that officials are just as likely to pursue their own interests while performing their duties as anyone else, then quite different conclusions can be derived. Just as firms freed from intense competition may have managements that recognize the scope for 'discretionary' behaviour (i.e. to pursue their own objectives rather than those of their shareholders), so officials who face no competition at all[12] may be expected to pursue their own objectives rather than those of the general public. Opportunity for discretionary behaviour will be further improved by the 'control loss' that many large organizations structured on hierarchical lines are known to suffer. For example, if each level of a hierarchy only carries out a proportion of the instructions from the higher level because of the inability to control completely the actions of subordinates, the amount of control can rapidly fall. In a four-level hierarchy if only 85 per cent of instructions are carried through this means that at the fourth level only just over half are completed. In such a situation there may be a great deal of scope for discretionary behaviour. Formally the situation can be viewed as one of bilateral monopoly with the bureau/officials (the monopolist) offering a particular level of service in return for an agreed budget from the governing party (the monopsonist). Given the inclination and scope for discretionary behaviour, it has been argued that the officials will seek to maximize the size of the budget. This will allow them to satisfy their taste for empire building and all the related perquisites of office (Hartley and Tisdell, 1981). In the pursuit of this objective the officials will have a strong incentive to emphasize the benefits of their preferred projects in terms of increased employment, involvement with high-technology enterprises, contributions to the balance of payments, and so on, while at the same time underplaying the costs, particularly the external costs. Firms that are likely to benefit from such a programme will thus have an interest in lobbying for its adoption.

In the context of regulation this analysis suggests that officials will tend to be attracted to those policies that do most to meet their budget maximizing objectives rather than those that may perform the required task most efficiently. Hence regulation introduced basically on a 'public interest' or market failure ground may in fact have a number of indirect and hidden costs that the original theory ignored. The attempt by officials to increase budgets so as to enhance the scope for their own discretionary behaviour may be made worse, from the point of view of resource allocation, if the bureaux that they administer are inefficient. If firms operating in a market environment that shields them from effective competition can become x-inefficient, as is now widely claimed, there may be strong reasons to expect a similar performance from organizations such as ministries and regulatory agencies which by their very nature have no strong incentives to remain internally efficient. Furthermore if the theory of bureaucratic behaviour is correct in predicting that an identity of interests between officials and firms or groups likely to benefit from (regulatory) policies will emerge, then this would further strengthen the 'sectional' interest type of theory. In practice it may be impossible to distinguish whether an agency has been 'captured' by the group it is supposed to regulate or whether it simply recognizes a strong community of interest with it. Recent examples of this problem in the UK are the relationship between officials in the Department of Health and Social Security and, firstly, the monopoly supplier of oxygen equipment and, secondly, the monopoly supplier of surgical gloves to the National Health Service. It has been claimed in both cases that officials have shown unwarranted favouritism towards the existing suppliers.[13]

The conclusion, however, remains the same through whichever lens we view the regulatory process: once initiated there will be strong forces making for an expansion both in range and complexity.

III CONCLUSION

Since economic regulation takes so many different forms and affects industries in a great many ways, it is not surprising that no single explanation of how it arises and thus what are likely to be its major effects is wholly satisfactory. The theories that we have discussed in this chapter fall essentially into two groups: public interest and sectional interest theories. The former grows naturally out of the analysis of market failure and therefore predicts that regulation will be introduced where, for example, private and natural monopoly arise, where public good considerations predominate or where adverse externalities pose serious hazards. We observed that whereas antitrust policies, consumer protection and measures to control pollution could be interpreted largely as a response to market failure, there were many other cases of regulation that could not be explained in this way. Tariff and quota restrictions, heavy subsidies to individual firms and nationalization of industries having no natural monopoly characteristics are only some examples of regulation that bear only the most tenuous connection to market failure as usually understood.

The sectional interest theory, as proposed initially by Stigler, is built upon the usual assumptions of economic analysis. In essence he argued that under certain circumstances particular interest groups – firms in an industry, members of a particular occupation – will organize themselves to demand from the administration the use of its sovereign power to provide them with regulations that will enhance or maintain their earnings. In return they will provide funds, votes (and possibly jobs) for the administration and its members. The emphasis was on groups who may find it especially difficult to organize privately without official backing.

While the theory does help to explain more effectively why regulation often occurs in industries with many small firms and no threat of monopoly or where it has clearly operated to the advantage of existing firms rather than to new entrants or the consumer, like the public interest theory, it does not provide a complete explanation. In particular it does not explain those general measures to protect consumers or clean up the environment that have been especially prominent both in North America and Western Europe during the last twenty five years. Measures that are designed to keep unsafe products off the market by laying down strict quality and design standards or that ensure that lead additives are much reduced or completely excluded from petrol may impose significant costs on a comparatively small group (of producers) while generating relatively small benefits for a very large number of people. In such cases the public interest theory, or a variation that recognizes the objectives of most governments wider than that of simply maximizing economic welfare, is more persuasive.

The explanation of how regulations arose and therefore what their effects may be are thus likely to depend on the particular kind of regulation being scrutinized. In all cases, however, we need to be aware of the *indirect* as well as direct effects of regulation. Administering regulatory policies is not costless and an institutional setting may almost unwittingly be established that allows not only the pursuit by officials of their own objectives running counter to the 'public interest', but also encourages the wasteful process of rent-seeking.

3

The Scope for Regulation and an Outline of the Book

I INTRODUCTION

So far we have deliberately used a very general definition of 'regulation'. Any government policy that directly affects the operation of the market can be said to 'regulate' it in some degree. Thus product, input and profit taxes, controls on entry including tariffs and quotas, legal requirements for input and product standards or specifications, as well as the whole of antitrust or competition policy can be included in such a definition. Using a slightly different terminology, any policy that affects market structure conduct or performance can in principle be regarded as 'regulatory'. Interpreted in this way, therefore, it appears to cover practically the whole field of applied micro-economics. In order to strike a balance between theory and practical detail, as well as to keep the book to a reasonable length and within the competence of the author, we have to be highly selective in the topics treated in subsequent sections.

The selection process itself was not without its problems. It would have been desirable to have found a single unifying criterion for the selection of the topics to be discussed, but in the event this was not feasible. The ways in which regulations can impinge on the operations of markets are so varied (and often matched by the ingenuity of participants in trying to avoid them) that selection according to 'type of regulation' does not, at first sight, seem very helpful. However, if viewed in terms of 'type of policy instrument' employed, it does assist us in making the choices. Thus examples of regulation by *special laws* to protect interest groups such as consumers; by *special agencies* to monitor the market conduct and performance of firms in both the private and public sectors; and by the *control of entry* to certain industries will be included. On the other hand, measures aimed at changing relative input or product prices *directly* by taxes, tariffs and subsidies (e.g. regional, agricultural and parts of 'industrial' policy) will, generally not be included. Their exclusion is not to under-rate their importance but simply for reasons of space.

Despite the criticisms made in the previous chapter of market failure as the source of economic regulation we will find that in many of the topics discussed below it provides a useful starting point for the analysis. Furthermore we can use the market structure, market conduct and market performance (SCP) framework developed by Bain (1968), to analyse industry, to illustrate in a compact form the contents of the book.

II AN OUTLINE OF THE BOOK

The subsequent discussion is divided into three main sections: information and consumer interests; monitoring firms' behaviour and performance; and regulating natural monopoly.

We have already noted that although in many economic models it is assumed that information is perfect, in practice nearly all markets suffer from a greater or lesser degree of ignorance on the part of buyers. In some markets it may simply amount to ignorance of the precise current terms of trading that can be easily (cheaply) overcome by making contact with a number of market participants. At the other extreme the costs of either informing customers of the qualities, locations and prices of certain products or, on the other hand, of discovering whether producer claims for a product are genuine may be prohibitively high. Part II of this book (chapters 4 and 5) is concerned with such problems, seen mainly from the point of view of the final consumer where they take their most acute form. Intermediate buyers (of capital goods or components) often have as much, if not more, information about the products they require as the sellers and therefore the need for direct regulation may not be as great. However an interesting question, which we take up later, is that of such buyers find it worthwhile to provide themselves with sufficient information while final consumers very often apparently do not.

In industrial economics the market structure, conduct and performance framework is used to highlight the inter-relationships between key aspects of market structure (such as the number and size distribution of firms), market conduct or behaviour (such as price and product policies) and market performance (such as technical and allocative efficiency). In the present context we can use this terminology to show how government regulation may impinge on different aspects of the market. The details are shown in table 3.1. For example, under part II of the book, concerned with information and consumer interests, the policy objective is the improvement of information and product quality. The policy instruments used in this case bear largely on market structure and market conduct. In the UK, for example, a number of important laws such as the Trade Descriptions Act and the Consumer Credit Act try to ensure that fuller and more

Table 3.1 Market regulation by government

Section of the book	Objective	Market structure	Anticipated effect on market conduct	Market performance
Part II Information and consumer interests (chapters 4 and 5)	Information improvement Product quality maintenance and improvement	Quality of entrants maintained	Information disclosure and regulation Advertising standards maintained Trading terms improved	More efficient consumer purchases and trading relations
Part III Monitoring firm behaviour and performance in the private sector (chapters 6–8)	Maintaining/stimulating competition	Concentration levels contained or reduced Entry conditions eased	Reduction in: dominant firm anti-competitive practices and joint price fixing	Improved allocative, technical and x-efficiency
Part IV Regulating natural monopoly (Chapters 9 and 10)	Protecting the consumer Maintaining and improving technical, allocative and x-efficiency	Entry prevention or restriction Concentration levels maintained	Prices and price discrimination controlled Anti-competitive practices reduced	Improvements in technical, allocative and x-efficiency

accurate information is available to consumers prior to purchases. In addition, the Consumer Affairs Division of the Office of Fair Trading has the responsibility of monitoring the market conduct of firms, especially when complaints from consumers have been received. There are also a number of restrictions on the content and media usage of advertising messages – another way in which regulation can affect market conduct.

Part III, monitoring firm behaviour and performance in the private sector, is concerned with the control of market power. As table 3.1 shows, a major objective of antitrust policy is the maintenance and stimulation of competition. The main way in which this form of regulation may affect market *structure* is by preventing or limiting mergers. In principle it is also possible for the antitrust agencies to change the structure of the market by ordering the break-up of a dominant firm, but in practice this remedy has been unused in the UK and very sparingly used in the US. Much more attention in practice has been paid by the antitrust authorities to the market conduct of dominant firms, especially the wide variety of ingenious pricing policies that may inhibit competition (chapter 7) and, particularly in the UK, to their market performance as reflected in their profitability. Where production is less heavily concentrated firms may nevertheless seek to suppress competition by mutual agreement. Also included in table 3.1, therefore, as an important aspect of market conduct regulation is the control of price fixing which is discussed in chapter 8.

In the case of natural monopoly the main policy objective is to maintain efficiency. Until recently in the UK this mainly took the form of setting financial targets for the industries concerned and guiding their price and investment policies. The situation has been complicated because successive governments have used the nationalized industry sector as an instrument of anti-inflationary policy and in effect controlled their prices. This aspect of regulation is recognized in table 3.1 in the 'conduct' column by the effect on price and profit levels. We should note, however, that this policy was not part of the formal system of regulation, although in the 1970s it must at times have seemed so (chapter 9). A puzzle that we also discuss is why natural monopolies, if they really have the characteristics assigned to them by economic theory, require the prevention of entry by new firms. As table 3.1 shows the structure of the market on the sellers' side was for a long period maintained inviolate by legislation. Not only were new firms prevented from entering the industry but the nationalized firms were debarred from diversifying into other industries which may have been more profitable. The uninitiated may rightly ask why, if the core of the problem with natural monopoly is that the first entrant wins and can thereafter exploit its position and the public, it is necessary to debar firms by law from entering the industry? The answer usually given to this question is that it is to protect the nationalized industries, which have social obligations, from 'unfair competition'.

Entry conditions are a major concern in chapter 10 where we consider the effect of entry regulation in a number of industries such as telecommunications, gas, and air transport. Attitudes and policy towards such industries have been changing rapidly in the last few years, especially in the UK and US. Industries with a long history of regulation have found themselves at the centre of a debate on the whole rationale of regulation, and in some important instances in the UK over their *public* enterprise status. The main focus of the debate has not been whether service quality and safety can be assured by regulation – most observers now seem to feel that it is not necessary for these purposes – but whether the internal efficiency and dynamism can be maintained in a protected market. On this issue there is far less unanimity.

The final chapter of the book assesses the relative achievement of different forms of regulation and suggests a number of possible criteria for establishing those kinds of regulation that are appropriate for different markets. The last few years in the UK and US have been periods of attempted de-regulation. In view of Olson's (1982) thesis on the development of blocking distributional coalitions, we would expect the de-regulation movement to meet strong resistance. For if he is right, the UK and US, with the longest periods of uninterrupted social and political stability, have generated very powerful interest groups which will not give up their privileges without a struggle. It is doubtful, for example, whether the privatization of a number of UK industries will lead to increased competition rather than simply to a change in ownership, with the capacity of these industries to earn monopoly rents left largely intact. The opposition of trade unions in these industries which was initially very strong may thus have been misplaced. Far from weakening their ability to improve the wages and conditions of their members, the change of ownership may actually enhance it.

Moreover the fact that de-regulation remains an important policy issue probably means that more resources are used for the purpose of rent-seeking (or perhaps more aptly in the present context 'rent-maintaining') than formerly when it was not on the agenda. These questions recur throughout part IV.

PART II

Information
and Consumer Interests

4

Information
and Consumer Protection

During the last twenty years or so there has been widespread and growing recognition of the consumer interest. It has been reflected in the creation of institutions publishing reports on consumer products (such as *Which?* in the UK and *Consumer Reports* in the USA), in the popularity of radio and television programmes and newspaper surveys that take producers to task for supplying faulty products or inferior services, and widespread changes in the law specifically designed to protect or enhance the consumers interest *vis-à-vis* the producer (for example a recent analysis of the subject lists at least 35 statutes passed between 1950 and 1980 having consumer protection as one of their main objectives (Borrie and Diamond, 1981).

A number of factors help to explain why this development took place. Partly it was due to the growing affluence of Western economies after the Second World War. The range of products that families earning only average incomes could afford was increased dramatically. Furthermore, many of the products, such as household appliances, television and stereo equipment and motor cars were increasingly complex and under some circumstances potentially dangerous. Laws that might cope adequately with the relatively rare instances when a horse was found, after sale, to be lame or more ancient than had been alleged, were considered inadequate to cope with a rising tide of cases arising from the sale of dud second-hand cars, of exploding television sets, or of holidays booked into half-completed hotels. At the same time the growing concentration of industry with, in many markets, only a handful of giant enterprises supplying the bulk of the output appeared to tilt the balance of advantage too much in the producers' favour to the possible detriment of consumers.

It was no coincidence that at the same time the economic analysis of the consumer's role in markets received an overwhelming amount of attention. As we shall see shortly a central focus of attention in the analysis has been the nature of 'information' and the operation of markets where information is less than complete. Stigler set the tone for much of the subsequent discussion when he remarked in a path-breaking article: 'One should hardly have to tell academicians that information is a valuable resource: knowledge *is* power. And yet it occupies a slum dwelling in the town of economics. Mostly it is ignored: the best technology is assumed to be known; the relationship of commodities to consumer preferences is a datum. And one of the information producing industries, advertising, is treated with a hostility that economists normally reserve for tariffs or monopolists' (Stigler, 1968). Much of the problem stemmed from the continued widespread use of the abstraction of perfect competition in analysing economic problems. Two key assumptions in the model are that in any market the products from all sellers are homogenous and, above all, there is perfect information amongst consumers about all of the characteristics of the products and terms and conditions on which they are available. Consumers are thus assumed to know before transacting everything about a product, where it is sold and at what price. It is perhaps not too much of an exaggeration to say that what one eminent theorist characterized as the 'decade of information economics' was an attempt to unravel the full implications, for markets, of modifying the assumption of perfect information, and even a cursory glance at the economic journals will indicate that the analysis is still far from complete.[1] If there was perfect information there would be no need for a 'consumer movement' and the law could concern itself with deliberate acts of fraud. However, since it is very difficult to conceive of any actual market where full information is available,[2] these reversals are unlikely to occur.

A closer examination of the main characteristics of information reveals that as a 'commodity' it appears to involve practically all of those sources of market failure that we mentioned in chapter 1 that lead to regulation. Indivisibilities, externalities and monopoly are *all* associated with information. While a steel plant may generate external diseconomies and electricity production involve indivisibilities leading to natural monopoly, these are single market failures which can be analysed in a relatively straightforward manner. However, with information every kind of market failure is likely to be present in varying degrees, according to the market studied.

Considerable ingenuity is therefore required to draw out all of the implications for the operation of markets when so many sources of failure are present simultaneously. Section two of this chapter contains a summary discussion of the main points to emerge from this analysis. In the light of this discussion we shall then be in a position, in section III, to consider the relative feasibility and efficiency of various policy approaches to consumer markets: whether, for example, the main emphasis should be on providing more information, so that consumers can make more skilful choices, or whether the government should lay down standards for product qualities and conditions of sale. The policies themselves, mainly in the UK and the US, can then be outlined and appraised in chapter 5.

II MARKET FAILURE IN CONSUMER GOODS MARKETS

The authors of a recent article on the efficient regulation of consumer information warned their readers at the start that 'information economics is perhaps the most confusing branch of the dismal science. Because the demand for information is derived from the demand for products, failures in one market feed back on the other in a circular fashion' (Beales *et al.*, 1981). The subject has engaged some of the most eminent economic theorists and has led on at least one occasion to diametrically opposed analysis and conclusions.[3]

A cursory glance at the respective incentives that both sellers and consumers have for obtaining or providing product information might suggest that policies designed to increase or regulate the further dissemination of information are unnecessary. For consumers, information about a product or service can help improve their decisions and ensure that they derive maximum satisfaction from the product eventually purchased. A wide variety of information sources for consumers already exist and include their own past experience, inspection of products to ensure that certain attributes are present, recommendations from friends, journals (including specialist publications like *Which?*) advice from specialists (e.g. car mechanics, surveyors, lawyers) and so on. Equally, sellers have a strong incentive for disseminating information about their product. In a market where there are many brands to choose from, in the absence of information about the respective merits of different brands consumers may view all of them as having 'average' quality. Sellers of above-average brands would thus have an incentive to publicize to consumers the superior attributes of their products. Consumers may then begin to assume that those brands for which they had little or no information were inferior, and this in turn would lead sellers of any remaining brands of above-average quality to disclose information about their advantages.[4]

As we have already indicated, however, it is wrong to conclude from this that consumers' desires to make efficient purchases and sellers' incentives to ensure that the true qualities of their products are known will lead to the optimum amount of information disclosure. The pervasiveness of market failures will ensure that this is rarely if ever the case. However, before we examine the nature of those failures in more detail we should make it clear that less-than-perfect information in a market does not automatically mean that the appropriate policy response is to ensure fuller information, just as a less-than-perfect market structure does not provoke antitrust authorities to attempt to remove all imperfections.

A comprehensive discussion of possible market failures in the 'information market' has recently been published by Beales *et al.* (1981) and we draw on their analysis in what follows. In chapter 1 we mentioned that in the case of public goods (such as defence, national parks and fire services) free markets would tend to supply less than the optimum because of the difficulties of ensuring that all who benefit pay for the service provided. A similar problem arises with information in consumer (and other) markets. The production and then the use of product information by some consumers who wish to be well informed is likely to generate competition amongst sellers for the custom of this group and as a result price or quality will improve. The benefits of this process will also go to those consumers who buy indiscriminately. As a result the market, left to itself, will tend to under-supply information.

The problem is compounded by the fact that once information about a product has been produced and sold, it can be passed on to other consumers at little or no marginal cost. Information thus shares this characteristic with a natural monopoly (where marginal costs are a very small fraction of total costs). If marginal costs of dissemination are effectively zero then there is a case for saying that it should command a zero price. However, since information, unlike tangible goods, can be used over and over again without deterioration it is probable that many consumers will receive it and be able to act on it without having paid anything for its provision. In other words they can free ride on the payment of others. Again this means that the market will tend to under-supply, and it accounts for the lack of private firms selling information on consumer products. Information, therefore, involves a complex tissue of externalities in the form of public good characteristics, near-zero marginal costs in distribution and free rider problems.

In practice sellers may attempt to overcome these difficulties by providing information, especially in the form of advertising; but as we might expect this, at best, offers only a partial solution and at worst creates additional policy problems. From an individual seller's point of view in a competitive market the provision of general information about a product class through advertising is likely to help competitors' sales as well as the seller's own. If the seller attempts to denigrate rivals' products this may either have the unfortunate effect of giving additional aid to them[5] or help to raise the sales of substitute products. Alternatively a seller may attempt to internalize the full benefit of the information supply by stating that their products have a particularly desirable characteristic (or lack an undesirable one) even though all products of the class, including those of competitors, share it. The tactics will only work, however, as long as other suppliers do not make the same claim.

So far we have assumed that all information is 'good' in the sense of making the market more perfect and therefore pushing it closer to the optimum. However, in the short-run, firms may have an incentive to disseminate false information or at least remain silent on negative characteristics that they know about but that the consumer could only discover at very great cost or after a long time interval. In the longer term the superior products of competing firms or the bitter experience of past consumers may tend to correct this situation, but in competitive markets there may be little incentive for individual firms to undertake an expensive positive information programme because any resulting benefits are likely to be widely dispersed amongst other firms. On the other hand in an oligopolistic market for a product that is known (by producers) to have serious defects it may be in all their interests to remain silent about them. Tobacco is the most obvious example. No tobacco firm is likely to inform customers voluntarily of the potential health risks of using their products. As a consequence, we shall see later, government regulations may be required to force disclosure. Remaining silent about attributes of a product is not the same as making false claims and where competition from superior-quality products cannot be expected to eliminate inferior (or harmful) brands some kind of regulation may again be necessary.

Under the old legal doctrine of *caveat emptor*, consumers were expected, within certain limits, to make purchases with a keen concern for their own interest. There was little room for wrong deductions or mistakes. When we discuss the greatly increased volume of laws designed to protect consumers, it will be evident how narrow the concept has recently become. The development is really a recognition of the asymmetry of information that is present in many modern consumer markets between the seller and the buyer. Without experience of a particular class of product the buyer may under-estimate the value to himself or herself of actually acquiring more information before making the purchase. In many instances the detriments suffered as a result of making a 'wrong' purchase may be comparatively trivial: the consumer, in effect, at low cost learns from the mistake and any subsequent purchases are only made with fuller information. In other cases (even if we exclude for the moment products that may involve serious health risks) lack of information and a too hasty purchase may subsequently be regarded by the purchaser as an extremely costly mistake. One obvious example is a hire purchase agreement with very onerous terms. Consumers may, on the spur of the moment, and under pressure from a skilful salesman commit themselves to purchases and on terms that they quickly regret. Whereas the salesman is trained in the art of selling, the consumer may be relatively unskilled in buying, especially as to the amount of information required to make an optimal decision.[6] Although such decisions can be treated in the economic analysis of consumer behaviour as a change in consumer preferences for information, it is more productive to regard them as another aspect of the market failing to provide the 'correct' amount of information.

Both Nelson (1970) and Spence (1973) have drawn attention to the point that consumers may use the available information as a signal for the other attributes of a product. Thus, for example, the heavy advertising of certain brands may be interpreted as a sign of their quality. Genuinely high-quality brands will produce more repeat purchases from satisfied customers and therefore the firms selling them will have a greater incentive to advertise in order to maximize the probability that consumers make the initial purchase. However, there are a number of inter-related limitations that may result from this response. Once it is known that consumers in effect regard heavy advertising as a guide to value and product quality, producers of inferior brands will likewise have an incentive to advertise more heavily. The process then becomes self-defeating and may lead not only to an over-investment in market signalling but also eventually destroy the basis on which it was founded. In other words consumers lose confidence both in the information with which they are supplied and the attribute of the product on which it was focused. In view of the earlier conclusions that imperfections may lead to the *under*-supply of information, the exact balance of the forces is difficult, *a priori*, to determine. We are left with the unsatisfactory conclusion that the net effects of market failure on the one hand and 'signal' competition on the other, may lead either to an under- or an over-supply of information.

So far we have concentrated on the problem posed for consumers by the special characteristics of information and the 'information market'. We turn now to the ways in which imperfections in the supply of information may cause distortions in the related *product* markets. It has frequently been pointed out that a lack of information may give even a small firm a degree of market power despite an underlying market structure that is fragmented. Thus in his study of the US market for spectacles (eyeglasses) Benham (1972) found marked differences in the prices between states that allowed advertising and those which did not. There was also considerably greater price dispersion where advertising was not allowed. Similarly where information about the quality of a product is sketchy and costly to obtain, as in the case, for example, of non-prescription drugs, firms have an incentive to differentiate brands of what are physically the same product, with a consequent rise in the average price.

In general, drawing on the important result given by Akerloff (1970), if price is more discernible than quality, competition will tend to be focused on the cheaper end of the market. The result follows from the asymmetry of information that can develop between buyers and sellers, especially for complex consumer products. Thus for a product like the motor car the majority may be trouble-free and perform exactly as the seller claims. For a minority, however, termed 'lemons' in the US and 'Friday afternoon cars' in the UK, all kinds of faults and problems may develop that were not observable at the time of sale. Amongst new cars, therefore, perfect performers will sell at the same price as those that turn out to be 'lemons'. In the second-hand market for cars of, say, one year old, pressures will build up that will force the price to be some way below what could normally be expected for physical depreciation. The demand for second-hand cars will depend on their price and the probability of buying a 'lemon'. Cars a year old (or less) coming onto the market almost automatically set up the suspicion that something is wrong, otherwise why are they being sold? A low price for one-year-old models will tend to contract the supply and owners of good cars will reckon that it is not worthwhile selling. The net result of this process is likely to be that owners of 'good' cars will feel obliged to hold onto them because they cannot realize the 'correct' market price. Potential buyers are put off by the likelihood of getting a 'lemon' and the process therefore becomes reinforcing. The average quality of second-hand cars falls, as both supply and demand contract. As Akerloff says, the process is rather similar to Gresham's law: in this case bad products tend to drive out good. The lack of systematic information amongst buyers and sellers therefore prevents trading taking place that could have been mutually beneficial.

Again, if it is difficult (costly) for consumers to obtain information about product safety but easy for them to observe price, firms may gain an advantage by cutting the quality of their product as a means of reducing price and gaining a competitive advantage. Even in those cases where consumers would be prepared to pay extra for more favourable contract terms (such as extended warranty protection) they may be prevented from making the optimal choice by the difficulty of comparing alternative contracts often written in language of labyrinthine complexity and in print of a size designed to induce giddiness even amongst those fortunate enough to have purchased a pair of competitively priced spectacles. As Beales *et al.* conclude: 'Many traditional consumer protection problems – unsafe products, defective or poor quality services, or 'unconscionable' contract terms – may be the result of such lemons competition' (1981, p. 511).

In some instances producers may be able (partially) to overcome these problems by offering generous warranty terms or other conditions, such as money-back guarantees. The producer's willingness to offer such terms may then provide a good indicator of the quality or reliability of the product, since frequent replacements or repayments will be costly for the

seller. Hence with a generous contract the inference by the consumer may
be that relatively few of the contracts fail. However, as in most cases with
this subject we no sooner appear to have a remedy for the problems created
by inefficient information than others arise. In this case there may be
drawbacks from the sellers' point of view that prevent them from offering
terms that would lead to the optimum amount of trading. Just as the buyer
wants some assurance against the risk of being sold a 'lemon', so also the
seller would like to be confident that customers treat the product correctly.
Unfortunately generous warranty terms or other conditions may tend to
undermine such confidence. The literature on 'moral hazard' is now
replete with examples of customers behaviour that can deteriorate after
purchase has taken place and the seller's guarantee (or risk-bearing)
given.[7] Similarly the more comprehensive the seller's terms in a contract,
the more they may attract customers who are careless in their use of the
product. There is therefore no guarantee that in particular cases the
balance of these opposing forces – warranties as a guide to quality and
good service, and moral hazard or adverse selection of customers inhibiting
sellers' terms – will lead to anything like the optimal amount of trading in
the market.

Having briefly surveyed the many and complex ways in which both the
'market' for information and for goods and services may fail, it is as well to
remind ourselves of a point made earlier that not every failure necessarily
needs a policy response. In some cases where a lack of information leads
initially to inefficient or insufficient trading by consumers the least-cost
correction may come from the consumers themselves without any
assistance from the law or the government. In such cases for the
government to compel the disclosure of more information would be
inefficient. On the other hand there are many instances where the market
left to itself will either provide a corrective only at very great expense or
suffering to consumers, or possibly no solution at all. The foregoing
analysis should enable us to assess more effectively which kind of remedy is
likely to produce the more efficient result in the particular circumstances.
In the next section we therefore consider a number of different approaches
that can be used to overcome the worst effects of information and related
failures in consumer product markets.

III DIFFICULTIES IN FRAMING REMEDIES

The previous analysis suggests strongly that there will be many instances
where some form of regulation of information is necessary. This is not to
deny that the two forces traditionally seen as furthering consumer interests
are not still at work. Indeed the natural good sense and caution of

consumers in looking after their own interest is probably stronger now than in previous periods. Competition amongst producers and regard for their own long-run reputation has also recently been reinforced by the growth of large retailers, equally jealous to maintain the high quality of products and the comprehensiveness of their service to consumers. There are a number of well known instances where the latter have used their undoubted bargaining power to ensure that quality is preserved.

However, as we have shown, information failures will often mean that this pursuit of long-term self-interest on the part of consumers and producers is inadequate. The problem is therefore to devise an efficient regulatory framework, and this is more difficult than the more extreme supporters of the consumer movement suggest. Broadly speaking two main kinds of policy can be used – those that seek to change the amount of *information* available in the market and those that seek to regulate directly product *standards* and terms of trading. In view of the previous discussion the first approach might seem more logical since it essentially provides an information remedy in response to an information market failure. There are strong grounds too for arguing that an information response will be more flexible and efficient. It will allow consumers to make up their own minds, based on more knowledge of the market than was previously available. In contrast a policy of specifying product quality or standards in effect forces the regulator to try to summarize what he or she sees as consumer preferences and this is likely to lead to a restriction of choice. As far as producers are concerned a market regulated to give fuller or better information allows them to respond to changing technology in whatever way they feel is appropriate. If the regulation turns out to have been mistaken an information remedy is likely to prove less costly than one that, by imposing standards, may have forced on producers changes in production and distribution methods that were unnecessary and therefore inefficient.

Despite the persuasiveness of this general point, as we shall see in chapter 5 much of the policy designed to regulate consumer markets has been of the second type: setting out quality standards, product specifications, and obligatory terms of trading. The explanation for why, on the whole, these remedies have been preferred even where they may be relatively inefficient is not altogether clear. Part of the explanation may be that politicians saw such remedies as the most effective response to lobbying by the consumer interest group. Regulations specifying product quality or standard are tangible and immediate. A requirement to make more information available about existing products and then leaving consumers to make up their own minds may be regarded as wishy-washy and inadequate. In other words the unspectacular and subtle modifications in consumer behaviour that might flow from a better informed market are lost amid political expediency. It is also the case, however, that the information remedies themselves are more complex than a preliminary analysis might suggest and in addition the actual technology of getting information across to consumers is still by no means fully understood. For example, a requirement to inform consumers that a product is rich in polyunsaturated fats may be regarded by some as a disadvantage, even though current medical opinion takes the opposite view.[8] A rather ludicrous recent example of how not to convey information, in this case to motorists and cyclists rather than to consumers, was given by the Department of Transport. As part of a campaign to reduce accidents to cyclists, hoardings appeared beside many roads. The message was to chastize both groups of road users for not keeping their eyes on the road. Unfortunately many of the hoardings were quite high up and the message quite long. The effect, therefore, was more likely to cause accidents than to prevent them.

It is possible to identify three main classes of information remedy and most of the remainder of this section is concerned with the difficulties of making them effective. The first category concerns the removal of restraints on the provision of information caused either by government regulations themselves or, more especially, self-imposed by existing members of an industry or occupation. The clearest example of such restraints occurs in the professions where it is usually the case that individual firms cannot advertise their services and particularly the prices they charge. In some cases publicity may be possible but only through certain media. To the extent that consumers are less well informed about available services and prices than they might otherwise be, it can be argued that they will make less efficient choices. If the more efficient firms cannot make their services and terms widely known there will be less scope for them to increase their market share or if they are only allowed to use less effective media, what information is made available will be more costly than it need be. For their part the professions using such restrictions argue that the quality of their services is maintained by preventing advertising (and price cutting). Equally they suggest that the public's confidence in their professional skills would be undermined if they advertised although, since this argument has more than a hint of disdain for the commercial practices usually associated with humbler goods and services, it has been heard less and less recently.

There have been some encouraging signs in the UK that the position is changing. We look more closely at some of these changes in chapter 5 but it is useful to note at this stage that since October 1984 it has been possible for solicitors to advertise their services (although not their scale of fees) in newspapers and on the radio, but not on television. All of the arguments in favour of such restrictions were rehearsed in a recent report of the Director

General of Fair Trading (1981) into the competitive conditions prevailing in the UK in the supply of optical services. Unlike the solicitors whose restrictions were self-imposed, by the rules of the Law Society, most of the restrictions that opticians operated were derived from the Opticians Act 1958. Since 1981 it has been possible for opticians to give prices in their window displays but they still could not advertise their services.[9] On the whole the climate of opinion has shifted markedly in recent years in favour of increased freedom to provide information for a whole range of services where previously this was regarded as unprofessional and even demeaning.

The discussion in the earlier part of this chapter suggests that removing restrictions on basic information covering price and conditions of sale will improve the efficiency of consumer purchases. In another case however, the benefit is less clear-cut. The Consumers Association protects information published in its journal *Which?* giving detailed assessments of a wide range of products and services. No firm is allowed to quote in its own publicity the verdict of *Which?* reports. The Association would argue that if its assessments were used in this way, perhaps prominently displayed in the advertisements of individual firms, consumers would tend to lose faith in its validity and the independence of *Which?* would be compromised. On the other hand there is no doubt that the information would reach a much wider public if included in the national advertisements of individual firms. Given that the costs of testing products had been incurred and that the resulting information can be used repeatedly without deteriorating, it can be argued that it should be disseminated as widely as possible. The problem might be overcome if instead of being privately funded by subscription and donation, the Association was publically funded and the results then made freely available.[10]

The first type of remedy thus aims to remove restrictions on information and thereby allow normal market forces to ensure that the amount of information available to consumers increases. The second and related type refers to measures aimed at increasing directly the amount of information. The most widely known example in the UK is probably the tar rating and health warning that has to be carried on cigarette packets and advertisements, but other examples are the type specification for car tyres and the ingredients for a wide range of food products (as well as their weight and volume).[11] If lack of information is seen as a major problem in a particular consumer market an automatic response may simply be that a governmental agency should ensure that 'information is increased'. The difficulty, however, is to devise an efficient way of doing just this. Consumer markets vary so enormously that it is not possible simply to lay down some general disclosure rules that can be applied with equal effectiveness to all of them. In addition, in any particular market consumers may differ as to which product attributes they would like more information.

A general requirement, for example, that food products should carry a weight label so that consumers can more easily compare real prices of different brands, fails in this objective if the leading manufacturers all choose different weight systems.

Emphasis on the product attribute that is rated or scored may lead to the downgrading of other equally important attributes that are more difficult to measure. If consumers begin to use the rated attribute as a guide (or signal) for other non-rated attributes this emphasis by sellers will be reinforced. The effect may then be that consumers make less rather than more efficient choices, since there may be no correlation between rated and unrated attributes as far as overall quality is concerned. Before the introduction of a new rating system, therefore, it is important to consider carefully the likely inferences that consumers may make. Just as new products are 'test marketed', so new rating schemes can be tested for consumer response and the side-effects on producers. As there is likely to be a direct relationship between costs of using a rating system and the degree of precision required actually to measure the attribute, it is also important to have a clear idea of the significance attached by consumers to the attribute (and therefore the benefits they would receive from a rating) and all the costs involved in introducing and then using a rating system. A system that is too precise may be too costly to introduce (i.e. the benefits are less than the costs), on the other hand, one that is relatively crude (for example, classifying brands into, say, three grades) may be cheap to introduce but give little benefit and actually weaken producers' incentives to improve their products. As long as they remain in the 'highest' category for the product, even though this may be on its lowest threshold, there is no inducement to improve quality.

Information provided by sellers can, of course, be supplemented by government-funded information campaigns stating what is known about the negative attributes of some classes of product. In the UK most national campaigns of this kind have been concerned with road safety (including the dangers of drinking too much alcohol) rather than particular products. However, some attempt has been made to inform the public of the dangers to health from tobacco, using the most effective medium – television – from which cigarette advertising has been banned; but the governments' budgets for such campaigns have usually been dwarfed by the marketing budget of the tobacco industry. This question is taken up again in chapter 5.

So far we have considered two ways in which consumers may be helped to make more informed choices: by reducing impediments to information provision and by encouraging or requiring increased dissemination of information. A third general way in which consumers can be assisted is by the prevention of false claims. Whereas the first two policies, therefore, lead to an *increase* in the information available to consumers, the third will often lead to a reduction, although strictly speaking if the policy is effective what is reduced is *misinformation*. If a claim made by a seller about a product can be shown to be false, then it is clearly desirable to prevent the dissemination of the claim. Consumers would benefit and make better informed choices without the claim than with it. Unfortunately, as many dissatisfied consumers can testify, for most products it is practically impossible to prove *for certain* that a claim made for a product is untrue. The best that can be done in most cases is to show that there is a greater or smaller probability that the claim is false. Whether the product has performed according to the reasonable expectations set up by the claim has usually depended on the courts. Despite the venerable case (known to all law students) of *Carlill* v *Carbolic Smoke Ball Co.* heard by the Court of Appeal in 1892,[12] which ended with the manufacturer having to pay the customer who had acted in good faith on the extravagant claims made for the defendant's influenza treatment, many cases still arise where consumers have apparently made bad choices based on false claims. Although legal precedents may help to ensure that sellers' claims are toned down, the consumer's position might be considerably strengthened if product tests were carried out by a government funded agency. Like many other aspects of information, product test results have the characteristic of a public good. The costs of testing are incurred only once but the results can be used repeatedly by consumers when choosing their purchases. It is important to note, however, that although such testing would provide valuable and objective information to set beside a manufacturer's claims for the performance of his products, the issue is still a complicated one. Since the absolute truth of a claim cannot be established it is necessary to decide what level of probability that a claim is true should be acceptable. In most cases increasing probabilities (one way or the other) will require more and more subtle and costly testing procedures and clearly there will be a point where the marginal benefits to consumers to be derived from increased confidence in purchasing will be outweighed by the marginal costs of ever finer testing. The probable benefits (and costs) from increased testing are likely to vary considerably from product to product. For example they will probably be greater in the case of complex, infrequently purchased products where claims cannot be verified prior to purchase than in the case of frequently purchased products which a consumer's own trials can effectively test. Consequently it is not possible to lay down in advance precise criteria for what constitutes an 'acceptable' performance claim by a manufacturer. For some products, because of the relative benefits and cost of testing, a probability of, say, 0.6 that a claim is true may be acceptable. In other cases a probability of 0.8 or more may be required.[13]

Despite the complexities there may nevertheless be a good case for centralized funding of testing agencies in order to provide a check on the validity of producers' claims with the further possibility of injunction if they are found to be unsupported. Not only would the information produced have the public good characteristics already referred to but it would avoid an important side-effect. If producers themselves had to bear directly the costs of testing particular attributes featured in their marketing campaign and which may subsequently be challenged, they are likely either to reduce significantly the claims made for their products, or shift the emphasis onto other, perhaps less important attributes.[14] In either case consumers will have less information than previously on which to base their purchases.

IV CONCLUSION

The central importance in much neoclassical theory of assuming perfect information is only really appreciated once market behaviour is examined without the assumption. A Pandora's box of market failures is opened up that raises many issues for regulatory policy. The nature of information makes it extremely difficult to establish well defined property rights and as a result it is likely to be under-supplied. On the other hand it can usually be disseminated at next to no cost and therefore raises well-known problems associated with natural monopoly, as well as setting up the presumption that it should be distributed amongst as many people as possible. Neither the caution of utility-maximizing consumers nor the self-regard of competitive producers jealous of their long-run reputation can therefore be expected to generate the optimal amount of trade in information. However, the issue is so complex that it is not possible to determine *a priori* whether too much information or too little will be produced.

Not surprisingly the problems surrounding information itself also set up a related series of difficulties in the associated product markets. An asymmetric distribution of information may affect both consumers and producers. For consumers, awareness of the dangers of buying a 'lemon' may constrict trade to below the optimal level, while for producers, anxiety to promote high-quality products by offering generous service terms, may invite careless or irresponsible consumer behaviour and eventually have the same result.

In principle the problems arising from information failure should be amenable to an information remedy. Thus abolition of the constraints on the supply of information by producers attempting jointly to maintain their market power might be expected to improve consumer choices. Measures to persuade or oblige suppliers to increase the amount of information about their products, although more complex to implement than might at first be thought, should also allow more discernment. On the negative side false or misleading claims can be made unprofitable for producers if it is clear that they will be subjected to government-financed scientific testing, and possibly then challenged by a body like the Office of Fair Trading.

On the whole, therefore, the theoretical analysis suggests that for many products the more efficient policy will be one that improves the quality and quantity of information in the market, compared with one that lays down product standards or conditions of sale. However there are some very important exceptions which we discuss more fully in chapter 5.

5

Regulating Consumer Markets

Advertisers for a number of food manufacturers have recently used as the theme of their campaign the idea that their products have all the wholesomeness, simplicity yet nutritional value of those of a former era, before factory farming and chemical additives. The advertisements, skilfully shot as though in a slight haze, often feature horse-drawn ploughs, rustic kitchens and rosy-cheeked children. Having done their market research, the advertisers are presumably responding to the frequent complaint by consumers that modern food is bland, homogenized and, above all, does not taste as it used to.

For anyone familiar with the law relating to the adulteration of food, such advertisements are especially ironic. Some of the first modern legislation dealing with consumer product standards was concerned with food and medicines, and was the result of the widespread use of alarming, pre-chemical additives: 'The addition of water to milk and beer was commonplace. Exhausted tea leaves were added to fresh tea, the exhausted leaves being glazed with black lead. Coffee had roast vegetable material, such as acorns, added to it. Bread was bulked up by inclusion of mashed potato and alum was added to bleach. Mustard was adulterated by the addition of wheat flour, pea flour and much else. Sand was added to sugar' (Smith and Swann, 1979, p. 101). As the authors conclude, these are just a few examples from among the many that could have been mentioned and they date from the 1860s and 1870s, the apparent golden age conjured for us by the advertising agents.

Since the original Adulteration of Food and Drink Act of 1860 there has been a continuous stream of legislation, growing into a flood in the last twenty years or so, both in the UK and the USA, aimed at protecting the consumer from the potentially dangerous product, the unscrupulous seller, or the consumer's own folly. Although there may be widespread agreement on the need for regulation of dangerous products and in some respects of unscrupulous sellers, there is much less agreement on the third category. Compulsory wearing of safety belts in cars is probably the best known example of a controversial regulation that seeks to protect consumers from folly. Opponents saw it as an unnecessary infringement on their personal freedom and could point to the different approach employed to regulate the use of another potentially lethal product, tobacco. In this case regulation takes the form of information about the dangers of smoking, but leaves the final decision up to the individual consumer. On the other hand, failure to wear a seat belt when travelling in the front of a car in the UK is now an offence punishable by fine. Critics of this and other cases that we mention below also argue that in some respects the urge to regulate has gone too far. Either the wrong *form* of regulation has been introduced, as in the seat belt example, or regulations now exist that in a more robust age would have been left to individual decisions (e.g. ingredient specifications in certain products: in the US products labelled 'beef with gravy' must contain at least 50 per cent cooked beef, whereas 'gravy with beef' requires only 35 per cent cooked beef (Weidenbaum, 1981)).

The distinction made previously between regulating information flows as opposed to regulating standards or behaviour directly, is maintained in our discussion in the present chapter of regulatory practice. It is tempting to suggest that where the potential physical dangers to consumers from products were greatest (medicines, food, complex electrical products) regulation has taken the form of standard setting, whereas for market failures with less dramatic possible outcomes, regulation has been largely through increased information. The distinction can, by and large, be made for the earlier legislation. More recently, however, the position has been much less clear-cut and it can be argued that some regulation of standards produces an inferior result compared with that for improved information requirements. The analysis of chapter 4 can therefore be used to assess the relative efficiency of the different kinds of regulation now in use. A major contribution of that analysis is the way it emphasizes the *indirect* as well as the immediate and direct effects of regulation. Thus if certain inputs into a product are restricted in the interests of raising quality, this may not only deny (low-income) consumers lower-quality products but also change production methods and alter relative input prices. In this way it forces recognition of the fact that regulation not only generates the direct benefits but simultaneously sets up a chain reaction of increased costs.

The subsequent discussion of this chapter is arranged as follows. In section II we outline consumer regulation by setting standards of one kind or another. The scope of these regulations is now very wide and we shall therefore confine our remarks to the main areas affected. In section III we consider the provisions for regulating the quantity and quality of information to consumers, including those dealing with deception and fraud. This is followed in section IV by a brief summary of the powers of the Director General of Fair Trading in the field of consumer protection.

II REGULATION BY SETTING STANDARDS

In the UK the state first assumed responsibility for protecting consumers from the injury that could follow from consumption of impure or debased food and drink in the latter part of the nineteenth century. Alerted by the press and by coverage in medical journals to the dangers, governments passed a series of Acts in the period 1860–75 that established a framework of regulation and that much subsequent legislation has developed and extended. The relevant current legislation is the Food and Drug Act (1955) and the Medicines Act (1968). The former makes it an offence to sell for human consumption food that is injurious to health. The provisions of the Act cover both additives (of the kind illustrated in the introduction to this chapter) and adulteration where products are supplied with smaller proportions of essential ingredients. Ministers were empowered to make regulations governing standards for particular products and machinery at local government level was established to ensure that the provisions of the Act were carried out. Local trading standards officers monitor the composition of food products and local public health officials test the hygiene of food premises. They have comprehensive powers to enter shops, depots and plants, to take samples of products and to have them analysed. All local authorities are required to appoint analysts. Prosecution may follow in the courts and substantial fines and/or imprisonment can result for proven offenders. Before a regulation under the Act is laid before Parliament, the Minister will have had a detailed report from the independent Food Standards Committee (established in 1947) and received comments on it from the public and any interested parties. Writing in 1979, Smith and Swann recorded that regulations had been made concerning the composition of ice cream, cheese, sausages, meat pies, sausage rolls, fish paste and jams.

The regulation of drugs under the 1968 Medicines Act is, if anything, even more severe than for food and drink. All new drugs have to be licensed by the Medicines Division of the Department of Health and Social Security (DHSS) which in turn is advised by a Medicines Commission. In the wake of the thalidomide disaster, what had been voluntary collaboration between the Commission and the drug industry was changed into an obligation to carry out pre-market tests under certification from the DHSS for all new drugs and to convince the Commission[1] of their effectiveness, and above all, safety. Only if the Commission is satisfied is a marketing licence granted. In effect the decisions of the Commission have the authority of a licensing law (Smith and Swann, 1979).

Controls over food, drink and drugs not only have the longest history but in many ways are the most fundamental and illustrate many of the central issues of regulation. It is useful at this point, therefore, to consider how the analysis of the previous chapter can be applied to this area of regulation. There are strong economic arguments for monitoring closely the hygienic conditions under which food and drink are produced and sold, as well as their fitness for human consumption. A high standard of health in society is frequently given as a prime example of a public good. Left alone unregulated markets are unlikely to deliver such high standards of public health because the benefits (of lower risks of infection) will accrue to everyone, regardless of whether or not they happen to participate in the markets concerned. For producers in an unregulated market therefore, there is less incentive for them to maintain standards of hygiene and product purity than is economically desirable.[2] The public good argument alone may be regarded as sufficient reason for the public provision of the means to monitor and maintain standards. However there are other, purely economic reasons for which the self-interest of firms in their long-run reputation and the self-preservation instincts of consumers are inadequate to cope with the problem. Clearly some firms, even in the absence of regulation, would seek to maintain standards but as the evidence of the pre-regulation days indicates many others would not. Preserving high standards almost certainly raises costs, at least in the short-run, and in an unregulated environment firms pursuing this objective would be at a competitive disadvantage *vis-à-vis* their less scrupulous rivals. Although it might be argued that in the long-run firms with high standards would eliminate their rivals or force them to change, where it is difficult for consumers to judge in advance the cleanliness of manufacturing and selling establishments and the purity of products, not only might the 'long-run' amount to a very long while indeed, but for some consumers it may be too late. (Even with the kinds of regulation we have described above successful prosecutions take place every year. So regulation does not eliminate the problem altogether, but significantly reduce it.)

Again, in the absence of regulation, some consumers would undertake their own investigations, and even pay to have products scientifically tested before using them. The incentive they might then have to publicize the results of the tests would allow others to 'free ride' at their expense. However, as we argued in the previous chapter, there are clearly large resource savings to be made if such testing and monitoring is centralized and carried out by specialists,[3] rather than the tests being made repeatedly for the same products for different consumers.

On the whole, therefore, a majority of economists (in common with a majority of the population) favour the kind of regulation of standards for these products that applies in the UK, the US and most Western European countries. There is room for disagreement on detail but not on general principle.

The reader may wonder in this case why there should be any debate on the matter, as most people are convinced of the case for regulation where such basic considerations as consumer health and safety are concerned. The reason is that there is an influential minority who, although not going so far as to recommend the abolition of regulations, do contend that the controls may be too severe and have consequences not necessarily foreseen when they were introduced. In the case of drugs, for example, it has been argued, especially in the US, where regulation is administered by the Food and Drug Administration (FDA), that the delays involved in the regulation process have had two harmful effects. First, drugs that are successful in curing or alleviating illness become available later than they otherwise would, and in the meantime some patients have died or endured severe pain that the drugs would have cured. Secondly, the certification process (including the delays) raises the costs of developing and marketing new products and as a result fewer new drugs are introduced. The criticisms were especially strong in the wake of accumulating evidence following an amendment to the US drug regulations in 1962. The amendment raised the hurdles that new drugs had to clear before they could be introduced. However, the fact that it was only passed after the thalidomide disaster serves to illustrate the complexity of the issue. Because American controls even prior to 1962 were more stringent than in some European countries (including the UK) this meant that the number of pregnant women who took the tranquillizer thalidomide[4] was very small, since the drug was used only for research purposes and had not been given clearance by the FDA. Supporters of strong regulatory controls could thus claim that Americans had been largely protected from the tragedy that some Europeans had had to endure. On the other hand the more stringent controls did appear to cause a dramatic slowing down in the rate of certification of new drugs.[5] There is clearly an awful dilemma facing any body charged with controlling the introduction of new drugs: will the benefits from increased certainty about new drug's safety that results from more stringent pre-market clinical tests outweigh the detriments in the form of patient suffering and possible death that follows from the delays involved in obtaining clearance? In some cases, adverse effects of drugs may not show themselves for months or even years after they have been taken so there can be no definitive time period laid down for the trials of new drugs. The regulatory bodies both in the UK and the US are under strong pressure from the pharmaceutical industry to streamline the certification procedure and thus shorten the time-lag between discovery and widespread use, which in

America can now be up to a decade.[6] While most observers accept the need for making the procedure as efficient as possible, they would not want any relaxation of standards and argue for a greater concentration on monitoring the post-introduction performance of new drugs, provisions for which were included in the 1968 Medicines Act in the UK.

As far as food and drink are concerned, while there is broad agreement on the need to regulate basic purity and hygiene standards (at least partially on the economic grounds given above) there is much more controversy over extending controls into product composition. Critics argue that it is one thing to ensure that ingredients are fit for human consumption, but it is quite another to specify that, say, sausages, jam or ice cream have to contain certain amounts of particular ingredients, and yet this is precisely what the Food Standards Committee in the UK may be asked to decide. If sausages *have* to contain a given percentage of meat before they qualify to be called sausages, this may mean that consumers who actually prefer low-meat-content sausages or who cannot afford the higher quality may have their choice reduced as a result of regulation. By their regulatory endeavours some bodies (such as the Food Standards Committee) may inadvertently be led to establish standards that reflect their own preferences rather than ensure that the public is protected from contaminated or unhygienic products. Opponents of such extensions of regulation therefore argue that as long as basic standards are maintained and in addition the final products' composition is clearly stated on the package, then *caveat emptor* should take over, as this will allow the maximum choice to consumers and also cause the minimum distortion in production methods. While it may be comparatively easy to define adulteration of basic commodities like tea, coffee, sugar and milk, problems abound when this concept is carried over into more complex products made from a variety of ingredients in different proportions. A much larger element of subjective judgement rather than objective scientific evidence is then likely to be involved.

Although this section is primarily concerned with standard setting it is convenient to note at this point the role played by the Food Standards Committee in improving the information available to consumers through date-marking. Leading food retailers had already begun to use such a system for products with a relatively short shelf-life by the time the Committee reported in 1971 and 1972. It recommended that from 1975 food to be consumed within at most three months should bear a 'sell-by' date on a prominent part of the label, for the benefit both of the retailer and the final consumer. It is not illegal to sell food after the stated date but if the food is unfit for human consumption then the provisions of the Food and Drugs Act apply (Smith and Swann, 1979).

The most immediate dangers to consumer well being may come from contaminated food or unsuitable drugs but consumer safety may also be imperilled by defective electrical and mechanical products or inflammable clothing. Indeed the Moloney Committee on Consumer Protection was so alarmed by the hazards that were involved that it issued an interim report, out of which came the 1961 Consumer Protection Act. Part of the concern of the Committee arose from the delays in dealing by statute with the recognized shortcomings of a wide variety of products. The Act therefore empowered the Minister for Consumer Protection to regulate the sale of products that could cause injury or even death, by the much speedier procedure of Statutory Instrument. Under this provision regulations were made about cooking untensils, oil heaters, fireguards, electrical wiring colour codes, carrycot stand safety, paint on toys and flame resistance of children's nightwear and toys (Smith and Swann, 1979, p. 127). Amending legislation in 1971 made it a criminal offence for a trader to sell goods that do not comply with standards established by the Minister. Regulation in this area has been further strengthened by the Consumer Safety Act (1978) which provides a streamlined procedure for banning the sale of dangerous products, allows the Minister to require distributors of dangerous goods to publish warnings about the possible dangers involved and obliges Local Authorities to enforce the standards established under the Act.[7]

A similar development in the US has been the creation of the Consumer Product Safety Commission (CPSC) in 1972 with the primary purpose of protecting 'the public against unreasonable risks of injury associated with consumer products.' The Commission not only monitors a vast amount of information on potentially hazardous products but carries out its own detailed analysis of how products might be improved so as to reduce risks. It claims a major success, for example, in eliminating injury or even death to young children by establishing, after painstaking research, the optimal width of slats in the sides of cots. Apparently by establishing the standard that the width should be no more than six centimetres, 95 per cent of all infants could be protected from accidental strangulation. On the other hand attempts to lay down standards for ladders 'consumed tens of thousands of man hours; reams of paper, and hundreds of thousands of dollars belonging to both industry and government' (Greer, 1983, p. 441).

On the whole the standards established to protect the consumer from injury relate to products where the danger is not directly apparent. Thus standards are not required for a whole range of everyday household utensils and tools (e.g. knives, forks, screwdrivers and saws) where the dangers from careless use are readily seen. On the other hand the dangers to a child from sucking toys coated with lead-based paint or from oil heaters posing a high fire risk even when used normally are not evident unless the product is subjected to the kind of testing that consumers do not usually expect to carry out. In such cases there is thus a strong probability that the benefits to consumers from reduced risk of injury more than outweigh the detriments to producers and distributors in the form of increased costs that the compulsory standards impose (although it may be extremely difficult to demonstrate this empirically).[8]

In view of their increased importance in the national economy it is not surprising that regulations concerned with maintaining or improving standards in consumer *services* have been growing very rapidly. A large number of statues now regulate the qualifications of persons in particular occupations, license firms providing specified services and establish rules for the methods to be used in supplying certain services. Smith and Swann give a lengthy (although merely illustrative) list of occupations where qualifications are now regulated: architects (under Acts of 1931 and 1938); dentists (1957); doctors (1956 and 1969); opticians (1958); other medical practitioners (such as chiropodists, dieticians and physiotherapists; 1960); solicitors (1933, 1949, 1958 and 1974) and insurance brokers (1977). The usual procedure is for a Registration Council to be set up under the relevant Act which then ensures that all practitioners have passed the specified examinations and have the requisite amount of experience. It is usually then an offence for an unregistered person to use the titles of the profession and attempt to practise within it.

The main purpose of the legislation is ostensibly to ensure that the standard of competence of practitioners is maintained at the appropriate level.[9] At least this is its original purpose but whether ultimately that is its main effect has been challenged. For example, we have referred previously[10] to Friedman's point that if *maintaining* competence was the main objective, then practitioners should be subject to periodic re-examination. There is no provision for this in the legislation and, as far as we are aware, no professional association has insisted on its introduction. While ensuring, therefore, that newcomers to a profession have initially reached a certain level of competence, regulation also serves to restrict the number of entrants. Naturally members of the regulatory councils appointed under the various acts tend to be drawn from senior practitioners. The danger is therefore that Council members can approve a tightening of entry standards in order to preserve or increase the incomes of existing practitioners. The law may thus serve to underpin the restrictive tendencies of a professional association. In one of the original studies of the effects of regulation in the US, for example, Stigler found, with admittedly imperfect data, that licensed occupations maintained higher incomes than unlicensed occupations (Stigler, 1975). In its general report on the effect of restrictive practices maintained in the supply of professional services the Monopolies Commission (MMC, 1970b) recognized the danger and concluded: 'We think that it is against the public interest that the unqualified should be barred from offering a service except where the service involves risk of a specially serious kind and degree to clients who are unable to assess the danger of using the services of unqualified practitioners, or to the interest of third parties' (paragraph 310).

One of the most interesting and controversial cases concerns the supply of optical services: interesting because it raises a number of important issues concerning the indirect and possibly unforeseen effects of regulation; controversial because moves to end the restrictive policies of the Association of Optical Practitioners, following a report from the Office of Fair Trading (OFT) have met, not surprisingly, with stiff resistance from the industry. The Opticians Act of 1958 provided for the creation of the General Optical Council which became the regulatory body for the industry. Attention has focused on the joint effects of, first, the statutory monopoly conferred by section 21 of the Act on registered medical practitioners and registered opticians and, second, the rules on publicity for the sale of spectacles made by the General Optical Council under section 25 of the Act. At this stage we will consider mainly the first restriction, reserving until later in this section comments on restrictions on advertising, although it is clear in the OFT report that the two restrictions interact to affect the performance of firms in the industry. What prompted the OFT enquiry[11] was not only complaints from the public that the price of spectacles was too high but also two reports by the Price Commission. The first, on the prices of private spectacles and contact lenses, concluded that 'it is quite clear that dispensing private spectacles is a very profitable activity' (Price Commission, 1976). The second was the prices and margins of the leading firm in the industry, Dollond and Aitchison, which had earned very high profits on its optical operations (Price Commission, 1979).

As a result of its enquiries the OFT considered that the effect of section 21 was clearly to keep unregistered sellers from the market, and that if the rules were revised a number would begin to sell ready-glazed spectacles. They estimated that the market share gained by unregistered sellers might amount to between three and five per cent (which in 1981 would have represented 250–400 thousand pairs of spectacles). However, since they also considered that the new entrants would be able to supply at prices below those of opticians and 'in some cases, significantly below' (para. 14.7) the estimate might be unduly modest. The case is particularly interesting because most of the arguments for restricting entry to an industry supplying professional services are set out in report but in fact are resisted in the final conclusions. Also, although the report does not mention the criterion for assessing the public interest in such cases suggested by the Monopolies and Mergers Commission (MMC) and indeed under the terms of reference was precluded from considering whether the restriction operated against the public interest, the OFT seems, implicitly at least, to have used it in arriving at their conclusions. They decided that 'there was almost unanimous agreement among those who gave evidence to us that inaccurate spectacles could not cause permanent damage to the eyes but there exists the possibility of minor discomfort. Such discomfort could be eliminated by removing the spectacles and the problem resolved by the substitution of a more satisfactory pair. No evidence was presented during the review to support the proposition that inaccurate spectacles from self-prescribing could lead to additional accidents' (OFT, 1982, p. 159). Because of the terms of reference the Director General did not consider it appropriate to make recommendations but it is clear that he considered that a widened consumer choice and lower prices would follow from de-regulating the service (subject to safeguards in the provision of spectacles for children).

Exactly two years after the report was published, it became legal for ordinary retailers to supply spectacles to customers over sixteen, as long as they had a prescription signed by a doctor or ophthalmic optician (December 1984).[12] The expectations of lower prices seem from the preliminary evidence to have been borne out. It is thus probably correct to conclude that regulations having as their prime purpose protection to the consumer from injury actually did more to protect the incomes of qualified opticians.

The regulations that we have discussed so far have been largely concerned with protecting the consumer from physical injury (from debased or contaminated food and defective or dangerous products). More controversial has been the extension of regulations governing all aspects of the provision of credit to consumers. With only slight exaggeration we can perhaps think of this as protecting the consumer from the psychological injury suffered at the hands of unscrupulous salesmen or loan sharks. One reason for which this development is more contentious than other measures is precisely that the consumer may suffer only financial hardship or loss rather than physical injury. It is difficult, for example, to extend the MMC criterion of the public interest to such cases where no physical danger is involved. Some may therefore be much more inclined to argue in favour of the *caveat emptor* doctrine for such cases rather than rely on standard setting through an elaborate system of licensing.

The whole system of credit provision for consumers which had expanded very rapidly in the 1950s and 1960s suffered a severe jolt in the UK in the early 1970s when several secondary banks collapsed. Reform of the law, anticipated with the appointment of the Crowther Committee in 1968, thus became inevitable. The resulting Consumer Credit Act (1974) was a comprehensive attempt to regulate the intricate and varied institutions and arrangements that had developed, particularly during the postwar consumer boom. In the present context we will focus on a central feature of the Act: the Licensing and Control procedure for all regular providers of consumer credit.[13] Under the Act the Director General of Fair Trading[14] is given the power to license all firms and institutions that provide consumer credit on a regular basis, and it is now a criminal offence to continue to make credit contracts without a licence. In itself, a licensing procedure will be ineffective unless the licensing authority has sanctions against those infringing the law. The Act places the onus of ensuring compliance upon the Director General who is given very wide discretion in the granting of licences and, more to the point, can revoke a licence if he considers that the individual or institution is no longer fit to trade. The threat of withdrawal of a licence therefore acts as a very strong incentive to comply with the law. Prior to the 1974 Act the worst that could befall an unscrupulous trader in this area was a private lawsuit brought by an individual aggrieved consumer. Although the trader might lose the case and receive a certain amount of adverse publicity there were no further sanctions, and little to make him mend his ways. The withdrawal of a licence and the loss of livelihood that this would entail is clearly a much stricter sanction.

How does the Consumer Credit Act actually seek to protect the consumers interest in credit transactions? The Act is extremely complex and covers a great deal of ground, as it attempts to carry out the wholesale reform of consumer credit trading recommended by the Crowther Committee. Our comments will be confined to some of the major provisions. In two ways the Act directly extends consumer rights in contracts involving credit. The first aims to protect those vulnerable to the blandishments of the doorstep salesman by allowing a 'cooling-off' period of five days (after receiving the statutory second copy of the contract) during which the consumer may withdraw and also recover any preliminary payments made. The provision thus amounts to an exception to the general rule that contracts once made cannot be unmade (although strictly speaking no agreement has been completed). Secondly, in hire purchase agreements the Act gives greater protection to consumers than previous regulations allowed. In a hire purchase agreement title to the goods does not pass to the debtor until all payments have been made. Before the 1974 Act it was possible for creditors to reclaim goods if the debtor defaulted on payments, even though a major part of the total debt had been paid. The Act makes it much more difficult for the creditor to repossess goods (e.g. where the debtor has paid one-third or more of the total price, repossession can only be made after a court order has been issued and entry by a creditor into the debtor's premises can only be made with the latter's consent or with a court order).

The Director General of Fair Trading in collaboration with local

Consumer Protection or Trading Standards Officers has the responsibility of ensuring that these provisions are carried out. If he is not satisfied with the conduct of traders he may, as we have seen, withdraw their licence. He also has the duty to monitor other major sections of the Act that are concerned with increasing the *information* available to consumers about the exact terms and conditions of contracts involving credit. Although information provisions are strictly speaking the subject of the next section, in this case the two aspects of the policy (standard setting and information provision) are so inextricably mixed that is better to deal briefly with them both at this stage.[15] Failure to comply with the information requirements may again, for example, be grounds for withdrawal of a licence as well as rendering any agreement unenforceable unless a court order can be obtained. Thus while the licensing procedure is designed to help maintain standards in the provision of consumer credit, an important part of the assessment of whether satisfactory standards are being maintained is by monitoring the information provided by traders.

The 1974 Act incorporated and extended provisions of earlier legislation dealing with hire purchase agreements.[16] Consumers now have to be provided, prior to signing the agreement, with information on the cash price of the good as well as the hire purchase price and the true rate of interest to be charged (calculated according to a formula laid down in the Act). The last provision was seen by many as especially important since it was thought that consumers had often been deceived in the past by interest rates calculated on the basis of the purchase price rather than rates adjusted in line with the declining amount of the outstanding balance. Research from the US also indicated that about two-thirds of consumers had little or no idea of the annual percentage rate of interest paid in hire purchase agreements. They were often confronted with a bewildering range of methods of calculating interest rates which made comparisons of costs between different suppliers of credit extremely difficult. Since 1969 the so-called 'Truth-in-Lending' Law in the US has required disclosure by providers of consumer credit of both the total amount paid to obtain the credit and the annual percentage rate of interest. Comparisons between credit sources are thus much easier to make.

Another provision of the 1974 Act is likely to be of considerable importance in the future, as more and more firms make use of computerized credit ratings of consumers. Negotiations for a hire purchase contract may be abruptly halted if the creditor receives information from a firm specializing in making credit ratings that the consumer is a bad risk. Before the 1974 Act there was little a consumer could do to rectify this impression because he or she could not get access to the information supplied by the firm. Mistaken or out of date information was thus likely to remain and the consumer be condemned to a credit-less existence. In the

US, consumers can gain access to the information on which their credit rating is based under the powerful Freedom of Information Act. In the UK consumers now have a similar right as a result of the Consumer Credit Act. Thus consumers may apply to the creditor company, after negotiations have ended, for details of any firm consulted about their credit rating. Failure to comply with this request is a criminal offence. The credit rating firm must similarly furnish the consumer (on payment of a nominal fee) with any information supplied about their credit-worthiness, a duty also backed by a criminal sanction. Finally if the credit rating firm refuses to amend any information considered incorrect by the consumer, the matter is referred to the Director General of Fair Trading who has the power to authorize whatever remedy he feels is appropriate.

All of these measures may be interpreted as attempts to restore the balance of power between consumers and producers or suppliers which many see as having been upset by the growing concentration of industry. It can also be argued that, in any case, markets operate more efficiently when information central to trading relations (especially on prices) is readily available. Consumers can make more efficient decisions if, for example, the real price at which credit is offered by different firms is uniformly published. Those firms concerned about their long-run reputation in the industry may provide clear information on the real costs of credit, even without the threat of legal sanction, but the experience prior to the 1974 Act[17] suggested that there were others for whom the incentive was not strong. In the absence of legislation therefore it may have taken an extremely long time before annual percentage rates were given as a matter of course in the industry and in the meantime many consumers would have paid more for credit than was necessary. The fact that some recent research into consumer behaviour suggests that many consider the amount of monthly or weekly repayments as paramount, rather than the real rate of interest, underlines the point rather than refutes it: there may be a considerable lag in consumers adjusting their behaviour to improved information in the market. The legal requirement may therefore help to speed up the process making for more efficient consumer decisions.

There is clearly an important qualitative difference between measures designed to protect consumers from injury or disease discussed earlier in the chapter, and those that allow consumers to avoid being overcharged for their terms of credit. The difference is reflected largely in the method of regulation used in each case: control of product quality compared with monitoring the conduct of firms (part of which includes conformity with legal information requirements). The element of paternalism is stronger in the latter case, where it could be argued that consumers should be prepared to decide for themselves which firm gives the best credit terms, or that consumers who default on a hire purchase contract have only themselves to blame and should not be given the special protection of the law. On the other hand Smith and Swann contend that it is a legitimate aspect of consumer protection to assist the vulnerable, those on low incomes and even those who may not be entirely without fault.

III INFORMATION PROVISIONS

In our discussion in chapter 4 of information and consumer protection we concluded that there were likely to be many instances where increasing the flow of accurate information into a market would not only improve the efficiency of decisions made, but also give a superior outcome compared with a regulatory standard. We have already suggested that the requirement to give uniform information about the cost of credit should lead to more efficient trading in this market. An alternative policy of specifying rates that must be charged or not exceeded would be likely to make the market very inflexible and also pose severe problems for monitoring firms' performance. In general, therefore, information remedies can be used as supplements to or substitutes for standard setting in a variety of instances affecting different industries.

Under the auspices of the Food and Drug Act (1955), for example, the Food Standards Committee has made regulations for the labelling of many pre-packed foods. They must contain a list of ingredients, a description of the food enclosed and the name and address of the food packer. Similarly under the Weights and Measures Act (1963, amended 1976) certain specified foodstuffs, fuels and some other goods must have labelling that discloses the quantity. It is also possible under this act to specify the precise measures that *have* to be used in selling certain products (e.g. alcohol in public houses).

Although this information can help the discerning consumer to choose between products (if say the ingredients of one brand are preferred to those of another) an efficient choice may still be hindered by the complexity of weights and packaging employed by different producers. Classifications such as 'economy', 'jumbo', 'family' and 'extra large' may assist the producers' marketing effort but do little to help the consumer decide which gives the best value for money, especially if one brand is given in grams while another is in pounds and ounces (including fractions). One response is that skilful shoppers (with a calculator) can easily verify which pack gives the best bargain. In fact during the discussion in the US of the proposed Fair Packaging and Labelling Act (1966) which aimed to introduce some standardization, commercial opposition was cast in precisely these terms.[18] Eventually it was passed in a somewhat diluted form. Under the Act net quantities have to be stated in a suitable unit of measurement, in a uniform and prominent position on the packet and if 'servings' are mentioned the net quantity of a 'serving' must also be stated. The Act did not, however, include a provision for 'unit pricing' that many consumer groups in different countries regard as a major aid to efficient shopping. By specifying the quantity of a product in pence per gram or per 100, for example, unit pricing makes inter-brand comparisons relatively easy, but only Germany and Switzerland have introduced the system on an extensive basis. In 1982 eleven states in America had adopted unit price regulations while in the UK it has been applied (under the Weights and Measures legislation) to products such as meats, fish, cheeses, fruit and vegetables although the intention is gradually to extend the list. In this respect too, those stores jealous of their reputation for high standards have introduced unit pricing on a wide range of products, and since they tend also to be commercially successful it can be argued that there is no need for formal regulation since market forces bring about the change in any case. However, if the regulation speeds up the process the benefits to consumers will be derived sooner. It is true that the costs (of calculating the unit price and then displaying it on the packaging) are shifted from consumer to producers, but since the calculation only has to be performed once, rather than hundreds or thousands of times by individual consumers, and because the incremental packaging costs are minute, the net welfare effect of such a regulation is very likely to be positive (even when incremental enforcement costs are included in the assessment). The only adjustment forced on (some) producers will be a minor change in the labelling of their products which for the more efficient will, in any case, probably lead to increased sales.

The most controversial aspect of information in consumer markets concerns advertising. The fiercest opponents of much modern advertising would probably deny this on the ground that it contained no genuine information at all but simply attempted to bamboozle, flatter or persuade reluctant consumers into buying brands or products that they do not really want. Apart from the simplest classified advertisement stating price and major characteristics of a standard product, there is probably a greater or lesser degree of attempted persuasion in all advertisements intertwined with useful information. In view of this it may come as a surprise to many readers that for the UK at least 'there is relatively little formal control of the form or content of advertising' (Smith and Swann 1979, p. 144). Apart from some important exceptions which we shall mention shortly, regulation of the advertising industry is self-imposed and administered by the Advertising Standards Authority. The Authority was established in 1962 by the Advertising Association (the trade association of the advertising industry) for the purpose of monitoring the industry's voluntary code of practice. Perhaps sensing increased pressure for more government-sponsored regulation, the Association has in recent years been running its own expensive advertising campaign to inform the public about the code of practice and inviting them to write to the Authority if they have been affronted by any advertising. Since the number of complaints sent to the Authority has also recently risen sharply we may assume either that advertising about advertising is successful or, perhaps less plausibly, that there has been a deterioration in its quality.

The Association has made the keynote of its campaign that all advertisements should be 'legal, decent, honest and truthful' and conform to normal standards of competitive behaviour. It is quite acceptable to make comparisons with other products, as long as they are fair and not designed to mislead or simply denigrate competitor's products. The Association argues that the voluntary regulation allows them to maintain high professional standards in advertising, even in areas involving public decency and taste which may be particularly difficult for the law to handle in a satisfactory fashion.

Although it is doubtful whether a formal code of practice laid down, say, by the OFT, would differ very profoundly from that of the Association what would differ would be the sanctions available if an advertisement infringed the code. At present all sanctions are administered by the advertising industry itself and some may feel that this is inadequate for such an important subject. However, the Authority can ask for any advertisement failing to meet the code of practice to be withdrawn. Persistent refusal to comply with their requests may eventually lead to newspapers and magazines declining to carry their advertisements. In addition the Authority would itself buy advertising space to publicize its findings. On the whole, therefore, few firms are likely to stand out against such pressure, even though it does not have the backing of the law.

More restrictions are imposed on perhaps the most effective advertising medium, television. The best known example is the complete ban on cigarette advertising on television. More generally the governing body of the commercial television channels, the Independent Broadcasting Authority (IBA), has overall responsibility not only for programmes but also for advertising and the criteria it uses to maintain advertising standards are subject to the scrutiny of Parliament.[19] In contrast with the control exercised by the Advertising Standards Authority, which at present carries out no pre-publication scrutiny of advertisements, the IBA has the power to reject scripts (of both programmes and advertisements) on grounds of unsuitability or ask for amendments. This provision is clearly a much more effective sanction than those of the Advertising Standards Authority, since the 'damage' created by a substandard advertisement may occur before the Authority is alerted and before it is withdrawn.

We have already noted in the previous section the information requirements under the Consumer Credit Act, particularly with regard to real rates of interest. The government also insists that all cigarette advertising should carry a health warning. Together with the comparatively minor provisions mentioned above, these broadly constitute the only requirements for *positive* information and firms thus retain a very wide discretion over the form and content of advertising of their products.

On the other hand, as we mentioned above, almost all advertising has been banned in the optical industry since 1958. Under the Opticians Act (1958) responsibility for the industry was given to the Optical Council and the rules of trading it laid down were so strict that only the most meagre information could be provided by registered opticians to their existing customers.[20] A major part of the OFT report was concerned with the effects of these restrictions and the conclusions were more than enough to warm the heart of any advertising agent. In fact they read like a litany of the adverse consequences that result from a denial of information to consumers in the market. Because consumers had inadequate knowledge to make an informed choice the report concludes that individual opticians were able to fix prices (there was evidence of different prices charged by different opticians for identical products) and had little incentive to reduce their costs. The rules also made it more difficult for new firms to enter the industry (reinforcing the licence requirement) as well as possibly acting as a deterrent to innovation. The central conclusion, therefore, was that the advertising restrictions resulted 'in prices being significantly higher and efficiency significantly lower than they would otherwise be' (OFT, 1982, p. 161).[21] Largely as a result of the report and parliamentary pressure, the severity of the rules has recently been modified (cf. p. 61 above).

The analysis of the effects of severely restricting advertising in an industry may, however, have a wider importance than is at first apparent. In the past advertising has received a great deal of adverse comment[22] and its potentially favourable effects have been underplayed. Given the official nature of the OFT's report and its almost unqualified support for freeing firms from restraints on their advertising, a precedent may be created for other regulated industries or professions.

There are, however, considerable legal impediments to the provision of false or deceptive information. The general stance of the law, created for example, by the Misrepresentation Act (1967), the Theft Act (1968) and especially, the Trade Descriptions Act (1968) is to prevent traders gaining from false statements. Criminal penalties can follow from a false description of a good or service made by a trader and prosecution under the Trade Descriptions Act is usually carried out by the local Consumer Protection or Trading Standards Officers. The definition of what constitutes a description is very widely drawn by the Act and can apply, for example, to quality and size; method of manufacture and composition;

fitness for the stated purpose; place or date of manufacture; and history, including previous use (Swann, 1979). The definition applies to both oral and written statements and thus affects misleading advertising.[23] The Act also contains very specific provisions with regard to misleading statements about prices. First, it is an offence for a trader to advertise a product at a price lower than the actual price. Thus, for example, if a poster on the window of a supermarket advertised a special offer for a branded washing powder, while in the shop all special-price packets had been sold and the usual price was being charged, this could constitute an offence. Secondly, false comparisons between a manufacturer's recommended price and the price actually offered constitute an offence. Thus if the good on offer differs as to quality or standard from the one whose recommended price is being displayed, an offence is committed. Finally, it is an offence falsely to convey the impression that prices are lower than they previously were. For example, in the past stores may have offered goods at 'special' or 'sale' prices apparently with huge discounts, when in fact they have been specifically purchased for the occasion and not previously sold at the higher price. Under the Act price discounts in this form can be offered as long as the trader has actually been selling the goods at a higher price for a continuous period of at least 28 days in the previous six months.

There is clearly room for considerable disagreement about the necessity for the price provisions of the Trade Descriptions Act. Adhering to the view that consumers are the best judge of their interest, it can be argued that it is entirely up to them whether or not an advertised price is regarded as offering a good deal. Given the other provisions already mentioned, which protect them from illness or injury, they might then be regarded as quite competent to judge the merits of a particular price, whether or not it is surrounded by dubious discount claims. More especially it may be argued that in this respect the enforcement costs (monitoring all and prosecuting the minority) may well outweigh the benefits derived by consumers from the removal of misleading claims. On the other hand consumers, bewildered by an array of special offers, discounts and spectacular bargains, a proportion of which are bogus, may tend to lose confidence in price competition and treat even genuine price reductions with scepticism – a variant, in other words, of the 'lemons' argument mentioned in chapter 4. To the extent that this holds it will make it easier and more attractive for sellers to compete in non-price ways. Consumers may thus tend to place more reliance on, for example, the quality and intensity of a firm's advertising campaign than on their products' prices.

Misleading or deceptive information in the provision of services has led to a number of problems. It is an offence to make a false or reckless statement about a wide range of characteristics of a service.[24] However whereas in the case of a false or deceptive description of *goods* or their prices there is strict liability, i.e. the prosecution does not have to prove that deception was deliberate on the part of the seller, the *fact* of the deception is sufficient, in the case of services it is apparently necessary to show that the false or reckless statement was made knowingly and deliberately by the seller. The position has been made somewhat ambiguous, however, by the subsequent decisions of the Courts which have generally given a narrow interpretation of what constitutes a false statement, while interpreting very widely evidence of *intent* on the part of a seller. Thus a number of important decisions under Section 14 of the Trade Descriptions Act have concerned travel and holiday accommodation where sellers publish in advance detailed brochures of what customers will receive. Where the customers' expectations have been dramatically disappointed, the Courts have had to decide whether statements in brochures about the future quality and characteristics of holiday accom- modation and other services amount to an infringement. Unfortunately for the consumer who has relied on promises of spacious accommodation, exotic food and a convenient swimming pool, the Courts have in effect determined that a forecast or promise of such facilities that is not borne out does *not* amount to an offence under the Act. Only where a false statement of *current* fact is made in a brochure will an action be successful.[25] In effect consumers have to rely on their own wariness induced by some widely publicized cases of half-finished and over-crowded hotels. However, in an important case concerning the well-known practice of over-booking by airlines who rely on subsequent cancellations to ensure that customers can be satisfied, the House of Lords decided that by *confirming* a seat reservation the airline was making a factual statement about the future availability of a seat. When it transpired that the seat was not available, it amounted to a false statement and the airline was liable under the Act.[26]

As far as establishing the intent of the seller, on the other hand, the Courts interpretation is so wide that it seems to be in danger of including the innocent as well as the unscrupulous. Instead of taking 'recklessness' to mean a statement made without regard to a risk of which the accused is aware, the Lord Chief Justice has stated that 'it suffices for present purposes if the prosecution can show that the advertiser did not have regard to the truth or falsity of his advertisement, even though it cannot be shown that he was deliberately closing his eyes to the truth, or that he had any kind of dishonest mind' (quoted in Smith and Swann, 1979, p. 160). In this respect, therefore, it is difficult to see the distinction between the strict liability set out in the Act for goods and the qualified liability (the need to show reckless or fraudulent intent) for services. There is thus much to be said for the conclusion of an OFT group reviewing the workings of the Trade Descriptions Act in 1976, which recommended that the two provisions of the Act should be made comparable.

Although we deal with the Consumers Protection Advisory Committee in section IV below, it is appropriate at this point to mention what effect it has had on deceptive practices. Soon after its establishment under the 1973 Fair Trading Act it was asked to investigate the practice by some traders of first displaying notices purporting to exclude or diminish consumers' rights under the Law that could not legally be so modified; and secondly of advertising items for sale without disclosing that they themselves were traders. The Committee agreed with the Director General of Fair Trading (DGFT) that both practices were intended to deceive consumers, in one case as to their legal rights and in the other as to who was making an offer of sale. Both practices were subsequently made the subject of prohibitive orders under the Act[27] and thus became criminal offences.

Preventing the supply in the first case of misinformation should in principle allow consumers to make more efficient decisions, in the sense that they may be more inclined to pursue a complaint arising out of a faulty product if they believe that they have a legal claim. On the other hand in practice it might be argued that reputable dealers would not display misleading notices in the first place, while the less reputable may still rely on false statements to deter a consumer from pursuing a claim. Consumers who would be deterred by a printed notice may be just as likely to be deterred by the erroneous pronouncements of a plausible rogue.

IV THE ROLE OF THE DIRECTOR GENERAL OF FAIR TRADING

Many of the statutes dealing with consumer protection mentioned in this chapter pre-date what can be called the modern consumer movement. There was, therefore, no Ministry with overall responsibility for ensuring that the diverse legislation was working effectively. In fact, the first Minister charged with that specific task was not appointed until 1972, and then it formed only a part of his responsibilities. However it was while Sir Geoffrey Howe was Minister for Trade and Consumer Affairs that probably the most important move was made to provide an effective central focus for consumer protection. With the passage of the Fair Trading Act in 1973 and the creation of the OFT with the Director General as its head, British policy came of age. Since that time successive governments, some of which have been unsympathetic to the consumer movement, have recognized the importance of the consumer work done by the OFT and particularly by the Director General, and there has always been a Minister responsible for Consumer Affairs.[28]

We have already referred to the Director General on a number of occasions in the previous pages and it is now useful to summarize his role in relation to consumer affairs. Smith and Swann distinguish six separate functions for the Director in this field. First, he has a general responsibility to keep under review all trading relationships between firms and consumers in order, if necessary, to be able to investigate more fully practices that may adversely affect the consumers' interest. Secondly, and clearly related to the first point, he receives and collates evidence concerning practices that may affect consumers, including those affecting their health and safety. Thirdly, he can make references to the Consumer Protection Advisory Committee (CPAC) which was also established by the 1973 Fair Trading Act and which includes some members with knowledge and experience in the supply of goods and services to consumers, some with particular experience in the enforcement of consumer legislation such as the Trade Descriptions Act and some members closely associated with consumer organizations. A reference to the Committee can be made where the Director considers a trade practice adversely affects the economic interests of consumers.[29] For the purposes of a reference, a 'trade practice' is widely defined and can apply to the terms and conditions of a sale, the way in which the terms are communicated to the consumer, the method of promotion and sale, the way goods are packed, and finally the methods of securing payment. Under certain circumstances a reference can contain recommendations for an order regulating or forbidding the practice. Thus a reference can be made where it appears to the Director that a trade practice is likely to have the effect of (a) misleading or confusing consumers as to the nature, quality or quantity of goods purchased, (b) misleading consumers as to their rights and obligations, (c) subjecting consumers to undue pressure, or finally (d) making the terms of consumer transactions so adverse as to be 'inequitable' (Borrie and Diamond, 1981). The terms of any reference to the CPAC must be published, so that objections by affected parties may be heard and the report has usually to be made within three months. Recommendations from the Director that are agreed (possibly with modifications) by the CPAC may then form the basis of an order by the Minister.[30] We have referred above to two such orders made under this procedure, one concerning the display of notices that purport to remove from the consumer inalienable legal rights and another concerning the practice of traders advertising goods for sale without disclosing the fact that they are traders rather than private individuals. Both practices thus became criminal offences under the terms of the Order. Borrie and Diamond suggest that as only four orders were made between 1973 and the end of 1979, this aspect of the Director's powers has had a much more limited impact on improving the position of consumers than was originally envisaged. They argue that establishing economic detriment to consumers is difficult and that the Minister has only 'limited room for manoeuvre'. However, they do not indicate the kind of practices that are widespread and that should fall within this area of the Director's authority.

On the whole it might be more effective to use this power selectively rather than risk having it discredited by over-use and then abolished by a future government persuaded by business lobbying that efficient trading was being impaired by an over-zealous Director and a plethora of regulations.

Fourthly, Section III of the Fair Trading Act contains important provisions for the Director to take action against offenders who continuously infringe their legal obligations to consumers. One of the conclusions of a recent report on consumer policy over the last ten years from the OECD(1983) was the need for much more progress to be made in follow-up and enforcement powers if the impetus of consumer policy was not to be lost. The UK was singled out in the report as one of three countries where significant advances in this direction had been made. Under Section III the Director can seek an Order from the Restrictive Practices Court[31] against a trader who has persistently broken the criminal or civil law in respect of his obligations to consumers (e.g. under the Trade Descriptions Act or the Sale of Goods Act). Thus an Order might be sought against someone who persists in illegal activity even in the face of prosecutions and fines brought by trading standards authorities and who refuses to give to the Director a written undertaking that he will desist. An Order from the Court will direct the trader to stop using the objectionable trading practice and failure to comply makes him liable to imprisonment. The presence of this ultimate sanction had probably helped, by 1980, to persuade the 200 or so traders at the more recalcitrant end of the market place to sign written assurances to the Director. As Borrie and Diamond point out this power helps to bridge an important gap in the previous laws whereby a trader could probably rely on the individual consumer not being prepared to pursue at his own expense (and time) an action in the County Court for an infringement of, say, the Sale of Goods Act. As a result many offences probably went unpunished and there was little incentive for the unscrupulous trader to change his conduct.

Fifthly, the Director has the duty to encourage the use of codes of practice amongst trades and although these are not legally enforceable there is a good deal of agreement that they have helped to standardize and raise accepted 'good practice' in a number of trades (OECD, 1983, Smith and Swann, 1979). The codes are usually drawn up in consultation with the OFT and although they naturally vary from trade to trade, frequently include provisions about advertising, price information and labelling, repairs and complaints procedures. Nothing in the code can affect the statutory rights of the consumer, but consumers dealing with a signatory to the code will have the additional reassurance that in the case of dissatisfaction they can refer the case to the Trade Association which will, presumably, want the terms of the code upheld. Amongst the twenty or so trades where codes have been established are motor dealers, domestic laundry and cleaning services, travel agents, electrical appliances, double glazing, shoe manufacturers and retailers, and furniture makers and distributors. As with any voluntary system a weakness is that firms do not *have* to subscribe to the code. In some cases, notably travel agencies supplying package holidays, there has been in recent years so much publicity given to the advantages of dealing with a member of the Association of British Travel Agents (often in the wake of some calamitous experiences of holiday-makers in the Mediterranean) that there is a strong incentive both for consumers to ensure that a firm belongs to the trade association, and equally for traders to use membership as an added point in their favour.

This brings us, finally, to the role of the Director as a disseminator of information and advice to consumers, much of it freely available from citizens advice bureaux, trading standards departments, public libraries and so on. For example, summaries of the main points of the codes practice explaining consumers rights have been prepared, as well as booklets setting out in plain terms the important provisions of the Consumer Credit Act with a description of the total charges for credit that can be made and an explanation of how these changes are converted to an 'annual percentage rate'. Although less spectacular than some other activities of the Director to which we refer below, the dissemination of information about consumer rights under the law and how consumers can make the best deal, may in the long-run, if the analysis of chapter 4 is correct, prove to be amongst his most important functions.

We have so far concentrated on the role of the Director in the field of consumer protection. However, a major part of his activities is concerned with the promotion of competition and the control of monopoly. In a very real sense, of course, these activities too are central to consumer interests. A competitive private sector will help to ensure that consumers are supplied with well-designed up-to-date goods at low prices. Monopolies, on the other hand, may have scant regard for innovation, may allow their internal operations to become slack and serve the consumer ill by charging high prices. The regulation of firms in the private and public sectors is the main focus of attention of parts III and IV of this book and consequently we postpone a detailed consideration of these issues until then. However, for the sake of completeness at this point, it is appropriate to note that the Director plays a leading role in this regulation. He can, for example, refer firms with a market share of one quarter or more, or firms engaging in 'uncompetitive practices' to the MMC which reports on whether they have been acting against the public interest.[32] He maintains the register of restrictive agreements (cartels) between two or more firms and can refer them to the Restrictive Practices Court where he would put the case *against* the continuation of the agreement.

The Director, backed by the OFT, thus forms the focal point for coordinating and promoting activities designed to improve the operation of markets in the interest of consumers.

V CONCLUSION

Although laws to safeguard the consumer from contaminated or diluted food and untested drugs have been on the statute book for more than a century, growing concern with the consumer interest over the past 25 years or so has lead to a vast expansion in protective measures. Not only has the scope of the law for establishing *standards* for certain products been extended and strengthened (e.g. the Food and Drug Act, the Medicines Act and the Consumer Safety Act) but major provisions of the Trade Descriptions Act and the Consumer Credit Act now mean that consumers generally have available to them much fuller and more reliable *information* on which to base their purchases or acquire credit. It is now much more difficult for an unscrupulous trader to deceive an unwary customer into buying goods under a false description or on terms involving onerous rates of interest.

An important role in these matters has been assigned to the specially appointed DGFT who has overall responsibility for ensuring that the laws on consumer protection are operating correctly. He also has the important power of licensing firms wishing to provide consumer credit, and he can be instrumental in making certain trading practices illegal if they are considered to affect adversely the economic interests of consumers. One area of great interest to consumers that the Director can keep under general review but where there are relatively few *legal* controls is advertising. Although countries as diverse as the Netherlands, Ireland, Sweden and the US have all recently passed laws to protect consumers from deceptive advertising, the UK has no such general provision (although television and radio advertising is subject to the control of the IBA). Instead it relies on the advertising industry regulating itself – a procedure that, despite a good deal of scepticism from many critics, has on the whole worked well. However, the sanctions that may be used against an advertiser who persistently infringes the code of practice are inadequate, especially as there is no provision for compelling the offender to publish correcting information, as there now is in the US.

PART III

Monitoring Firm Behaviour in the Private Sector

6

The Economics
of Competition Policy

I INTRODUCTION

Competition policy in the UK is of comparatively recent origin despite an almost unanimous view in the economic literature that markets left entirely to themselves will not necessarily work to the consumers' advantage. Adam Smith spoke darkly of meetings between groups of traders, ending in conspiracies against the public. During the period that is often regarded as the golden era of laissez-faire capitalism, much British manufacturing was subject to formal or informal agreements on prices and other terms of trading, some of which were short-lived, but others survived to a venerable age (Clapham, 1938). The Depression in the interwar period gave an even greater impetus to cartels and cooperation (between government and large firms) which were seen as ways of alleviating the worst effects of unemployment. Thus 'by the outbreak of the Second World War it is probable that the majority of the leading British industries were familiar with devices for restricting competition and public and official opinion had veered round in favour of monopoly and its familiar associate planning' (Allen, 1968, p. 55). Against this background it was thus clearly a dramatic departure for the first postwar government to introduce a measure of monopoly and cartel control. The policy has developed considerably since then but it has never been without severe critics both from those who are strongly in favour of unfettered market forces guiding the allocation of resources, and at the other extreme from those who wish to see the market largely superseded.

In this chapter, which serves to introduce the detailed discussion of part III of the book, we therefore review the main sources of controversy surrounding competition policy. What, for example, should be the objectives of such policy? Is it sufficient to aim for the efficiency of industry? Efficiency has a number of different aspects and the achievement of one (e.g. technical efficiency) may be incompatible with another (allocative efficiency). Even if they can be reconciled in principle, it may be extremely difficult in practice to implement an effective policy. Furthermore it has also been argued that in some circumstances the efficiency objective should give way to considerations of limiting economic (and political) power and the need to preserve a decentralized economy. In the US, for example, antitrust decisions have sometimes had the effect of preserving competitors and a more fragmented market structure at the expense of the greater efficiency that would have resulted from a more heavily concentrated structure. The issues may be further complicated if it is considered that competition policy should also concern itself with the distribution of income, the level of (local) unemployment, or the promotion of exports. In sum, the form that policy takes will depend very much on objectives and unless these are clearly set out from the start inconsistencies will result.

At the core of the policy is 'competition' itself. However, even at this late date there is still considerable debate about how 'competition' should be viewed for policy purposes. Should the main emphasis be on the structure of the market and thus on the number of existing firms and the conditions of entry to the market (together with a number of other characteristics that we mention later) or should the primary concern be with the *forms* that rivalry takes on, for example, pricing, promotion and product innovation?

Thus ambiguity surrounding the concept of competition and the conflicting predictions to which they give rise (which we discuss in section II) lead not surprisingly to a number of different approaches to competition policy, the subject of chapters 7 and 8. What is particularly interesting, therefore, about a recent attempt to develop a more general theory of competition is the framework it appears to provide for an assessment of *all* forms of market structure. Indeed a central result of this theory, of contestable markets, is that under certain conditions an optimal economic performance can be attained by industries with as few as two firms. The implications of the theory for natural monopoly are considered in chapter 10. However in section III we also consider whether the new approach may be used in conjunction with the market structure, market conduct and market performance paradigm that has frequently been used in competition policy to isolate the most important features of a market and their likely consequences for the behaviour and performance of the firms concerned.

II THE NATURE OF COMPETITION

An apparently clear case of market failure occurs where monopoly arises in industries not subject to strong increasing returns. The interaction between demand and cost conditions are ostensibly consistent with a number of separate firms and yet either the industry shows a persistent tendency to fall into fewer and fewer hands or customers are confronted by such uniformity of terms offered by 'competitors' as to make even the most guileless observer sceptical of their true independence. Government intervention might then restore competition to such markets with resulting benefits to consumers in the form of lower prices and a more efficient allocation of resources.

Essentially the same view can be put in 'public good' terms. If competitive markets provide goods and services in quantities and at prices such that marginal social costs are just equal to marginal valuations, then any departure from this configuration caused by monopoly results in a welfare loss. In principle consumers could restore the equivalent of the competitive position by negotiating with the monopoly (or monopolistic group) and offering sufficient recompense to make the change worthwhile for both parties. This well known result is shown diagrammatically in figure 6.1. The lines D, MR and MC are the demand, marginal revenue and marginal costs for the industry in question.[1] A reduction in output from Q_c (competitive output) to Q_m (monopoly output) and an increase in price from P_c to P_m results in a loss of consumers surplus equivalent to P_cP_mAC. Of this loss an amount P_cP_mAB accrues to the monopoly in the form of a rent, while the residual, ABC, is lost entirely: the Marshallian 'dead-weight' loss. The equivalent areas to ABC in other industries represent the welfare losses to consumers that result from the presence of private monopoly.[2] Transactions or policy that restores prices (and outputs) to competitive levels would therefore yield the equivalent consumer surpluses across

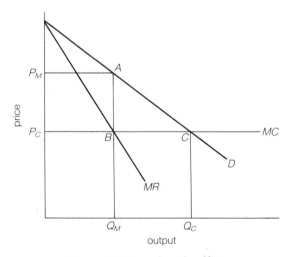

Figure 6.1 Monopoly and welfare

industries and the welfare gain that they represent. In principle it would be in consumers' interests to bribe the monopolist to increase output to Q_c and lower price to P_c. The gain in consumer surplus, P_cP_mAC, is more than sufficient to compensate the monopolist for lost revenue, and consequently the consumers and the monopolist would all be better off. Such negotiations, however, would only be feasible in a world of zero transaction costs, full information and no free riders. In practice, mobilizing consumers, who may number tens of thousands, and negotiating terms with a monopolist is likely to be extremely difficult and costly. Furthermore, many consumers may hope to gain an advantage (a 'free ride') by dissembling their own valuation of the good or service in question. Anyone waiting for a negotiated solution to the monopoly problem is likely to grow old in the process. By regulating markets through its competition policy the government seeks to attain the 'public good' that competitive markets thus represent.

It is one thing, however, to recognize the source of a problem but quite another to frame policies that ensure that they are overcome. Many agree that competitive markets amount to a 'public good' but disagree profoundly on how markets should be made 'competitive'. In the above analysis, for example, the price, P_c and output Q_c were those that would prevail under perfect competition. As is well known the results of this model depend on a long list of assumptions about the structure of the market. They include a group of buyers and sellers large enough to ensure that none has control of price, a homogeneous product, free entry and exit, and complete information amongst buyers and sellers about demand and cost conditions.[3] The model has undoubted uses in economic analysis and can be helpful in pinpointing those features of market structure whose presence or absence will make for more or less competitive markets. Furthermore much of the criticism of the model is misplaced. No economic model is intended to be 'realistic' in the sense that a photograph is an exact representation of its subject. If it were then it would be unmanageable and defeat the purpose of its construction. However, when attempts are made to apply the model directly to competition policy, criticism is more firmly based. The following points are thus not criticisms of the model itself, which within its assumptions is perfectly consistent, but rather criticisms of its use as a guide to regulatory policy that is seeking to establish 'competitive' markets.

Given the assumptions of the model there is very little scope for the kinds of competitive behaviour that most people would associate with business rivalry. All that profit-maximizing firms can do is to adjust their output to the point where (rising) marginal costs are equal to price (marginal revenue) over which they have no control. The large numbers assumption means that no individual firm can gain a price advantage, while the assumptions of product homogeneity and full information imply that firms make zero expenditure on advertising, marketing and product differentiation. While demand or cost fluctuations may mean that firms operate at greater than minimum unit cost and earn abnormally high profits in the short-run, in long-run equilibrium all such aberrations are eliminated. All firms will then operate not only where price (marginal revenue) equals marginal cost, but also where unit costs are minimized and only normal returns are earnt. Thus the conclusion is reached that long-run perfectly competitive equilibrium produces the maximum desired output at minimum resource cost.

Any regulatory policy taking its cue from such a model is thus likely to have a built-in bias against many activities that in real markets are regarded as normal attributes of competitive behaviour. Nearly all firms have some degree of discretion over the prices they charge for their products. As Lerner showed a long while ago the extent to which firms can raise their price above marginal cost will be inversely related to the elasticity of demand for the product (Lerner, 1934). Even quite modestly sized firms may recognize that they do not sell in a unified market but into a set of related but distinct markets which can sustain different prices not strictly related to costs. Again, very few consumer products are homogeneous and sellers may therefore channel much of their competitive effort into product differentiation to enhance their brands in the eyes of consumers and this may mean heavy advertising and other promotional activities. In chapter 4 we discussed the significance of imperfect information in the regulation of consumer market. Amongst producers, a lack of complete information will mean resources devoted to the new and alternative methods of production, organization and selling, (including innovations from entirely new firms or those originally operating elsewhere) which make the previous technology redundant. Although there is a role for entry (and exit) of firms in the long-run adjustment process of the perfectly competitive model, it is a completely automatic one. Existing firms can do nothing to stop entry in response to short-run abnormal returns. In practice, as part of their competitive strategy firms may take deliberate action on, say, pricing and product differentiation in an attempt to deter entry.

In short, because the assumptions of the model are deliberately designed to purge competition of all imperfections, real markets are bound to fall far short of this 'ideal'. However, it is a fallacy to conclude that the task of regulation should be to attempt to create markets as near 'perfect' as possible. Firstly, and most obviously, the technology of many industries may imply that only relatively few firms can serve the existing and foreseeable market efficiently. Technical economies of scale may mean that unit costs continue to decline until a substantial part of that demand is served from one plant. Technical efficiency may thus be incompatible with a large number of competitors. Competition policy that sought to maintain or re-establish a market served by many independent firms would, in such circumstances, have to sacrifice efficiency. Clearly in this case resource costs for any level of output would be higher under the structure induced by the policy than would have occurred in the free market. Whether or not prices would be higher or lower would depend partly on the extent of the scale economies and partly on the manner in which they (prices) would be established amongst the rival firms. Both of these are empirical questions that, it may be argued, a properly constituted competition policy might seek to answer. In some industries production economies may only allow scope for a few firms, while in others they may be compatible with many. In some cases the behaviour of individual firms may yield monopoly prices while in others it may induce prices close to costs.

Secondly, most firms do not sell products that are identical to those of their competitors and they will therefore regard branding, trademarks, advertising and product variation all as part of their marketing strategy. By contrast, because it can be shown that perfect competition (including, of course, the assumption of product homogeneity) will lead to an optimal resource allocation, a policy that relies, perhaps only implicitly, on the theory, will tend to be antagonistic to all marketing activities. In its extreme form this may lead to strong pressure for product standardization and the elimination of waste resulting from a multiplicity of sizes, specifications and brands of products. As Chamberlin pointed out long ago, however, if consumers derive utility from product heterogeneity – a plausible assumption – then it no longer follows that welfare would be increased following the greater output (from a given input base) of a more standardized set of products that such a policy might induce (Chamberlin, 1958). This is not to say that markets left to themselves will automatically produce the 'optimal' degree of product heterogeneity. Indeed some recent work suggests that they may not (Dixit and Norman, 1978). It is simply to point out that product homogeneity is not an ideal that policy should pursue and that many aspects of product differentiation should not therefore automatically be condemned.

The third point is probably the most important and concerns the assumption of full information on the one hand, and the static nature of the theory on the other. Hayek has taken particular exception to the assumption that sellers are in possession of full information about the best method of coordinating resources so as to produce and distribute, as efficiently as possible, products that consumers value most highly. In his view the assumption robs the whole concept of competition of its essence: 'What the theory of perfect competition discusses has little claim to be called "competition" at all and . . . its conclusions are of little use as guides to policy. The reason for this seems to me to be that this theory throughout assumes that state of affairs already to exist which . . . the process of competition tends to bring about' (Hayek, 1948, p. 92). The thrust of Hayek's argument is that competition consists of a process of discovery by producers of better ways of serving consumers needs. Successful discoveries for improving the coordination of scarce resources will then allow individual firms to improve their own position in the market. Others, less successful in their own attempts at reducing costs for existing products or in innovating new ones, will see their position decline. For Hayek, and others of the 'Austrian School', the crucial feature of competition is thus the *process* of finding out better methods or improved products, rather than the static concept of production by a large number of similar firms under conditions of full information. It is thus not surprising that a model like perfect competition, which starts with full information, is regarded by such writers as assuming away the whole process that it purports to describe. The emphasis on the roles of new information and change in competition allows us to link these ideas with those of Schumpeter who although differing from Hayek on a number of issues, nevertheless agrees on the central part of the argument. In the description of his famous process of 'creative destruction' previous positions of dominance in a market are sooner or later undermined by the creative use of new discoveries – in production, distribution, marketing, managerial organization – which for a time will lead to very high profits but which in their turn will be eroded by a continuation of the same process (Schumpeter, 1965). Their conviction that markets, free from artificial constraints (especially those imposed by government), are essentially self-regulating and efficient allows these writers to tolerate the presence of apparent monopolies. Schumpeter argued that high returns should be expected for the successful innovator, partly to recoup previous costs of research and development, partly to compensate for the special risks attached to initiating change, and partly as an incentive for channelling the exceptional energy that the whole process requires. In fact he and most Austrians were rather sceptical of the role of antitrust or competition policy in improving the performance of industry. In view of the context of our present discussion, that is, the type of competition that regulatory policy should seek to promote, some readers may find it ironic that in using Schumpeter's views on the competitive process to criticize the influence on policy of the theory of perfect competition, we may have simultaneously demolished the case for having any regulatory policy at all. Although this position is not without influential adherents it is not a view we share, as our later discussion indicates.

Schumpeter makes the following vivid comparison between the performance of an economy judged dynamically and one judged in static terms: 'A system – any system, economic or other – that at *every* given point of time fully utilises its possibilities to the best advantage may yet in the long run be inferior to a system that does so at *no* given point of time, because the latter's failure to do so may be a condition for the level or speed of long-run performance' (Schumpeter, 1965, p. 83).

III CONTESTABLE MARKETS AND WORKABLE COMPETITION

While in principle many would sympathize with Schumpeter's position, when it has to be made operational for policy purposes, difficulties arise. There are no clear-cut predictions as to precisely how much market power may be conducive to technical change, or how many centres of independent research initiative are necessary to generate an 'optimal' amount of new ideas. Writers of the Austrian School stress that the main source of monopoly power will be government inspired or supported in the form of special privileges, licences, restrictions and so on. Their central policy recommendation, therefore, is that many of these provisions should be abolished entirely leaving as much scope for the free play of dynamic competitive forces as possible. It is at this point that some of their ideas may be linked to the much more recent analysis of competition in contestable markets developed in particular by Baumol and his colleagues. The Austrians emphasized the strength of market forces in the absence of artificial constraints on the movement of resources imposed by government. As long as entry to markets is free in this sense, the long-run performance of industry will be the best attainable and this would be regardless of the number of firms that happened to be serving a particular market at any one time. There are a number of similarities between their approach and the policy implications that follow, and the theory of contestable markets, although it does not do to push the comparison too far. The ideas are especially relevant in the present context because they can be applied across the whole spectrum of industries – those that have hitherto been regulated (or nationalized) on grounds of natural monopoly as well as those to which the traditional weapons of competition policy have been applied. Our main concern in considering them here, therefore, is to assess how far they provide a more suitable framework for policy analysis than previous theories.

The most comprehensive development of the theory of contestable markets was published in 1982 by Baumol, Panzar and Willig but many of the ideas had already been published in a number of separate articles. The reader is referred paticularly to Bailey, (1981) and Baumol, (1982). Although Baumol is concerned with the importance and implications of the theory he is also anxious to demonstrate the extent to which it draws on and develops the previous analysis of many other contributors. The central ideas are straightforward even though the rigorous proofs of some of the detailed results are quite complex. A perfectly contestable market is defined as one where entry is completely free and exit is costless. Free entry, as Baumol stresses, is used in the way that Stigler has suggested. Potential entrants certainly have to incur costs, which in some cases may be considerable, but there are no costs that they have to undertake that incumbent firms escape. Potential entrants also find it appropriate to assess their prospective profitability in terms of the existing firms' pre-entry prices. Similarly, costless exit implies that firms have not incurred large sunk costs on entry and that any costs are readily recoverable if firms decide to leave the market. In such a market the price structure will be 'sustainable' if it has the following three properties. Firstly, the quantity of output demanded by the market at the established prices must be equal to the total of all outputs from firms serving the market. Secondly, the prices must yield revenues for the existing firms that are at least equal to the cost of producing the outputs. Thirdly there must be no opportunities, as perceived by potential entrants, for entry that would allow them to be profitable given the prevailing price structure (Baumol *et al.*, 1982). The key characteristic of such markets, as far as Baumol is concerned, is their vulnerability to what he terms 'hit and run' competition. The free entry and exit assumptions mean that even if profitable opportunities are very short-lived, entrants will be attracted since they can leave the market costlessly once the profit prospects disappear. In long-run equilibrium such markets with more than one firm[4] will also display similar desirable welfare properties to perfectly competitive markets with added advantages to which we return below. Firstly, the perpetual threat of new competition will ensure that all incumbent firms must remain efficient both technically and organizationally. Any hint, for example, of x-inefficiency will provide scope for successful entry and will thus be eliminated. For the same reason, secondly, existing firms will be forced to charge prices equal to marginal costs, since any higher price levels will again encourage new entry until the difference disappears. Thirdly, the corollary of the second attribute is that in long-run equilibrium all firms will earn only normal profits. Hence such markets display in long-run equilibrium all the characteristics of a Pareto optimal resource allocation. Baumol concludes that since such markets 'enjoy those three properties, the optimality of perfectly contestable equilibria ... fully justifies our conclusion that perfect contestability constitutes a proper *generalization* of the concept of perfect competition so far as welfare implications are concerned' (Baumol, 1982, p. 5; my italics). The result is general in the following very important sense. A perfectly contestable market with more than one incumbent firm will in equilibrium attain these results. The emphasis on a *large* number of firms in the theory of perfect competition thus disappears. Although a perfectly competitive industry is necessarily contestable, the reverse does not hold. In particular even a concentrated oligopoly, as long as entry is free and exit costless, will achieve an equilibrium consistent with optimal resource allocation. This result follows without any of the additional assumptions about response and counter-response by incumbent firms upon which most traditional oligopoly models depend to achieve a determinate outcome. More generally the theory gives a quite different perspective on market structures. A common inference drawn from theory is that there is a spectrum of market structures stretching from the perfectly competitive at one extreme, representing the ideal, through a variety of imperfectly competitive markets, to monopoly at the other extreme, representing the worst outcome. Progression along this spectrum as the number of firms in the market is reduced, is frequently taken to imply a deterioration in performance. In contrast, the clear inference from contestable theory is that as few as two firms are sufficient to guarantee optimality. Even in the case of single-firm monopoly, where under certain circumstances the firm may be able to adopt non-optimal prices,[5] the major conclusion of Baumol *et al.* is that the threat of entry is in most instances likely to induce the most efficient performance from the firm and lead to the optimal price structure.

Taken together the implications of the theory for regulatory and competition policies appear to be profound. Before considering these in more detail, however, some general observations are in order. Remembering the context of the present discussion, that is, which concept of competition is most appropriate as a framework for policy purposes, and recalling also the rejection of the theory of perfect competition on the grounds that its assumptions appeared to remove the very process it attempted to describe, the reader may be puzzled as to why we should be concerned with an equally abstract model. After all a *perfectly* contestable market requires the extreme assumptions of completely free entry and costless exit. Furthermore, although it is not made explicit, the assumption of full information on the part of incumbent and potential entrants firms does seem to be implicit in the analysis of competition in a contestable market. Is it not the case, therefore, that the theory has precisely the same shortcomings, as far as policy considerations are concerned, as that of perfect competition? Baumol addresses this issue directly. To derive the result that perfectly contestable markets will, in equilibrium, lead to an optimal resource allocation is not to say that 'they populate the world of reality any more than perfectly competitive markets do, though there are a number of industries which undoubtedly approximate contestability even if they are far from perfectly competitive' (Baumol, 1982, p. 1). Although perfectly contestable markets are not a description of reality, they do provide, in the judgement of Baumol and his colleagues, a benchmark for judging industrial organization that is much more flexible than that of perfect competition, and much more widely applicable. While, therefore, the fact that contestable oligopolies behave ideally and contestable monopolies may have a strong incentive to do so does *not* indicate that such oligopolies or monopolies exist, it does suggest that effective policy measures should aim to make actual markets more contestable. The focus of policy towards firms, whether publically or privately owned, is therefore shifted to entry and exit conditions. Where perfect competition seemed remote and where, as a result, regulatory measures appeared to lack coherence or consistency, the supporters of contestable theory would argue that the policy implications of the new approach are more compelling simply because they are more in accordance with actual markets.

As far as oligopoly is concerned Baumol acknowledges that the conclusions are little different from those that have found favour for a long while amongst Chicago economists. For example, a market with two firms may produce an optimal result. Similarly Fisher has argued that if existing firms are continually constrained by the threat of entry to charge limit prices, 'competition is doing its job' (Fisher, 1979).[6] To the extent that the conditions for contestability are met, oligopolists can only prevent entry by behaving in a manner that promotes efficiency in both technical and allocative senses. One inference that Baumol draws is that in industries with a high level of concentration, a record of no new entrants may no longer indicate an adverse performance – rather the reverse. It may signify that contestability in the market was forcing virtuous behaviour upon the incumbent firms just as the fear of hell-fire did upon our medieval ancestors. Any measure that removed or lowered entry barriers would assist contestability, although this is hardly a new result, as a number of commentators have been quick to observe. More problematical are measures that assist *exit* from a market. Although there has been some attention to the problem of exit barriers (see, for example Caves and Porter, 1977) the treatment has been slight compared with that given to entry conditions.

In the view of Bailey, one of the main contributors to contestability theory, 'its most dramatic results relate to natural monopoly' (Bailey, 1981, p. 178) where the policy prescriptions can be directly and readily applied.[7] As far as entry conditions are concerned the implications are the same for both oligopoly and monopoly but in the latter case they take on special importance since the effect of the regulations of such industries in the US has been to restrict severely, usually through licensing arrangements, the number of firms permitted to operate. Contestability points unambiguously to the conclusion that these restrictions should be swept away to allow free entry. In some natural monopoly cases, as Demsetz (1968) pointed out some time ago, the main deterrent to entry will not be economies of scale as such, but the very great sunk costs that such economies involve. The risks inherent in the large outlays necessary to set up sunk cost facilities will act to deter entrants when apparently profitable opportunities exist. The market power of an incumbent monopolist that has undertaken such investment only remains potent, however, as long as the monopolist has permanent and exclusive access to it. Thus Bailey concludes: 'the single most important element in the design of public policy for monopoly should be the design of arrangements which render benign the exercise of power associated with operating sunk facilities' (Bailey, 1981, p. 179). The actual method of achieving this objective will vary from market to market according to the nature of the sunk costs involved. In some cases it may be necessary for central or local government to shoulder the burden of sunk costs, just as they do for roads and airports. In others a more appropriate arrangement may be for a group of firms jointly to share in the cost, as in the case of communications satellites.

For those who have been following the debate about privitization of previously nationalized industries in the UK, much of this has a familiar ring. Many suggestions have been made as to how the exercise of monopoly power can be prevented in such industries if they are to be returned successfully to the private sector. Although the discussion has not, on the whole, adopted the terminology of contestable market theory many of the ideas coincide. In particular, it has been widely recognized that the actual monopoly element in a number of the industries may be less intractable than had previously been thought. For example, while the sunk cost element of the national grid in electricity supply may have to be centrally borne, local supplies may be provided by companies awarded a limited-period franchise; the track and related sunk costs of the railways may have to continue as a monopoly but with individual transport companies leasing track time and possibly rolling stock on a competitive basis; in telecommunications, while local domestic telephone systems contain unavoidable monopoly elements, long-distance commercial services may be much more amenable to competition or, in the new terminology, may be made contestable. In chapter 10, where we consider in more detail the problems of regulating dominant firms in the public sector, the recent experience of British and American industries can be compared in the light of these developments in contestable market theory.

As far as dominant firms in the private sector are concerned where no strong element of natural monopoly is present, the main contribution of the theory may turn out to be the firmer underpinning it gives to antitrust or competition policies which have hitherto drawn similar conclusions on an intuitive basis. Baumol acknowledges that, in this respect, the approach that comes closest to his own, albeit in a much more informal way, is that of J.M. Clark and the notion of workable competition (Clark, 1940, 1955). Clark set out to reconcile the facts of modern industry with the need to ensure that competitive pressures remain an effective force on firms' market behaviour and performance. He therefore attempted to identify the structural and behavioural features of markets that were necessary to ensure a 'workably competitive' performance in the private sector. Subsequent writers built on Clark's original initiative, and one indirect result has been the market structure, conduct and performance (SCP) paradigm mentioned in chapter 3 which dominated the economic anlaysis of industry from the mid-1950s until well into the 1970s (cf. Scherer, 1980, chapter 1). Clark was looking for a concept of competition that could be used for assessing the behaviour and performance of industry instead of the remote 'perfect competition', while writers such as Mason and Bain, who pioneered the SCP paradigm, had the wider objective of providing a framework for deriving testable predictions about the performance of industries, despite their seemingly impenetrable complexity.

The theory of contestable markets is still in a relatively early stage of its development and it is thus too soon to decide whether the revolutionary claims made for it by its authors are justified. However, it has been developed at a time when many issues concerning private market power and natural monopoly are being reappraised. It is therefore likely to be at the centre of this policy debate for some considerable time.

IV CONCLUSION

The guidance received by regulators of the private sector of industry from the economic theory of markets turns out on close examination to be limited and double-edged. Most markets tend to have quite strong elements of oligopoly and the policy inferences that can be drawn from the many alternative theoretical models are often unclear. Where they appear to give some guidance (e.g. on collusion to achieve a joint monopoly profit) the implications of a positive policy response may be ambiguous (lower profits may weaken the incentives for the most efficient).

An important cause of this problem is the unsatisfactory nature of the analysis of competition. For the purpose of policy analysis the static theories of perfect competition and monopoly appear to be of limited use. Quite apart from the extreme assumptions made about market structure, the assumption of perfect information amongst sellers and buyers appears to many to rob the theory of the very process it is trying to explain, i.e. how behaviour amongst rival economic agents (firms) leads to improvements in resource allocation. Although the attempt by Schumpeter to place the main emphasis in competitive theory on the creation and use of *new* knowledge was generally welcomed, it was too loosely formulated to be of much practical use to the regulatory authorities.

The debate has recently received a major new impetus with the publication by Baumol and his colleagues of the theory of contestable markets. The theory aims to provide an entirely new theoretical explanation of how, under certain (extreme) conditions, a market containing very few or very many firms can achieve optimal results. It remains to be seen whether the regulatory policies discussed in subsequent chapters (7–10) will undergo anything more than superficial changes as a result of this development.

7

Regulating Dominant Firms
in the Private Sector

In the light of the discussion in chapter 1 of market failure and the need for regulation it might appear that monopoly in the private sector gives the clearest case possible for intervention. The inefficiencies that can result from monopoly have been thoroughly analysed and are well known. Many of the exclusionary practices with which monopolists have been associated in the past have also been thoroughly documented. It remains true, however, that regulating private sector monopolies still gives rise to a great deal of controversy and conflicting analysis. One has only to think of some recent decisions of the US and British antitrust authorities to illustrate this point: the action by the US Justice Department leading in 1984 to the break up of the AT and T Company, for example, or the continued prohibition by the British Minister for Industry of the acquisition of The House of Fraser by the Lonrho Company.

Part of the problem of regulating private monopoly lies in transferring concepts that in pure analysis can be made clear-cut, such as monopoly, into the much more difficult realm of actual firms and their markets. The attentive reader may already have contrasted the use of 'dominant firms' in the title of this chapter with 'monopoly' in the text. It is comparatively rare in practice for any firm to have complete control of the market. Even an apparent share of 100 per cent may be a very misleading guide to the actual monopoly power enjoyed by the firm if other close substitute products are available in related 'markets' over which the firm has far less control. An initial problem, therefore, is to determine what, for regulatory purposes, constitutes 'monopoly' or 'dominance'. Even assuming the relevant market can be defined it is then necessary to determine when one firm is in a position to control the price and other terms of trading to its own advantage. Does this occur at 60 per cent or 80 per cent or much lower? Can a firm with a market share *now* of 65 per cent really be said to dominate the market if three years ago its share was 85 per cent. Alternatively in the recent past, it may have only had 40 per cent of the market but have won its additional share through superior management and innovation. Regulation of such an enterprise may reduce efficiency rather than increase it.

The position taken for the remainder of this chapter is that the main objective of competition policy should be efficiency and since the concept is a complex one, section II discusses it in detail. We can also note at this stage that even though the ostensible objective of the policy may be efficiency, achieved by competition, firms may attempt to use the policy for their own rent-seeking ends. Thus, a policy that interprets predatory pricing very broadly may allow firms to take advantage of it by bringing actions against (larger) rivals in the hope first of gaining relief from unwelcome competition and also (under US antitrust law) receiving a considerable amount in damages. The analysis of rent-seeking discussed in chapter 2 would lead us to expect firms to exploit such a situation, and as Baumol and Ordover have recently argued the more fully developed the policy, the greater the scope for such behaviour (Baumol and Ordover, 1985). We note in the next section that once rent-seeking is incorporated into the analysis, efficiency itself must be viewed in a different light.

Although the central objection to positions of dominance may be that they can lead to inefficiency, a major role for competition policy is to analyse the *means* used by firms to maintain their position. A complete list of possible exclusionary or anti-competitive tactics would take us too far afield and spread the discussion too thinly.[1] We therefore focus in section III on some of the more familiar kinds of allegedly exclusionary behaviour: full-line forcing (or tie-sales), predatory pricing and refusal to deal, drawing on recent cases when appropriate.

The final section of the chapter then considers how private sector dominance has been regulated assuming, that is, that the regulatory bodies have concluded that some action is required. A central problem to emerge is the possible conflict between achieving a higher level of allocative efficiency (by some regulatory solution – including the break-up of dominant firms) but only at the expense of some degree of technical efficiency. Since this is precisely the issue involved in many mergers that may create positions of dominance, it is appropriate also in this section to deal with merger control.

The appendix to this chapter contains a brief outline of the major provisions for controlling positions of dominance in Britain, the US and in the Common Market that are referred to in section III.

II EFFICIENCY AND DOMINANCE IN THE PRIVATE SECTOR

If the major objective of policy in the regulation of dominance is the improvement of efficiency, it is evident that the concept should be clearly defined and in a way that is generally acceptable. Problems have arisen in the past and are still common partly because the term is widely used in popular debate and partly because it has a number of quite distinct aspects when properly defined.

In the discussion that follows we will keep to the threefold distinction between technical efficiency, allocative efficiency and x-efficiency. The first two concepts are well established in the literature and generally accepted, the third, although it has been around in one form or another for many years, is more controversial. Indeed for economists of the Chicago school, as one of their most eminent authorities has recently claimed, the x-istence of x-efficiency is questioned (see Stigler, (1976) and Leibenstein, (1978) for opposing views). We will regard a firm as technically efficient if it produces its output from a plant or plants of an optimum size (given the state of knowledge in the industry) and therefore at minimum unit cost. Short-run fluctuations in demand, for example, may temporarily raise costs above the minimum, but most output can be produced at minimum cost. In other words a technically efficient firm will be producing at some point on the horizontal position of the long-run average cost curve. This is shown in figure 7.1 where we adopt the now widely used assumption that long-run average (and therefore long-run marginal) costs remain constant over a range of possible outputs. In the figure D and MR are the demand and marginal revenue curves respectively of the dominant firm. The long-run average cost curve is denoted by $LRAC$ and long-run marginal cost by $LRMC$. Long-run average costs become horizontal at an output Q_{MES}, which thus represents minimum efficient size. As long as the firm, operating on $LRAC$, produces an output of at least Q_{MES}, it can be regarded as technically efficient. If costs remain constant over a considerable range of output, as suggested by the figure, then clearly a firm may hold a dominant position without it being strictly necessary for technical efficiency. The relationship between demand and the minimum size of output required for technical efficiency will govern the degree to which it is compatible with a competitive market structure. In the case shown in the diagram, a profit-maximizing monopolist would restrict output to Q_M and charge price[2] B. On the marginal output Q_M, therefore, price (the equivalent of CQ_M) exceeds marginal cost EQ_M) by the amount CE. It is this divergence between price and marginal cost, which is central to the (static) concept of allocative inefficiency.

If the total output supplied to the market was Q_C the marginal valuation, as reflected by the demand curve, would just equal marginal cost.[3] In this sense the amount of resources devoted to production for this market could be exactly in accordance with the valuation placed on those resources by consumers and there would be no scope for further resource reallocation that could improve consumer welfare.[4] If the structure of the market was competitive and cost conditions remained unchanged (long-run marginal cost would become the aggregation of marginal costs for all firms supplying the market) then Q_C output would be supplied at the price A. The fact that the profit-maximizing monopolist charge a price B causes two important effects. First, and most important, there is a loss, triangle CEF, of consumers' surplus compared with the position under competition. Over the entire output range $Q_M - Q_C$ consumers who would have been prepared to pay a price greater than the marginal cost of production, are denied that opportunity because of the output restriction. Secondly, in the case shown in figure 7.1 the monopolist earns an excess profit, represented by $ABCE$, on the output Q_M, most of which would have formed part of the consumers' surplus under competition. The restriction of output thus will normally lead to an income transfer from consumers to the producer.[5] The central conclusion, however, is that allocative inefficiency results from the opportunity given to the monopolist to charge a price in excess of marginal cost. The additional resources that would have been employed in this market if it was competitively organized (i.e. to produce the output $Q_M - Q_C$) will be employed elsewhere but less efficiently.

Thus the firm shown in figure 7.1 may be technically efficient (at an output Q_M) but producing an allocatively inefficient performance because of the scope it has for charging above marginal cost.

There are many other points that could be made about allocative efficiency and positions of dominance and some of these emerge in subsequent sections of this chapter. For the moment, however, we will proceed to the third and more controversial aspect of efficiency, namely x-efficiency. Since a firm that is x-efficient will be operating somewhere on its normal long-run average cost curve, it is easier to define the concept by reference to its obverse, x-*in*efficiency. Under competitive conditions all firms will be constrained to be as technically efficient as possible. Those that through lack of managerial flair and energy do not keep up will eventually be taken over by others or forced to leave the market. In these circumstances there will be little scope for x-inefficiency. However, according to Leibenstein and others when a firm has attained a position of dominance, competitive pressures may not be so strong and internal operations both at managerial and shop-floor levels may become slack. Managers of firms that have persistently earnt high profits for a considerable period may subconsciously begin, in effect, to take part of those profits in the form of more relaxation and less stress. Supervision and

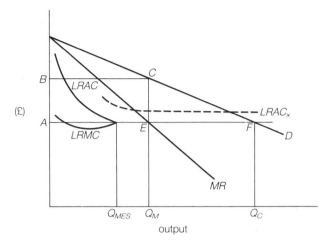

Figure 7.1 Monopoly output and costs

control on the shop-floor may similarly become lax. Diagrammatically this effect is illustrated in figure 7.1 by the broken curve $LRAC_X$ which lies above the conventional long-run average cost curve. While $LRAC$ may be technically possible, under the condition of monopoly, or more approximately of dominance, $LRAC_X$ becomes the effective cost curve, and the firm will make its price and output decisions accordingly. Since, for example, the intersection of $LRAC_X$ and MR occurs to the left of the point where $LRAC$ cuts MR, output will be even further restricted and price even higher with x-inefficiency than without it. In short, x-inefficiency consists of firms, sheltered from competition, operating at greater than attainable minimum unit cost.

A criticism of this interpretation is that if $LRAC$ cannot be attained, for whatever reason, under monopoly, then it makes no sense to assume that it is. On this view the effective cost-function, *given the monopolistic structure of the market*, is $LRAC_X$. The monopolistic output restriction that such costs imply can be measured in *allocative* efficiency terms and the reduction in costs that would result from a change in the market structure (following perhaps some regulatory action) can be interpreted as one of the benefits of increased competition. Viewed in this way x-inefficiency is the approximate counterpart of the reductions in costs that are often claimed to follow the reorganization of a competitive market into one dominated by a few much larger concerns that are able to achieve economies of scale unattainable by smaller firms.

From our point of view it is less important to insist on the use of a particular term (such as x-inefficiency) than to realize that the increased

competition that regulatory action can bring may improve not only
allocative efficiency, by narrowing price–cost margins, but also reduce costs
by eliminating internal slack.

It is appropriate to take up at this stage another recent development in
the analysis of efficiency, monopoly profits and regulation. We have already
discussed the notion of rent-seeking (as opposed to rent creation) in
chapter 2. If monopoly profits or rents are available in some markets it
seems likely that firms will expend resources either in trying to maintain
such rents if they already benefit from them, or alternatively in an effort to
gain rents from others. The precise form that the rent-seeking will take
depends on the source of the rent. Firms deriving rents from a unique
brand image and consumer loyalty built up over many years of investment
in advertising, clearly have an interest in preserving that asset in order to
keep competitors out and thus maintaining their rents. Alternatively, firms
that have gained special concessions from the government in the form of a
tariff or legislative protection from new competition will, through lobbying
and the media, continue to make the case for their continuation. In
addition other firms will be seeking to wrest part of existing rents from the
present beneficiaries or press their case for protection or privilege that will
create entirely new rents. In short, a competitive process will take place in
rent-seeking. However, unlike the competition that seeks to meet
consumers' needs at the lowest cost and that regulatory policy may seek to
achieve, this type of competition leads to income redistribution and waste.
The effects of the process can be illustrated diagrammatically, as in figure
7.2.

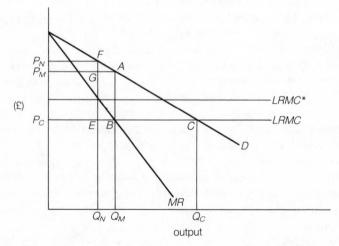

Figure 7.2 Monopoly and rent-seeking

The demand and marginal revenue curves of the monopoly are again shown as D and MR respectively. The long-run marginal cost curve is now shown as horizontal throughout its length in order to make the exposition clearer without affecting the central conclusions. Assume initially that the monopolist's marginal (and average) costs are given by $LRMC$ and it is x-efficient. Output is restricted to the level Q_M in order to charge the monopoly price. Compared with the output produced by the industry if it were competitively organized (with unchanged costs) Q_C, the monopoly configuration creates a dead-weight welfare loss of ABC due to allocative inefficiency. In the absence of rent-seeking (and x-inefficiency) this area measures the full extent of the loss resulting from monopoly. Indeed some early estimates of the likely extent of these losses in the US economy were embarassingly small, usually much less than one per cent of GNP.[6] Subsequent estimates were considerably higher but, more important for our purposes, they highlighted the multi-faceted nature of the likely inefficiences that could follow from dominance. In particular Posner (1975) pointed out that the competitive rent-seeking process described above meant that the probable resource waste was much higher than the strict allocative inefficiency loss represented by ABC. In the conventional analysis the monopoly rent $P_C P_M AB$ earned by charging the monopoly price P_M is treated merely as a transfer from consumers to producers. However, with rent-seeking the whole of this amount will be dissipated in the attempt to maintain or divert existing rents.[7] The full inefficiency that is likely to result is thus the much larger area, $P_C P_M AC$. Far from being the insignificant problem that some had claimed, using the original estimates of welfare losses, market dominance may on this view cause considerable inefficiency and waste. The argument is reinforced if instead of assuming x-efficient dominant firms, they suffer from internal slack. In this case the relevant cost curve is $LRMC^*$ and this causes the further output restriction to Q_N (and a price P_N). There is the further loss of consumers' surplus of $P_M P_N FA$, again representing some dead-weight loss and some resource dissipation through rent-seeking.[8]

Taken together, therefore, the three inefficiences and the attraction of rent-seeking may cause considerable losses to consumers. In a smoothly working competitive system, however, the above distortions would be short-lived. New entry would bring prices down, eradicate the technically- and x-inefficient, and undermine the incentive for rent-seeking. The purpose of the next section is to discuss a number of ways in which it is frequently claimed dominant firms can protect their position from the incursion of fresh competition and thus prolong inefficiency.

III EXCLUSIONARY PRACTICES

Some firms will grow to dominance in a market through a combination of outstanding management, luck and continued flexibility in the face of change. Williamson (1972) is prepared to accept that in a number of instances dominant positions will be retained because of market failure rather than through any positive action by the firms concerned. Much of the regulatory policy on dominance, however, is concerned with the issue of whether such positions have been created and maintained by deliberate exclusionary tactics. Thus a major part of the UK Monopolies and Mergers Commission (MMC) enquiries consist of an analysis of whether 'things done' by dominant firms (i.e. their market conduct) are intended to consolidate or extend their position and whether they operate against the public interest, which since 1973 has to be interpreted largely in terms of competitive effects (see the appendix to this chapter). Similarly a section II action under the US Sherman Act turns essentially on the issue of whether market conduct by a dominant firm can be interpreted as an attempt to monopolize the market, which is usually understood to include anti-competitive actions against both existing and potential rivals. Again, under Article 86 of the Treaty of Rome, certain practices employed by a dominant firm that are regarded as having distorting or anti-competitive effects on trade between member states of the European Community are prohibited.

In each case, given the market structure of one firm that may be technically efficient but that has a dominant share, the question is whether aspects of its market conduct unfairly weaken or exclude existing and potential competitors with the adverse effects on efficiency discussed above. From a policy point of view the analysis is complicated by the central assumption that the firm has discretion over price. For example, in most cases if the firm charges the full short-run profit-maximizing price entry will occur and its market share will be eroded. A response to new entry taking the form of a price cut may be interpreted as anti-competitive or even predatory. Alternatively the firm may act strategically and deliberately limit its price below the short-run profit-maximizing level in order to deter entry. Although this may be regarded as equally anti-competitive, in practice it may be very difficult for a regulatory agency to detect.

(i) Price Discrimination and Predatory Pricing

In a well known taxonomy of types of price discrimination Machlup once noted no fewer than nineteen (Machlup, 1955). Clearly it is impossible to discuss the practice in anything like that degree of detail. Interested readers are referred to the original article and also to the excellent, brief analysis in Scherer (1980, chapter 11). There are two reasons, however, for which it seems appropriate to begin our discussion of exclusionary practices with price discrimination. First, judging from the MMC reports it occurs in one form or another in practically all markets dominated by one firm. Secondly, although in a number of instances it is not seen as particularly harmful, in the extreme form of predatory pricing it may be of central importance. Recently predatory pricing has received a growing amount of attention from both theorists and policy makers.

For our purposes it is sufficient to use Stigler's definition of price discrimination as occurring when the same product is sold at different ratios of price to marginal cost (Stigler, 1966). It includes, therefore, the practice of selling different amounts to the same customers, in a given time period, at different prices. For example, the customer only pays a lower price per unit once a certain 'threshold' number of units have been purchased. This type of discrimination, usually termed second-degree discrimination, raises a number of important issues for natural monopoly pricing, but in the present context the more important form is third-degree price discrimination. Where a firm operates in a number of markets or market segments that have distinct and different price elasticities of demand and where resale between markets is impossible or extremely costly, then it will find it profitable to charge different prices, even though marginal cost per unit is identical. Thus in markets where actual or potential competition is greater and therefore price elasticity is higher, prices will be lower than where the firm is much more secure.

If we assume that the firm is producing on a large enough scale to achieve all available economies and is therefore technically efficient, our main concerns will then be, firstly, does the third-degree price discrimination lead to allocative inefficiency and, secondly, can it be used as a device to exclude or contain other firms? Unfortunately on the first point economic theory does not give a clear-cut answer. Whether or not output is greater or smaller with this form of price discrimination than with simple monopoly pricing depends on the shape of the demand curves in the different markets (Scherer, 1980). Despite the formal result, however, that output might be lower with price discrimination, the general view seems to be that there is a stronger likelihood of a larger output which would therefore be closer to the allocatively efficient level. This is partly based on the argument that firms will often use price discrimination to test the potential for selling in a new market segment, and at a low price. Also it is based on the observation that in practice the isolation of different markets is rarely as complete as the theory assumes. The possibility of some 'leakage' of supplies from one market to another will therefore tend to modify the price level in the most highly priced market.

The view is also carried over into policy, at least in the UK, where the MMC has concluded that price discrimination *per se*, being a widespread fact of industrial and commercial life, is generally not harmful unless it is accompanied by discount and rebate structures that have an exclusionary purpose (and to which we return shortly). For example, in a report on Joseph Lucas it concluded 'It would in our view be unrealistic that price differentiation for the purpose of meeting competition at the point where that competition is having most effect must be improper' (MMC, 1963). In contrast the European Commission (later backed by the European Court of Justice) came down firmly against United Brands which discriminated on price between national distributors of its bananas within the Common Market and prohibited any resale between markets. The resulting price differentials were considerable and were condemned as a violation under Article 86. The decision was clearly influenced by the over-riding objective of the Community to stimulate trade between members, although it has subsequently been severely criticized by observers who argued that enforcing uniform pricing would have an income redistribution effect against poorer members where demand would be depressed by the price increase (Merkin and Williams, 1984). Finally, although the US antitrust laws have many critics, probably their most persistent and vociferous censure has been aimed at the Robinson–Patman Act which, although ostensibly directed at price discrimination, was clearly intended to work in favour of the small shop against the chain store and to maintain fair or equitable prices for different buyers who also competed against each other as sellers. In view of this, decisions under the Act have often seemed to bear little relation to economic logic in general and efficiency in particular (cf. Posner, 1976, chapter 9; Bork, 1978, chapter 20).

The ambiguity that surrounds the theoretical results on output levels under third-degree price discrimination are thus reflected in the different conclusions of the regulatory bodies in the UK, the EEC and the US (although the EEC view was coloured by the aspirations for making the Community a uniform market). There has been, however, a much more unified response to those types of discrimination that appear likely to have the effect (and in some instances have also had the clear purpose) of binding customers more closely to the dominant seller and thus making it more difficult for other competitors to increase their market share. Indeed a more important form of price discrimination than different prices to sellers in different markets (with similar costs) may be cases where the *same* prices are nominally charged to different customers (with the same costs incurred by the seller) but where net prices are different because of the application of a discriminatory discount structure. Clearly there should be no objection to different discounts being given to different customers if real economies are achieved by the seller in meeting large orders. In fact it would be inefficient in such cases to charge the same price if costs differed; but where costs of supply are the same but realized prices differ the result may not only be resource misallocation but exclusion.

Two examples are loyalty and requirement rebates. In the first, buyers are rewarded by an additional discount if they do not deal with competing firms. Similarly, in the second, the size of the discount is geared to the proportion of the buyer's total requirements that are purchased from the seller. In neither case is there any apparent cost saving to the seller. The purpose, according to both the MMC and the European Court, has been to make it as difficult as possible for competing firms to find outlets for their products. The MMC, for example, applauded the Metal Box Company's detailed discount structure insofar as it was based on real savings for the company, but condemned the additional discounts based on 'requirement' (MMC, 1968). Similarly the requirement terms offered by Hoffmann-la Roche to customers, making it almost inevitable that they would take all of their supplies from the one company, were regarded by the European Court as an infringement of Article 86.

Despite the agreement between such authorities there has always been, however, a degree of dissent for those conclusions amongst some economists. Why should existing dominant firms give discounts to customers over and above those that can be directly justified by the costs of actually making the sales, unless the purpose was the preservation of their market power? Critics have offered a number of explanations. First, what is to prevent an actual or potential rival of the dominant firm from offering similar terms, if they are as technically efficient? If they are less efficient then competition is merely having the effect it is supposed to have. If the answer to this question is that the dominant firm is prepared, in effect, to offer part of its monopoly profit to its customers in order to exclude rivals, then so long as monopoly profits exist, unless it can prevent entry (which is a separate issue), competition will force it to concede more and more to its customers. If the dominant firm attempts to use discounts to such an extent that it is claimed that sales are being made below cost, then this would amount to predatory pricing which we discuss shortly. The argument that loyalty rebates or requirement discounts by binding retailers closely to the dominant firm 'forecloses' an important portion of outlets to rival manufacturers who are therefore unable to increase market share only holds if there are barriers to entry at the retail level. If effective barriers are present then they are the real source of any exclusion and the proper focus of regulatory action, not the rebates of the dominant firm. More positively it is argued that winning and keeping customers involves considerable transaction costs. Avoiding these then brings clear benefits to the firm and it is this that is incorporated in the extra loyalty or requirement discounts. Making them illegal therefore involves, according to Bork (1978), for example, some loss of efficiency. One interpretation of the decisions of the MMC and the European Court is that, without denying the possible efficiency effect that accrues to the dominant firm from having well established and reliable distribution outlets, nevertheless, given the existing structure of the (manufacturing) market the inhibiting effect on existing rivals and potential entrants more than outweighs the advantages. In markets less dominated by a single firm loyalty rebates and similar special discounts are likely to be less cause for concern. Competing firms of roughly the same size can then be expected to match such moves by a rival with no serious exclusionary consequences.

Where one firm with a sizable market share overall operates in a number of geographically or otherwise distinct[9] market segments and where it responds to different competitive conditions, as reflected in varying elasticities of demand, sooner or later it is likely to attempt or at least be accused of predatory pricing. In this sense, therefore, it is useful to view predatory pricing as an extreme form of price discrimination. It is perhaps the most widely used allegation made against dominant firms: they can cut prices to 'uneconomic' levels to drive out or coerce existing smaller rivals and frighten off potential entrants. In this way, it is claimed, they can continue to enjoy the returns brought by their dominant market position. The deceptively simple argument should immediately put us on our guard because it seems to raise more questions than it answers. For example, what is meant by 'uneconomic'; how frequently will it have to ward off competitors by charging very low prices; while it is charging these prices will it not make heavy losses, and so on? Any caution we may have will be reinforced, firstly, by the relative scarcity of well documented cases of predatory pricing and, secondly, by the sheer volume of (recent) literature, mainly in the US, which has run to several thousands of pages and generated perhaps a dozen different suggestions for regulating the practice.[10] Bertrand Russell once wrote that a proposition commanding general agreement – two plus two equals four, for example – requires little discussion and raises few emotions. One on which there is great disagreement rests on shaky foundations. Much passion is thus spent defending the different positions without unfortunately reaching an acceptable conclusion. A recent sceptical writer on the subject put it this way: 'Do we have so many theories because predation is a common but variegated phenomenon, curable by no single antidote? Or do we have so many theories for the same reason that 600 years ago there were a thousand positions on what dragons looked like? (Easterbrook, 1981, p. 264).

In the space available we can give only a brief introduction to the topic, beginning with a more precise attempt at a definition: 'Predatory pricing behaviour involves a reduction of price in the short-run so as to drive competing firms out of the market or to discourage entry of new firms in an effort to gain larger profits via higher prices in the long-run that would have been earned if the price reduction had not occurred' (Joskow and Klevorick, 1979, pp. 219–20). Without necessarily regarding it as ideal it does allow us to make a number of preliminary points that bring out the complexity of the issue. Firstly, the definition refers only to *pricing* behaviour as predatory. Although this is often regarded as the most common form, some recent discussions have emphasized that many other aspects of market behaviour can have a predatory effect. For example, a dominant firm subsidizing a very heavy advertising campaign in one segment of the market where it faces new entry of the growth of an existing rival may be interpreted as predatory. The campaign is 'uneconomic' in that it is not intended to bring any short-run return. Some have even argued that a proliferation of product innovations may constitute predatory behaviour if their main purpose is to protect an existing market position and exclude new entry (Salop, 1981). As most of the policy discussion, however, has been in terms of pricing behaviour we will confine our remarks to it while recognizing that in some instances predatory behaviour should be more widely interpreted.

Secondly, there is no mention of costs, which have frequently been suggested as the benchmark against which price cuts should be measured. If price is cut below a certain level of costs then it is likely to be predatory rather than a response to a fall in demand. The problem, of course, is to specify precisely which 'costs' are the relevant benchmark: those of the predator or the victim; short-run or long-run; average, variable or marginal? In the recent voluminous discussion an advocate of each concept can probably be found. In the article that sparked off the controversy Areeda and Turner (1975) argued, for example, that in principle the dominant firm's short-run marginal cost should provide the benchmark, as being most in accordance with economic analysis, but that for practical purposes, because marginal cost is very difficult to measure, they were prepared to recommend the use of average variable cost. Thus their cost-based rule was that regulatory authorities should compare dominant firm prices with their average variable cost. Prices equal to or greater than such costs should be regarded as competitive (and legal) whereas prices below this level should be classed as predatory and therefore illegal. Others have argued in favour of long-run marginal cost or average total cost as the benchmarks while, as we shall see shortly, some writers reject entirely the notion of a cost-based or any other rule (cf. Bork, 1978; Easterbrook, 1981).

Thirdly, the definition emphasizes the anti-competitive and exclusionary nature of predatory pricing. The predator is seeking to maintain a private long-run advantage, that is its ability to earn super-normal profits, by undermining competition. If successful, therefore, it will perpetuate allocative inefficiency. However, the definiton also allows us to point out the central regulatory dilemma. Active competition is expected to cause price reductions and generally 'low' prices from which consumers benefit. Yet predatory pricing will show itself in exactly the same fashion: prices cut to very low levels. There is thus the danger that a regulatory policy that is too harsh, identifying predation with every price cut by a dominant firm, will impair the very instrument that should help to improve allocative efficiency. On the other hand, a policy that is too lax will allow dominant firms to use low prices as a means of maintaining their long-run position, and thus hindering any alloctive improvement. The evidence, which we discuss briefly below, suggests that despite a general belief to the contrary, the occurrence of predatory pricing is probably comparatively rare. In view of this a fairly cautious regulatory policy may be justified to avoid the first of the dangers identified.

Finally, *short-run* behaviour is identified in the definition as a means of achieving a long-run objective. The sequence envisaged is one where the dominant firm first cuts its price in the short-run to eliminate a rival or prevent entry, and then subsequently raises price again to a monopoly level to restore its earnings. This is certainly the inference that can be drawn from those commentators, like Areeda and Turner, who emphasized a cost-based rule. They have been severely criticized, however, for not incorporating into their analysis the possibility that a dominant firm will act strategically, i.e. plan its entire investment and subsequent pricing policies with a view to preventing entry while simultaneously retaining its ability to earn super-normal profits.

It would be wrong to conclude from these points, however, that while there was considerable disagreement about the *means* of regulating this feature of dominant firms' behaviour, there was general agreement about its use and importance. A number of distinguished critics have argued either that a rational firm would never employ the practice[11] or that in those rare instances in which it does occur its effects are not damaging to competition and it can safely be ignored. (On the whole this is the position, for example, of Bork (1978) and Easterbrook 1981.) They argue that a firm with a large market share will have far more to lose than a much smaller rival or one attempting to break into the market. A cut in price to, say, below the dominant firm's average variable cost (the policy benchmark advocated by Areeda and Turner) will not only increase demand, but all of that demand will have to be met at a direct loss by the firm. Although the finance for such losses may be available from the firm's profits in other markets, since such funds clearly have a positive opportunity cost, the losses will be compounded. Furthermore the firm may have no guarantee that the policy of eventually raising price to a monopoly level once competition has been eliminated will materialize. Recouping present losses in the future may be very uncertain. If current 'victims' are aware of the predatory strategy they will also know that it must eventually be reversed. From their point of view they may judge that they can inflict the maximum damage on the predator by temporarily ceasing production, thus forcing it to meet all market demand at a loss. Even if some firms are forced to leave the industry permanently, their production capacity (unless purchased by the predator, making its losses even greater) will remain intact and available to other firms once prices rise. In industries with high ratios of fixed to variable cost a long period is likely to elapse before firms are eliminated from the industry because of the likelihood of heavy sunk costs. On the other hand, where the fixed–variable-cost ratio is much lower, firms may exit from the industry in the face of predatory pricing much more readily but, equally, entry to the industry is likely to be relatively easy. In this case any attempt by the predator to raise price to recoup previous losses will be met by fresh entry. Finally, it is argued that in an environment where horizontal mergers are tolerated, although a dominant firm may threaten predatory behaviour, a much cheaper option would be for it to acquire any troublesome competitors. However where antitrust policy effectively precludes such mergers (as in the US and UK for example) neither policy will be feasible.

For reasons such as these, as well as the considerable amount of resources that may inconclusively be devoted to attempts at control, Easterbrook decisively concludes: 'The antitrust offense of predation should be forgotten' (1981, p. 337). Along with Bork, he therefore recommends that any price cuts by a firm, dominant or otherwise, should be regarded as *per se* legal.

While conceding that predatory behaviour could be expensive for the predator and, partly for that reason, is likely to be employed only infrequently many observers have nevertheless maintained that in a small number of important cases predatory pricing will be used. They make two important criticisms of the above argument. Firstly, it under-estimates the scope that market dominance allows for *selective* price cuts in a small segment of the market and this may allow the predator to inflict maximum damage on a smaller rival or entrants at minimum cost to itself. The low price may thus only apply over a limited amount of output *not* over the whole the dominant firm's market share. Not only is this in line with evidence from the UK but in view of recent privatization policies, it takes on a special significance (see chapter 10). Selective and dramatic price cuts may also have an important 'demonstration effect' on potential entrants who observe the dominant firm carrying out its threats and who therefore change their plans (Milgrom and Roberts, 1982). In a world of perfect information, mobile resources and a very large number of potential entrants to all markets, the strategy of selective price cutting would fail because the subsequent price rise would quickly induce new entry. However, in the real world of imperfect information, sunk costs and a frequently limited number of potential entrants, the lags are likely to be long enough to enable a dominant firm to practice such a selective strategy with success. Antitrust policy has proceeded on this basis using some variant of a cost-rule.

Where some writers who recognize the potential importance of predatory pricing take exception to the way policy operates is in its failure to recognize the strategic behaviour of dominant firms. They argue that although price may never fall below marginal (or average variable) cost, a dominant firm may nevertheless be able to deter entrants or, if entry actually occurs, act so as to eliminate it. As Williamson (1977), in particular, has emphasized, a firm whose dominance has been built on achieving all available scale economies will be able to plan its production capacity in such a way that it can produce at minimum cost and earn abnormal profits, while still deterring entry. In what McGee (1980) has termed 'classical limit pricing', as long as the firm is content to price at less than the short-run profit-maximizing price, the interaction of market demand and scale economies will deter new entrants. One variant of such a limit price model is shown in figure 7.3. Demand for the dominant firm's product is given by DD and the related marginal revenue curve is DMR. Long-run average costs for the dominant firm and potentially for any other firm are shown by $LRAC$. Economies of scale are clearly significant in this market. The short-run marginal and average cost curves chosen by the

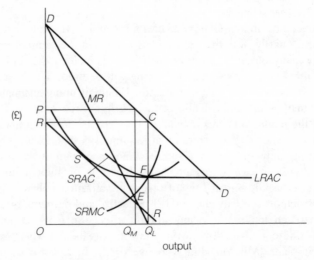

Figure 7.3 Limit pricing by a dominant firm

dominant firm are given by *SRMC* and *SRAC* respectively. If the firm maximized short-run profits it would produce Q_M at a price of *OP*. But in order to deter entry the firm deliberately chooses to lower the price to OR with the correspondingly larger output Q_L. Under these circumstances if the dominant firm maintains its output in the face of entry the only available demand exploitable by an entrant firm is the segment *CD* of the original demand curve or, displaced horizontally, the curve *RR*. We can now see the significance of the incumbent firm's decision to build a plant with average costs shown by *SRAC*. By producing an output Q_L, unit costs are minimized and the price of OR ensures that the best that an entrant firm could achieve would be to break even because the entrants' demand curve is tangental to *LRAC* at *S*. A marginally lower price than OR charged by the dominant firm would shift the residual demand curve down and there would then be no output at which a potential entrant could break even. If potential entrants continue to believe that the dominant firm will maintain output constant no entry will take place and the dominant firm will continue to earn abnormal returns, even though its price is below the short-run profit-maximizing price *P*. Thus the dominant firm is technically efficient but its market power and limit pricing creates considerable allocative inefficiency.

Writers on predatory pricing who have emphasized strategic behaviour have used some variant of the limit pricing model to argue that a regulatory policy based on a cost-rule, as suggested by Areeda and Turner, is inadequate to cope with the more serious cases. Our discussion is based on Williamson's analysis but a similar approach is suggested by Scherer (1976) and Baumol (1979) although their policy recommendations are somewhat different.

Williamson's purpose is to demonstrate that if the regulatory policy allows a dominant firm to continue unchallenged as long as its price is at least equal to marginal cost, the firm will optimize its position accordingly. In figure 7.4 *DD* and *DMR* are again the market demand and marginal revenue curves. Long-run average cost for the incumbent firm and for potential entrants is shown as *LRAC*. The dominant firm now plans its production capacity so as to meet the threat of entry. It builds plant with short-run average and marginal costs shown by *SRMC* and *SRAC*. Since it is assumed that the law allows price to fall to a level where it is equal to marginal cost, the dominant firm could, if faced by entry, expand output up to the point Q_L and price would fall to OR. An entrant firm would thus be faced with a residual demand curve *RR* which is flatter than in the case of 'classical limit pricing' (figure 7.3) because of the dominant firm's output response. The entrant is left with only the demand that the dominant firm does not meet. An output response to Q_L would just allow the entrant to break even: the residual demand curve *RR* is tangential to *LRAC*, at the

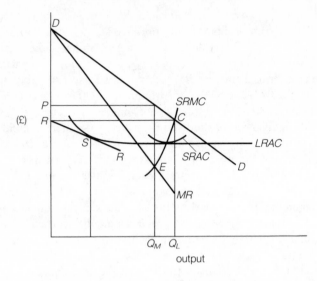

Figure 7.4 Output strategy by a dominant firm

point *S*. If any potential entrant believes that the dominant firm will respond to entry by increasing output and is thus deterred, then there is no reason for the dominant firm to forego short-run profits by charging a limit price. It can thus charge the short-run profit-maximizing price OP (where short-run marginal cost equals marginal revenue) and still deter entry. In this case not only is there considerable allocative inefficiency but also technical inefficiency. The dominant firm has deliberately built a plant larger than is required (as long as the entry-deterring strategy succeeds) and produces at less than minimum short-run average cost. It thus continually carries excess capacity in order to make its threat of increased output credible to potential entrants.

Williamson concludes, therefore, that a cost-based rule to regulate predatory pricing is inferior to one that would prevent a dominant firm from increasing its output if entry should occur. In this case technical inefficiencies would not arise because dominant firms would have no strategic reason for carrying excess capacity, although allocative efficiency might persist to the extent that limit pricing of the 'classical' kind could be maintained. Williamson thus recommends that dominant firms should *not* be allowed to increase their output for 12–18 months after entry occurs. Using a different approach but also emphasizing strategic responses Baumol (1979) suggests that dominant firms should not be allowed to rescind any price cut made in response to entry.

For all the ingenuity of the analysis there must remain a great deal of scepticism about the practicality of the policy suggestions compared with some analysis of costs. Although Williamson, for example, recognizes the problem of growing market demand by recommending that the output rule should make a suitable adjustment, there would still be formidable problems for the regulatory agency in the markets he has in mind. Prudent management requires all firms to plan ahead for a growth in sales. In a market where the dominant firm has 85–90 per cent of the market it would be extremely difficult, if not impossible, for an outside regulatory agency to distinguish between an increase in output that was due to an expanding demand from one due to an improved market share or to a strategic response to the threat of entry. A 10–12 per cent output expansion probably falls well within the range forecast by an ambitious management. As we shall see shortly markets where the dominant firm has a really substantial share may be precisely those most prone to predatory pricing but where tracking a strategic response may be most difficult. It is also not clear from Williamson's proposal whether a constant output would have to be maintained by the dominant firm as long as entry is occurring: would the entry of a second new firm mean that the output restraint period is doubled to two or three years? On the other hand if the dominant firm is released from any restraint after one year or so following entry by a solitary new firm, would not this alone be a sufficient deterrent? Twelve months of access to the market followed by a swift oblivion once the dominant firm can react may not be an attractive prospect for potential entrants. In short, there are many practical difficulties in applying rules of the kind proposed by Williamson[12], not least the fear that their implementation may bring greater damage to the competitive process than the practice they were trying to correct.

In the US, the UK and more tentatively in the EEC, antitrust bodies have used some form of cost-based test in their assessment of allegations of predatory pricing. The most striking example is provided by the US. Scarcely was the ink dry on the pages of the Areeda–Turner proposal in the Harvard Law Review before the Courts begun using it as a basis for their judgements, despite subsequent criticisms and a modification of their original view by the authors. While the test was widely cited, however, it was not adopted without qualification. In particular courts emphasized to different degrees the need to consider the level of entry barriers, the fact that a firm may be responding to price cuts by a competitor, and that average *total* cost, rather than average variable cost might be a more suitable test (Hurwitz *et al.* in Salop, 1981). After their detailed review of recent cases Hurwitz and his colleagues suggested that, contrary to expectation, the courts were moving towards a 'rule of reason approach'. The alleged simplicity of the average variable cost rule (the reason for the original proposal) had turned out to be rather elusive in actual cases. In contrast the courts had been willing to consider the complexities of entry barriers and even long-run strategic behaviour by dominant firms. They had thus found 'a somewhat more complicated approach – an approach more in line with most economists' proposals – to be both administrable and consistent with their own sense of where the greatest dangers lie'. (ibid. p. 140). So far, however, they have resisted the temptation to extend their interpretation of predatory behaviour either to innovation (on the grounds that it might have an adverse effect on incentives), or to promotion largely because of the complexity of much promotional activity.

The influence of Areeda and Turner's analysis may, nevertheless, have been significant by making it more difficult for a firm to convince the courts that it had been harmed by predatory pricing. Out of 23 recently determined cases reviewed by Hurwitz *et al.*, the plaintiff had won in only 2 and lost in 21. In comparison, a survey of 73 cases decided prior to 1971 found that the plaintiff won 45 cases and the defendant only 28 (Koller, 1971). The courts may therefore have tacitly accepted the basic premise of Areeda and Turner that predatory pricing was 'highly unlikely'.

The form of MMC enquiries in the UK allows the MMC to give due weight to all the factors involved. It is not bound in any way by previous conclusions and treats each case on its merits. What in one case, therefore, is judged to be predatory behaviour may in another, with many similar features, be explicable in terms of the interaction of competitive forces and the level of demand. Unlike US antitrust actions which may be concerned with the particular issue of predatory (or uneconomic) pricing as a means of monopolizing a market, the MMC is usually [13] concerned with the whole behaviour and performance of a dominant firm. Pricing may thus form only a minor part of a report, which often amounts to a monograph on the market concerned.

A close analysis of the reports on dominant firms, which have now been appearing intermittently since 1948, bears out the point made earlier that predatory pricing is probably *not* used frequently but that its selective use persists and can be effective. Examples can be found from the earlier cases, such as British Match (1953) and British Oxygen (1956) through to more recent ones like Hoffmann-la Roche (1973) and de Mulder (1985.[14] Although it is dangerous to generalize from relatively few cases, one striking point is that the objectionable price cutting was highly selective, either geographically (as in MMC (1953), (1981d) and (1985) or by type of customer (in MMC (1963) and (1973b). The losses incurred by the predator could therefore be contained while the price cuts could have their maximum effect on the entrants, struggling to gain market share. Clearly if the firms were forced to make such price cuts across the board, they would have second thoughts. Another characteristic of a number of the MMC reports dealing with this issue was the overwhelming dominance of the leading firm.[15] The success of a campaign of predatory pricing is likely to be achieved much more speedily in such a market than where the would-be predator faces a rival with a substantial market share. In the recent case heard by the European Commission, and which to date is the only clear-cut case involving allegations of predatory pricing under Article 86, the defendant company, AKZO, was accused of charging unduly low prices in the UK in order to force a rival out of a related market in Germany. Although the Commission came out strongly against AKZO, largely on the strength of some damaging internal cost evidence which referred to selling below cost in the UK (Engineering and Chemical Supplies Ltd, 1983), given the size of the victims (ECS's) market share in the UK of 35 per cent[16] compared with AKZO's 52 per cent, the success of its price cutting strategy was far from assured. A number of outcomes are possible with this market structure. For example, AKZO was likely to suffer heavy losses while the campaign continued because of the size of ECS's market share. The large customers may have been unwilling to see ECS weakened or eliminated to the benefit of AKZO, and therefore have been prepared to sign long-term contracts with ECS in order to forestall this possibility. Lying behind the European Commission's decision may have been the rather discredited 'deep-pocket' hypothesis. In the UK, AKZO and ECS had rather similar market shares but globally AKZO was much larger than ECS. The Commission may have concluded, therefore, that AKZO could finance a predatory campaign from its earnings in other markets although, for the reasons given, sustained action of this kind lacks credibility.

To rely almost exclusively on cost information in predatory pricing cases, as has recently been seen in the one significant EEC case, is not likely to provide a solid and consistent foundation for regulatory policy. Not only will potentially vulnerable firms learn to ensure that no damaging documents exist on their files but, more fundamentally, the complexity of cost allocations in multi-product firms makes much cost information misleading. As Easterbrook concludes, a different treatment of investment in research and development, human capital or advertising from the one appearing in the firm's books may 'make the difference between a finding of predation and a finding of no liability' (Easterbrook, 1981, p. 334). The MMC has recognized these problems and although it has in recent cases[17] examined cost data it has not been prepared to make its final judgement on pricing policies on that information alone but has assessed the competitive conditions taken as a whole.

One final point can be made about predatory pricing in the context of recent UK policy. If, as we suggested above, the markets most prone to predatory behaviour are those almost completely dominated by one firm, then the policy of privatizing intact monopoly enterprises that were previously state-owned (and therefore subject to a measure of direct regulation) is likely to magnify the problem. Predatory pricing may not only occur intermittently in those parts of manufacturing and services that have always been in the private sector but also in those important industries newly released from state ownership and control. The Civil Aviation Authority recognized the potential seriousness of this problem in the case of British Airways (CAA, 1984a). However, its proposals for generating more competition in the industry were largely ignored by the government aiming to sell off the airline for the highest price to relieve pressure on public borrowing. The broader issues of regulation raised by privatizing monopoly enterprises are considered more fully in chapter 10.

(ii) Refusal to Sell and Exclusive Dealing

A central tenet of a free enterprise system is that traders themselves should be free, within the law, to trade with whoever they wish. Indeed an important part of the efficiency with which such a system allocates resources consists of individual traders' using the information they have about the market and their own judgement to make contracts with the best suppliers or customers available. Any general interference with this freedom of contract would, therefore, be likely to reduce efficiency. The obvious corollary of the freedom to make contracts would appear to be the negative right to refuse to make contracts with certain traders or customers. It would be inefficient, for example, if a manufacturer was prevented by regulation, or law, from refusing to sell to a retailer who it judged to be uncreditworthy. Similarly if the size of the orders received from some customers was so small that it was uneconomic for the manufacturer to make the deliveries it would be inefficient to force the firm to do so.

Other cases may arise, however, where the intention and effect of a refusal to sell may be to inhibit competition and buttress monopoly power. Suppose, for example, a manufacturer with a large market share and well established pattern of distribution threatens to refuse to supply distributors if they begin to stock the products of a rival manufacturer or new entrant. If the threat is successful the dominant firm by denying the rival access to perhaps the best retail outlets is thus helping to preserve its own position. Although it may be claimed that as long as there are no restrictions on entry into distribution, rivals and entrants could distribute their products through their own retail network, unless there are real economies to be had from such vertical integration this solution would be inefficient and also make barriers to entry to the industry higher than they would otherwise be. The fact that the leading firm in the example was not vertically integrated implies that such economies were not available. Clearly if the threat of refusal to supply came from a manufacturer with only a modest market share it would be unlikely to carry much weight with distributors and would thus fail through lack of credibility.

A case very similar to the hypothetical one just sketched occurred in the MMC enquiry into the supply of clutch mechanisms for road vehicles (MMC, 1968). The dominant supplier, Automotive Products (AP), had, at the time of the report, a market share of about 85 per cent of the UK market. It had operated a system of discriminatory discounts in favour of those of its designated wholesalers who remained 'loyal' to AP and did not stock the products of its only rival in the replacement market, Quinton Hazell. When the latter company did actually integrate vertically and purchase a wholesale group that had carried AP's clutches, AP enforced a policy of initially withdrawing the special 'loyalty' discounts and then effectively ensuring that no supplies were made available to Quinton Hazell's subsidiary. The MMC summarized AP's behaviour as follows:

(1) AP adopted a two-tier selected distributor policy which involved refusal of direct supplies to a large number of wholesalers from buying from these distributors;
(2) AP imposed a condition of sale to prevent its distributors and their customers from selling to certain specified wholesalers for resale by the latter. (MMC, 1970a).

Not surprisingly the MMC concluded that the distribution arrangements restricted existing or potential competition and operated against the public interest, and recommended their abandonment.

A more difficult type of case to determine is where a dominant firm refuses to supply distributors on the grounds that they are known price cutters. The manufacturers may reason that if he or she supplies the price cutting firms there will be increased pressure from other distributors for improved terms in the face of intensified competition. Existing distributors may threaten to boycott the manufacturer's products if he or she supplies the discount firms, although given the dominant position assumed, the threat may not carry much conviction. More importantly some manufacturers may argue that they have a genuine interest in retaining the high-quality brand image of their products which in part may depend on distributors supplying a proper range of before- and after-sales service. For this they require an appropriate margin. Price-cutting retailers may do away with the services while consumers use the specialist retailers to gain information and advice but make their purchases at the discount store, in effect getting a 'free ride'. Eventually the high-margin specialists will leave the trade and consumers will then receive inadequate advice about proper use and maintenance of products. In the long-run the manufacturer would suffer a loss of sales. The classic reference on this type of argument is

Telser (1960), and was essentially concerned with the distinct but related issue of resale price maintenance which has been effectively illegal in the UK since the operation of the 1964 Resale Prices Act. An important provision of that Act was to make it illegal for a manufacturer to refuse supplies to a distributor on the grounds that the latter would cut prices. Clearly if resale prices could not legally be maintained[18] by manufacturers it would be inconsistent if they could nevertheless withhold supplies because they objected to the prices being charged by certain retailers. Unfortunately an additional clause was added to the Act that allowed a firm to avoid the previous condition by adding some other reason for withholding supplies. According to the MMC this amounts to a 'virtual invitation to suppliers whose reason for refusing supplies is to influence resale pricing either to invent some other reason for doing so or, if they have another reason which standing alone is, or may be too weak, to exaggerate its importance with a view to discouraging legal proceedings' (MMC, 1970, paragraph 45).

In effect the offending clause contributed to the emasculation of this section of the 1964 Act since no proceedings had been brought against a firm for withholding supplies by the time the MMC reported in 1970, and one of its major recommendations then was to try to make amends by revising the Act.[19] In the event only with the passage of the 1980 Competition Act, which made provision for referral of 'anti-competitive practices' to the MMC, was an attempt made to fill the loophole.

Unfortunately the very first case examined by the MMC which was concerned with precisely the issue of refusal to supply appears to raise more issues than it settles. Under the 1980 Act a two-stage procedure was established for investigating anti-competitive practices which were defined as courses of conduct that have the effect of 'restricting, distorting or preventing competition in connection with the production, supply or acquisition of goods in the United Kingdom' (section 2). The Director General of Fair Trading may carry out an investigation of a suspect anti-competitive practice and publish the results. If he concludes that such a practice is being operated he refers it to the MMC which then has to decide whether or not it operates against the public interest.

The first case concerned the refusal by T.I. Raleigh to supply its bicycles to certain distributors such as Argos, Asda, Tesco, Comet, House of Holland and Woolworth, all of whom were not specialist bicycle retailers but who had the reputation for selling at low prices. Raleigh's marketing strategy had tended to emphasize the high quality of its machines, distributed through specialist outlets which could give customers full pre-sales advice and post-sales service. They argued that both of these would suffer if Raleigh bicycles were distributed through discount stores interested in high volume with a minimum of service. Both the Director

General and the MMC in their report concluded that the refusal to supply was an anti-competitive practice under the 1980 Act. The MMC decided that it was against the public interest but they recommended *not* that Raleigh should be required to supply the stores with their bicycles but rather that Raleigh should make available to them bicycles manufactured by them and of an equivalent standard to their branded products and that could be termed 'made by Raleigh' rather than 'Raleigh bicycles'.

What both the Director General and the MMC appear to have neglected in this case is the effect of Raleigh's policy on themselves, the stores they refused and the ultimate consumer. At a time when the demand for bicycles was booming Raleigh's share of the market fell from a peak of 67 per cent in 1972 to 40 per cent in 1980, when it actually lost £7 millions. A large part of the lost market share was undoubtedly due to the discount retailers and other more specialist stores turning elsewhere, especially Austria and West Germany, to meet their growing demand. As a result imports which accounted for only one per cent of the market in the late 1960s had increased their share of the market to 36 per cent by 1980. The major sufferer, therefore, from Raleigh's marketing policy appears to have been Raleigh itself. The discount retailers obtained substitute goods from abroad which they sold to meet the growing consumer demand. Far from constituting an exercise of market power Raleigh's refusal to supply appears to have undermined its market share and led it to the verge of bankruptcy.[20]

As Kay and Sharpe (1982) point out a large part of the problem lies with the very loose definition of 'anti-competitive practices' in the 1980 Act. When the MMC concludes that 'Raleigh's policy of withholding supplies from some retailers therefore had, or was likely to have, the effect of restricting competition in the retailing of Raleigh bicycles' (MMC, 1981c) it comes close to saying that *any* refusal to supply, for whatever reason, is likely to be considered an anti-competitive practice, regardless of the effects. However, clearly this is not a viable position because it would place firms in the impossible situation of having to deal with customers, for example, whose creditworthiness they distrusted or who were not prepared to meet the basic requirements for distributing the product. It is not part of antitrust policy to protect firms from making bad commercial decisions. In the Raleigh case its refusal to deal was commercially disastrous. Under American antitrust law a firm is free to refuse to deal with others 'unless the refusal is intended to support another illegal restraint or constitutes an attempt to monopolise' (Bork, 1978 p. 344). Since Raleigh's action directly led to a weakening of its market position it is fairly certain that it would not have been seen as infringing American law.

The contrast with the earlier AP case is clear. Given the structure of distribution for motor vehicle clutches and AP's dominant share it could effectively bolster its position by a tight system of refusal to deal. In this case other manufacturers seeking outlets for their products would have to build up their own alternative distribution network, thus raising entry barriers. Raleigh attempted to use market power that it did not really possess, owing to the plentiful availability of alternative supplies from imports. In fact, as the MMC admits, if Raleigh had recognized the fundamental changes that were taking place in retailing methods it would also probably have seen that its own best interest lay in supplying the discount retailers.

A subsequent case involved an attempt by Sheffield Newspapers (SN) to prevent the successful entry of a competitor (supplying 'free' publications, financed by advertising, much of which previously went to SN) by threatening to stop supplies to distributors who handled the entrants' products. The Office of Fair Trading concluded that it constituted a clear anti-competitive practice and subsequently the MMC decided that it was against the public interest in that it attempted to exclude a potentially more efficient form of advertising. However, if the entrants' methods were more efficient the threat by SN is likely to have failed. It could either have made an improved offer to existing distributors or used direct distribution methods which have been successful in other parts of the country.

As far as the future developmnt of UK policy is concerned it is clearly important to establish that only those practices that ultimately affect consumers' interests adversely by preserving or enhancing market power are anti-competitive.

A closely related practice is exclusive dealing.[21] Under this arrangement a manufacturer contracts with distributors in such a way that in consideration of the generous margins offered they will handle its products exclusively and not those of rival suppliers. In some cases the exclusive dealing may be accompanied by an exclusive franchise whereby the manufacturer agrees to restrict the number of distributors who will handle its product in a particular area or delineate a particular region or class of customer to which a distributor will be the sole supplier.

Clearly such arrangements are restrictive in that they limit the range of products carried by some distributors and in effect give distributors a monopoly over the supply of a particular manufacturer's products in a city or region. In trying to determine the impact of the practice on competition and market power we should recall, however, that we are only concerned with dominant firms. If a manufacturer with a small market share attempts to enforce exclusive dealing arrangements, it is likely to meet either with a limited response from distributors[22] or, even if successful, have only a marginal impact on competition, since by assumption a large portion of the retail trade must still be open to competing products. There may be a number of advantages to both manufacturers and distributors from an exclusive dealing agreement. Firstly the manufacturer will be assured of a single-minded selling effort from distributors whose livelihood will depend on it. The improved selling performance may make it worthwhile for the manufacturer to provide special training in handling and servicing complex products. Secondly, costs may be reduced for both manufacturer and distributor as a result of the reduction in the total number of transactions. The handling, selling and even production costs are likely to be reduced for a manufacturer supplying a given volume of output to, say four distributors, instead of 20. In their turn distributors' transaction and inventory costs will be lower if they receive all of their supplies from a single firm. Thirdly, for risk-averse firms uncertainties over product demand (for the manufacturer) or product supplies (for the distributor) are likely to lead to a lower all-round output making both parties worse off (Blair and Kaserman, 1983). Both should, therefore, be prepared to pay a premium to have the uncertainties reduced. Such influences are likely to be particularly apparent where secure and uninterrupted supplies are essential (as in steel production and electricity generation).

To the extent that these cost savings are realized and are passed on, at least in part, to consumers, exclusive dealing can be considered desirable. The need for some kind of regulation of the practice appears to arise if no benefits are actually transmitted to consumers and the practice is used as a device to exclude entrants. The argument is normally put in terms of 'foreclosure'. Clearly an exclusive dealing agreement cuts the number of distributors available to an entrant. A dominant manufacturer, realizing the kind of economies mentioned above through a series of exclusive contracts, will simultaneously be limiting the number of existing outlets that can be used by a new supplier. To be sure the newcomer could also enter distribution, but unless integrated production–distribution brings economies *additional* to those achieved through contract it will simply raise barriers to entry. Nor in practice is it likely that a newcomer to the field will be able to win away from the dominant supplier distributors that had previously had an exclusive arrangement but whose contract had expired. As Williamson (1975) has argued, at the time of a *first* contract all manufacturers may be equal in relation to distributors, but once a contract has been signed and then run its course, the successful firm will be at a great advantage thereafter. It has learnt the special requirements and idiosyncracies of the distributor and can tailor its offer accordingly. Competition at contract renewal time is unlikely, therefore, to be an equal contest.

In the UK the MMC has had to consider the practice on a number of occasions. Although usually claims have been made for its efficiency effects, the Commission has almost without exception decided that the main impact had been exclusionary and therefore operated against the public interest. Thus in its report on industrial and medical gases (MMC, 1956) the MMC condemned the practice by British Oxygen (BOC), which had almost a complete monopoly, of insisting on exclusive buying as a condition of supply to its larger customers. It concluded that the purpose of the restriction 'can only be to preserve BOC's monopoly position, and in our view it limits the customer's freedom of choice to an extent which is contrary to the public interest' (paragraph 252). In almost exactly the same terms the MMC condemned the practice of the leading wallpaper manufacturer (market share 79 per cent) of insisting on exclusive dealing before customers could qualify for discounts[23] (MMC, 1965): 'We have no doubt that the exclusive arrangements formerly operated were intended to maintain the Group's hold on the market by depriving its manufacturing competitors of access to the distributional outlets concerned and that they had this effect' (paragraph 155). More recently the MMC concluded that exclusive purchasing imposed on franchised retailers inhibited new entry at the manufacturing stage (MMC, 1982).

Despite the consistency of the MMC's view on the practice, very much seems to depend on how one views the flexibility with which markets can respond to changed circumstances. The MMC clearly regarded the practice by an already dominant firm as one means of maintaining its position. In principle it might be true that as long as there is no other impediment to entry at the distribution stage, then a newcomer is not absolutely excluded from the market. If it can offer better terms to those well-placed distributors who have signed exclusive contracts with the dominant supplier, then the entrant remains free to do so. To this extent Blair and Kaserman's conclusion that exclusive dealing cannot create exclusionary power – 'it can only be a means of implementing such power as already exists' (Blair and Kaserman, 1983, p. 174) remains true. However, given the degree of dominance with which the MMC is often confronted it has, correctly in our view, decided that the likelihood of successful new entry is considerably reduced or at least very much delayed by exclusive dealing and has therefore opposed it. The judgement is reinforced when considered alongside the further conclusion that breaking up dominant firms may not be feasible as a remedy in competition policy (see section IV below).

(iii) Tying Arrangements and Full-Line Forcing

A tying arrangement exists where the supplier of a product A (the tying product) stipulates to customers that they must also take product B (the tied product). Frequently the products may be complementary (such as photocopying machines and toner or ink, colour film and film processing, petrol and lubricants) but in other cases they may be part of a range (e.g.

beer and soft drinks, main feature films and 'B' features). The latter case is similar to the practice of full-line forcing where the supplier insists on customers taking a complete range of products rather than individual items.

A dominant firm may have a variety of motives in seeking to tie its sales in this fashion and the general view now seems to be that only in special circumstances will the effect be exclusionary. It was originally argued that a dominant supplier of a product by tying could extend its dominance into the second market. Although there may be cases where this could occur they are likely to be rare, and in any case the regulatory action should be against features other than the tying arrangement. Thus, for example, if a dominant firm supplying A attempts to extend its dominance to product B by tying, it will fail as long as there are other uses for product B and other suppliers. It may be able to insist on the tie but independent producers of the tied product will retain the rest of the market. Nevertheless the dominant firm will be able to add to its monopoly profit for product A whatever additional profit it is able to obtain by tying at least part of the related product market. Only if the dominant firm for product A is in the fortunate position of supplying a major share of the tied product B will it be able to exclude competition. However, in this extreme case the firm effectively has an integrated monopoly of the two products and tying will hardly be necessary to secure exclusion. Regulatory policy in such a case should concentrate on the real cause of dominance, which may of course turn out to be perfectly legal, such as a patent. Furthermore where products A and B are complements used in variable proportions the dominant producer of A will be able to raise its profits by a tying arrangement above the level they would be if the products were priced independently. This follows from the ability of the tying firm to take account of all interdependencies in the variables affecting its profit-maximizing output position (see, for example, Blair and Kaserman (1983, chapter 4)).

A more familiar case is where the dominant firm uses tying as a means of achieving price discrimination and so increasing its profits. A firm renting out photocopying machines might find it difficult to discriminate between customers whose demands are very different. One customer with relatively light demand will be charged the same rental as the customer with a very heavy demand for photocopying. If, however, paper supplies are tied in with the deal for the photocopying machine, not only can the tied product be priced so as to bring a high return but the quantity supplied acts as a metering device which the company can use to adjust rental charges in a discriminatory fashion. The effect is to cream off part of consumer surplus in the form of a monopoly profit.[24] As we have already seen, however, the case for regulating price discrimination that enhances profits but that does not exclude is ambiguous. Depending on whether the discrimination results in a more or less widespread use of the product, consumer welfare will be improved or worsened. On the whole, in the UK at least, a regulating body like the MMC is unlikely to condemn a tie that has only this effect.

A dominant firm may thus have a variety of profit motives for adopting tying agreements but they are unlikely to be the cause of its dominance or explain its continuation. Moreover the regulatory issue is made more difficult by two further factors. Firstly, it is frequently claimed that a tying arrangement is necessary to ensure that complex products are used and serviced properly. If a complicated piece of electronic machinery, for example, is damaged by using inferior or unsuitable complementary products or by being overhauled by untrained personnel, then the reputation and goodwill of the manufacturer may be undermined. The firm clearly has a legitimate interest in maintaining the reliability and performance of its products and an important method of achieving this may be by tying. Whether the claim is actually substantiated will depend on the particular technology of the industry concerned. For example in the report on Rank–Xerox by the MMC (1976) it was found that the tying agreement (whereby rent for a photocopying machine also covered servicing, toner and other supplies such as filters, drums and developer) was reasonable where use of unauthorized materials could adversely affect the perform-ance of the machine but not where no adverse consequences would follow from the use of other products (as in the case of toner).

Secondly there may be economies in marketing and distribution where a tying arrangement is in force. In the above example distribution costs will be lower if the servicing engineer also delivers new supplies of other materials used by the machine. Again, a supplier of bulk storage or handling equipment to farmers may be able to offer favourable terms if feed, chemicals and fertilizers are also purchased (MMC, 1981b).

The difficulties of unravelling the complex series of motives and effects that may be involved in a tying agreement are reflected in the UK regulatory experience. The authoritative *Review of Restrictive Practices Policy* (1979) cited a number of MMC cases condemning the practice as against the public interest. Apart from the Rank–Xerox case mentioned above the Commission had found that Kodak's practice of selling its colour film at a price to include processing was objectionable; that Metal Box's policy of giving favourable terms to customers using their can-closing machines on condition that they used cans exclusively supplied by the company, was against the public interest;[25] and finally that the practice of film distributors sometimes tying the hire of a popular film to that of other films was contrary to the interest of cinema-goers. Largely on the basis of these cases the *Review* concluded that it was likely that tying arrangements usually had damaging effects on competition and that there might be a case for a complete prohibition. It was therefore recommended that the MMC should be given, as soon as possible, a general reference on tie-in sales (Review, 1979 p. 42). The reference was duly made in 1979 and the report submitted two years later.

Far from concluding that the practice should be prohibited completely, after calling for submissions from interested parties – a call that went largely unheeded – and reviewing the evidence, the MMC decided that 'the number of cases in which the practices (full-line forcing and tie-in sales) do *not* operate against the public interest is substantial' (MMC, 1981b, p. 42; my italics). It was therefore considered inappropriate to introduce any general ban. Under the 1980 Competition Act, however, it is perfectly possible for the Director General of Fair Trading to investigate particular cases of tie-ins as a possible 'anti-competitive practice' (see the appendix to this chapter) and then make a reference to the MMC if he considers it appropriate.

Although this conclusion was surprising in view of the presumption made by the earlier *Review*, the MMC, in its final summing up, did suggest that where considerable market power existed for the tying good 'the anti-competitive effects of tie-in sales and line forcing are likely to be much more significant if the practices are associated with an insistence on exclusive dealing' (MMC, 1981b, p. 45). This is in line with our comment in the previous section on exclusive dealing that where a supplier has a very dominant position in a particular market, practices that in other circumstances may be unobjectionable could unduly weaken or retard the competitive entry of other firms. Where a dominant firm in market A is seeking to strengthen its position in related market B by tying and exclusive dealing there is thus a strong probability that entry to the second market may be made unnecessarily difficult.[26] The position in the EEC is broadly similar to that suggested in the 1981 MMC report (MMC 1981b), except that the distinction between acceptable and unacceptable cases is made more clear-cut. Thus the Commission's policy is to permit tying under competitive conditions but effectively to forbid it in cases of dominance.

The eclectic, or 'rule of reason', approach to tie-in sales recommended by the MMC has not found much favour in the American attitude to the problem. Although the original stance of the American antitrust authorities of, in effect, treating tie-ins as *per se* illegal has been modified, most observers consider that it still lags a very long way behind the conclusions of current economic analysis. One of the most severe critics concludes 'Antitrust treats (tying arrangements) as utterly pernicious, despite the increasingly obtrusive fact that it has found no adequate grounds for objecting to them at all' (Bork, 1978, p. 365).

IV DOMINANCE, MERGERS AND REGULATION

Investigations by the MMC reveal that the greater the discretion firms have over prices, as revealed by their large market share and lack of a close rival, the greater is their profitability, *ceteris paribus* (Utton, 1986). One inference from these results may be that such firms were therefore generating considerable allocative inefficiency by persistently holding prices above average costs. To the extent that they could exclude rivals by the types of behaviour discussed in section III then the inference is correct. On the other hand it has been increasingly argued, especially for firms located in an economy like the UK, that in many markets technical efficiency inevitably results in dominance. To achieve *all* economies of size to operate efficiently in the UK and in overseas markets, firms have to be relatively large. Indeed, as we saw in the introduction, the next step in this argument is that leading firms owe their position to technical efficiency and would lose it soon enough if they became slack. For this reason regulators of private sector dominance, even in the US, have been reluctant to use the remedy, advocated on a selective basis by Williamson (1972b) amongst others, of dismantling large firms. The trade-off involved is, in principle, an improvement in allocative efficiency and possibly x-efficiency resulting from the increased competition in the market, against a loss of technical efficiency caused by the break-up of the largest firm into a number of separate components. In practice, as the recent AT and T example demonstrates, it is likely to be far more complicated.[27] To the probable loss of technical efficiency, broadly interpreted, must be added the resource costs of preparing and carrying out the break-up.[28] Furthermore the benefits of increased competition may be a long time arriving. A market re-structured largely from new firms created from parts of the previous leader, and presumably with many of the previous managers who had been colleagues, is unlikely to produce intense rivalry immediately. As we shall see in the next chapter it is frequently difficult to ensure active competition in oligopolistic markets between firms that have been always independent of one another. They frequently find methods of 'mutual accommodation' which may amount practically to collusion. The likelihood of such behaviour amongst firms managed by men and women who were previously all members of the same enterprise is probably much higher.

In consequence, even for a country like the US with its strong antitrust tradition the 'break-up' solution to dominance has met with comparatively little success (Posner, 1976, pp. 85-8). Admittedly there were some important instances prior to the First World War: Standard Oil, 1911; American Tobacco, 1911; and duPont's control of explosives, 1912. But in different ways these early cases highlight aspects of the general problem. In the Standard Oil case it was possible to dissolve the holding company which controlled the different operating companies with the minimum of disruption but also, initially, with a minimum of increased competition. Dissolution of a fully integrated company is likely to be much more difficult. Indeed this was precisely the view taken by the Court in 1953 when faced by the proposal from the government that the United Shoe Machinery Company (USM) should be broken up into three separate companies. The Court noted that all of USM's machines were made at a single plant so there was no feasible way of dividing it into viable parts. It therefore refused the divestiture proposal. American Tobacco *was* broken into three separate companies but their subsequent collusion was condemned in a later antitrust action, and again the re-introduction of competition was minimal. By the time that duPont was forced to sell off about half of its explosives interests, they accounted for only a fraction of its total turnover, and in any case many of the divested plants produced a material that shortly became obsolete (Posner, 1976, p. 86). The problems caused by the delays of the law and changing economic circumstances are also illustrated by the Aluminum Co. of America (ALCOA) case. Based on evidence up to the outbreak of the Second World War the Court had decided that ALCOA was guilty of monopolizing the aluminium industry. The final decision in the case, however, had to await the disposal by the government of productive capacity built up during the War. By 1950, compared with its prewar share of 90 per cent of primary aluminium capacity, ALCOA had just over 50 per cent with two new companies holding the remainder. The changed structure of the industry and the fact that ALCOA only had two primary production plants (one of which was not viable on its own) persuaded the Court that divestiture was not economically desirable, even though ALCOA had been found guilty under section 1 of the Sherman Act.

In view of the difficulties and previous decisions it is all the more remarkable that the most spectacular divestiture in US history was agreed in 1982, ending a suit that had begun in 1974. At the time of the announcement of the agreement between the antitrust division and the American Telephone and Telegraph Company (AT and T) over divestiture, the company was ranked first on the Fortune list with assets of $155 billions, revenue $65 billions, 84 million customers and about one million employees. It was a completely integrated company, not only providing a full range of short- and long-distance telephone services, but also manufacturing and researching telephone equipment for its supplying companies and handsets for final customers. Since the granting of the first patents in 1876, the company had dominated the US industry and had been able to use its regulated status to promote its own interests and deflect antitrust action.[29]

Most commentators are agreed that two factors played an important part in easing a path towards divestiture which thirty years ago would have seemed impossible. The first was a series of the Federal Communications Commission (FCC) and Court decisions which opened up to competition a number of markets that AT and T had previously supplied exclusively, and the second was the gathering momentum of technical change in the related areas of telecommunications and data processing and transmission. We look briefly at these developments in turn.

Until the late 1950s the attitude towards regulation of the industry had been governed by conventional notions of natural monopoly (discussed in chapter 1 above). Since then and until the consent decree[30] of 1982 the attitude of the FCC was one of 'managed competition' (Besen and Woodbury, 1983). The erosion of AT and T's monopoly of long-distance communication began in 1959 when the FCC allocated part of the radio frequency spectrum to users wishing to construct their own private microwave communication systems. It continued when Microwave Communications Inc. (MCI) attempted to enter the private long-distance line market, in competition with AT and T which had previously had a monopoly. AT and T denied MCI access to its local distribution facilities, employing a dual argument that paralleled its response to the competitive challenge it was also facing in the equipment market. The first part of the argument was that the integrity of the whole system had to be protected from inferior equipment which might cause serious damage. It was thus necessary for the *whole* service to be provided by one supplier. Secondly, high returns on the long-distance services which MCI wished to enter, were necessary in order to help support the less densely used services. In this market, as in the equipment market, both arguments were rejected by the FCC and it became clear that the decision could apply equally to other firms wishing to enter the conventional long-distance market. AT and T's response was to make it as difficult as possible for new entrants to be connected to the local services and also to use selective price cuts where competitors were trying to establish themselves. The ensuing controversy involved claims by entrants about predatory pricing and counterclaims by AT and T about inefficient, high cost new entrants.

Similar points were made by the company to try to preserve their position in the equipment market, again with very little success. An important outcome of the FCC's previous acceptance of the technical case that the 'integrity of the system as a whole should be preserved from defective equipment' was that the monopoly supplier of telephone services was also able to maintain its monopoly of equipment. When this position was challenged in the mid-1960s by the Carter Electric Company (Carterfone), claiming that the AT and T restriction was an infringement of the antitrust laws, the FCC decided in Carterfone's favour on the ground that AT and T had failed to establish that their equipment would damage the system. It was again made clear that the same would hold for other suppliers.

As in the long-distance case, the response of AT and T was not unnaturally to try to protect its position. Customers wishing to use equipment from independent suppliers were required to use an interface device, supplied by AT and T, ostensibly to insulate the system from damage in the event of a malfunction.[31] It was subsequently claimed by independent equipment suppliers that the prices of the attachments were often so high as to make their use uneconomic. It was also pointed out that AT and T equipment which had the same characteristics as that of the independents did not require special attachments.

The FCC response was eventually to introduce a registration system for telephone equipment. All equipment meeting the FCC standards could be registered for use with the AT and T system without an interface attachment. Note that, unlike the recently introduced British scheme whereby equipment has to meet with British Telecom approval (and can lead to considerable controversy, as we see below in chapter 10), in the US registration is carried out by the independent FCC. An important barrier to competition was thus removed from the telephone equipment market and a considerable number of new suppliers subsequently entered.

Thus in both the long-distance and equipment markets the FCC rejected AT and T's technical case for the protection of their system and new competition emerged. It was less successful, however, in dealing with the second argument, that cross subsidization was required if AT and T was to continue to supply all markets. In the equipment market the company maintained that it required high returns for equipment supplied to business customers (the section most attractive to new competitors) in order to keep prices relatively low for domestic consumers. In fact AT and T's pricing policies developed into an issue of central importance as some of its markets became accessible to new competition. What previously might have been regarded as an unexceptional (albeit paternalistic) policy of cross-subsidization was now regarded, especially in the long-distance market, as predatory. AT and T's defence was essentially that it should be able to meet competition and ensure that high cost new firms could not successfully enter, as this would be inefficient. In the late 1970s, therefore, the FCC found itself having to decide what constituted a predatory price. As we have seen in the previous section, the issue is extremely complex even when confined to relatively simple models. When applied to a predominant, well-established and multi-product firm like AT and T it becomes practically impossible. Not surprisingly, therefore, the FCC effectively abandoned the task (Besen and Woodbury, 1983). The experience should be a sobering reminder to the newly constituted OFTel in the UK that monitoring pricing policies in telecommunications markets is extremely complicated but nevertheless crucial if new competition is to develop.

Despite the problems, the combination of the FCCs and the courts' decisions helped to erode some of AT and T's monopoly positions. A second influence was the growing pace of technical change which served to obliterate very rapidly the old divisions between one market and another. The development created a new series of problems both for the FCC and AT and T. Under a previous antitrust action in 1956 which was settled by a consent decree, AT and T was prohibited from entering the computer industry. While the telephone industry was regulated, the computer industry was not. But as the information technology and computer revolutions gathered momentum in the 1970s it became increasingly difficult for the FCC to determine which part of AT and T's service should be properly regulated and which should not, and indeed whether AT and T could legitimately supply some 'unregulated' information services, given the terms of the 1956 settlement. From AT and T's point of view, the growth of the computer market and all of its ancillary developments looked increasingly attractive, especially as some of its traditional markets were being eroded. In addition it was excluded from participation in communications satellites, while from 1972 onwards its competitors were not, under a deliberate policy by the FCC of allowing them a 'headstart' in order to prevent AT and T extending its monopoly further by cross subsidization.

By 1980, therefore, the combination of a fundamentally changed competitive and technological environment had made divestiture a serious possibility and two years later an agreement was reached between the antitrust division and the company. Under the divestiture the former AT and T was divided into eight separate enterprises, but the essence of the division was between local telephone services and 'the rest'. Thus 22 local telephone companies were reformed into *seven* regional holding companies while the *eighth* company, AT and T with assets reduced to a 'mere' $43 billions, retained control of the long-distance services, the manufacturing companies (Western Electric and American Bell), the research facilities (Bell Laboratories) and the overseas sales company (AT and T International).[32] Thus those parts of the enterprise that recent experience had shown could be made competitive were separated from those parts (local services) where strong elements of natural monopoly persist. Both the new regional companies and the still dominant AT and T continue to be closely regulated, but competition will continue to intensify in all but the local markets now that the formidable entry barrier from the integrated concern has been removed. The local companies will no longer have any incentive to give preference to AT and T long-line links or indeed to the sale of their equipment.

For AT and T a significant inducement in the divestiture negotiations was freedom to enter the computer market for the first time where it may eventually form a suitable counterweight to IBM whose dominance has also caused severe antitrust problems.[33] But given IBM's lead it may take a considerable time before AT and T, for all its acknowledged prowess in research, can mount a serious challenge. In general the feeling is, however, that the divestiture, together with the intensified competition and the reduction in regulation, provide a much improved market environment for the rapid application of technical advances in the whole of the information technology sector.

Despite this spectacular precedent, 'break-up' solutions to problems of dominance are likely to be used very sparingly in the US and probably not at all in the UK. If this is correct, merger policy is of central importance. Considering the ease with which large market shares can be built up by a series of acquisitions effective regulation of mergers was late to develop in both the US and the UK. It is true that the US Clayton Act of 1914 had provisions for the control of mergers but the wording of the law made it largely ineffective until it was amended in 1950. Since then the antitrust authorities have been prepared to challenge all but the totally insignificant mergers. In the UK, although investigation of dominant positions has been possible since 1948, mergers were not made subject to this procedure until 1965,[34] at the culmination of the first of two postwar merger waves that had a profound effect on the structure of UK manufacturing industry.[35]

Confining our attention for the moment to horizontal mergers (i.e. between firms operating in the same market) the regulatory issue involves a trade-off similar to that mentioned above. Horizontal mergers of size may simultaneously increase market power, because of the larger market share created and the elimination of one independent competitor, while at the same time promise improved technical efficiency through reorganization. In principle, as Williamson first argued in relation to US antitrust policy, if the benefits from increased efficiency outweighed the disadvantages of enhanced market power, then the merger should be allowed to proceed (Williamson 1972a). Under US law if a merger 'tended to increase monopoly' the courts would strike it down, even if substantial scale economies seemed likely to result. The MMC in its merger enquiries can, of course, take account of all factors it considers relevant, including potential cost reductions,[36] but since 1973 has been expected to pay particular attention to the competitive effects.

It is now probably also true to infer that, despite the neutral stance that the MMC must take at the beginning of an enquiry,[37] it is sceptical of the public benefits that might flow from a horizontal merger that substantially increases the market share of the 'acquiring' company. Members of the Commission will be aware that since the early 1960s mergers have substantially increased levels of concentration in a large number of markets and also that the weight of the evidence on the effect that mergers have on firm performance is still probably adverse, although this is the subject of a lot of controversy.[38] The fact remains that a large market share gained through internal growth will have been achieved in the face of competition whereas one purchased through acquisition will not. The dangers, therefore, of both allocative and x-inefficiency are likely to be considerably greater in the latter than in the former.

In view of the total number of mergers that have been occurring in the UK in recent years the number that have actually been directly prevented as a result of MMC enquiry and recommendations is extremely small. Table 7.1 gives a breakdown for five-yearly intervals of 'all'[39] mergers and the numbers referred to the MMC. Although the number of proposed mergers falling within the legislation (according to the criteria given in the appendix) has risen dramatically over the past decade to more than 40 per cent of the total, compared with only about 10–12 per cent in the period 1965–74, the percentage referred to the MMC has remained roughly constant at between 2 and 3 per cent. (As a proportion of *all* mergers the number referred is much less.) Compared with the first decade in which mergers could be referred, the second decade saw a decline in the *number* of mergers but a considerable increase in their size. Together with an increasing concern about the likely effect of mergers on industrial structure and performance, this resulted in a sizable increase in the absolute number of references over the period 1980–4.

Not all of the mergers shown in table 7.1 were horizontal where the likely increase in market power is at its greatest. Indeed, at the peak of the merger boom in the early 1970s the largest mergers were conglomerate, a category that includes all cases where the firms concerned appear to have no markets in common nor to stand in a consumer – supplier (or vertical) relationship. Of mergers referred to the MMC horizontal cases predominate but a significant minority have been conglomerate. The details are set out in table 7.2 showing the number of different kinds of mergers referred and the eventual outcome. A majority, 45, of mergers referred to the MMC did not take place either as a result of the final recommendations or because the parties decided to abandon the attempt after a reference to the Commission had been made. This amounts to under two per cent of all mergrs in the period that fell within the scope of the Act.[40] To this we should add an unknown number of other merger possibilities that were not pursued because of the presence of an active investigating procedure. Of those mergers referred to the MMC, 61 per cent were

Table 7.1 Merger activity and referrals, 1965–84

Period	Within the legislation	Referred to the MMC		All known mergers
		Number	Per cent	
1965–9	466	10	2.1	4423
1970–4	579	19	3.3	4595
1975–9	903	19	2.1	2250
1980–4	987	31	3.1	2338

Source: Annual Reports of the Board of Trade and the Director General of Fair Trading.

Note: the criterion of minimum assets to be acquired was raised from £5 millions to £15 millions in April 1980 and to £30 millions in July 1984.

Table 7.2 Mergers referred to the Monopolies and Mergers Commission, 1965–84

Merger type	Referred	Abandoned	Public interest conclusion	
			Against	Not Against
Horizontal	48	10	17	21
Vertical	6	1	1	4
Conglomerate	25	11	5	9
Total	79	22	23	34

Source: Review of Monopolies and Mergers Policy HMSO, 1978, updated.

horizontal, 31 per cent conglomerate and 8 per cent vertical. Horizontal mergers formed almost exactly the same percentage of mergers challenged in the US, although the distribution between the other two categories was more evenly balanced than in the UK.

The rationale for referring sizable horizontal mergers to the MMC is reasonably clear-cut, even if, as we have seen, there are considerable problems in carrying out the analysis. Rather similar market power considerations may apply in vertical mergers, especially if a dominant firm, at one stage of the production process (say, manufacture), wishes to acquire a substantial firm at another stage (for example, distribution) where there are already barriers to entry (licensing restrictions on retail outlets). The third category of merger, however, which has received increasing attention over the last decade or so, is much more controversial. By definition conglomerate mergers involve firms that have no markets in common. They may share similar expertise: for example both may have experience in marketing (different) consumer goods or both may maintain considerable research and development laboratories in different areas of knowledge, but on the face of it, no question of market power is involved. Indeed if some economies are thought likely to arise from the merger and there is no countervailing increase in market power, the merger should result in a net social gain. Yet nearly one third of all mergers referred to the MMC have been conglomerate, and the majority of these have been abandoned or found likely to operate against the public interest. What is the explanation for this?

The basis of the regulating authorities' uneasiness about large conglomerate mergers lies in their overall financial strength which may be derived from many different markets. It is thought that this strength may be used in a number of ways that will impair the normal competitive process. In particular, in an interesting reversal of the arguments previously used in connection with predatory pricing, it has frequently been suggested that in a conglomerate merger the larger firm will be able to cross-subsidize the prices (or advertising campaigns) of its new acquisition to the detriment of other firms competing in the market. As Needham (1983) has recently pointed out, the arguments in this case are exactly the same as those used in the analysis of predatory pricing, the only difference being that the low prices now come from an 'entrant' (albeit through acquisition) rather than from an existing dominant firm. For the reasons given in section III(i) above the logic of the argument is difficult to sustain and furthermore there is an almost complete lack of evidence in support of the contention in conglomerate cases.[41]

More recently there has been a change of emphasis away from such 'long-purse' arguments to those highlighting the poor subsequent performance of acquired firms. Although there is still some dispute about the interpretation of the evidence,[42] there are quite strong indications that the profitability of firms taken over in conglomerate mergers deteriorates. The conclusion has been tartly summarized recently by Scherer thus: 'if one invested $1000 in June 1968, at the peak of the U.S. conglomerate merger boom, in each common stock of the 13 most active conglomerate acquirer firms, reinvested all dividends, and sold the portfolio in June of 1974, one would have received $5,669. An equivalent June 1968 investment of $13,000 in the Standard and Poor's 425 industrials portfolio would have yielded $14,340.' (Scherer, 1985). He goes on to argue that not only is there little indication of real economies made by such mergers but also that there is now considerable case study evidence that far from acquiring badly managed firms with a view to improving their efficiency, conglomerate acquirers have tended to take over well-managed companies with above-average profitability that subsequently decline.

The implications of these doubts for regulatory policy are that much closer attention should be paid to conglomerate mergers than an analysis of their immediate effect on market structure might suggest. In other words since the evidence suggests a fairly strong probability that conglomerate mergers may worsen the efficiency of the acquired firms they should therefore be challenged and, at least in the UK context, the acquiring firm should be asked to give detailed estimates of what it considers the social advantages of the merger will be.

Unfortunately for those who take this view of the evidence, regulatory authorities in both the UK and the US appear to have moved recently *away* from stricter control of conglomerate mergers, while retaining a firm control of horizontal mergers. Although not made explicit the Ministerial statement in 1984 on future merger policy clearly had this implication: 'my policy has been and will continue to be to make references (to the MMC) primarily on competition grounds' (*British Business*, 1984) Similarly, despite proposals made, for example, by the Federal Trade Commission in 1979 for greater regulation of large conglomerate mergers, the economic philosophy of the Reagan administration tends to favour large size on the grounds of efficiency and this is reflected in the attitude of the antitrust authorities.

Before leaving the subject of merger control it is appropriate to mention briefly the position in the EEC. Although the underlying rationale of the entire Common Market is for competition to prevail freely throughout the whole territory and Articles 85 and 86 sought to ensure the maintenance of competition by proscribing cartels and the abuse of positions of dominance, no special provision for the control of mergers was set out in the Treaty of Rome. Despite a key decision in 1973, this gap continues to cause problems for EEC merger regulation. An important point of principle established by the Continental Can case (1973)[43] was that article 86 of the Rome Treaty *did* cover mergers by a dominant firm in the Community. The plaintiff had argued that the article was intended to deal purely with the abuse of an existing position by a dominant firm and not with increases to market share that may occur as the result of merger. The Commission and then the European Court both took the view, however, that it would be inconsistent for article 85 to strike at cartels if firms could then seek to attain a similar control of the market by merger, free from any action under article 86. Although the Court accepted the principle that mergers involving dominant positions could thus be challenged, it nevertheless reversed the Commission's finding against Continental Can, largely on the grounds that the Commission had failed to substantiate the company's dominant position.

Perhaps fortunately for the Commission, since the establishment of the principle it has not been fully tested. Proposed mergers that have caught the Commission's attention have been abandoned when it has intimated that dominance and a potential for abuse were present (Merkin and Williams, 1984). It is widely accepted that the current position is highly unsatisfactory for a number of reasons. Compared with the situation in the UK there is no systematic procedure for notifying and receiving clearance from the Commission prior to merger which means that in the last analysis a challenged merger would have been completed and an adverse final decision would result in divestiture. Furthermore since proceedings would take place under article 86 only mergers that involved a prior position of dominance can be challenged. Mergers creating a dominant position for the first time would remain immune. For the same reason it remains unclear whether the procedure can be applied to vertical and conglomerate mergers.

Perhaps the most common refrain of observers of the workings of the EEC is that 'political factors prevent an improvement in economic policies'. This is also true of merger policy. Since 1973 detailed proposals, in the form of a draft regulation, for EEC merger control, prepared by the Commission, have been before the Council of Ministers, having been passed by both the European Parliament and Economic and Social Committee. The amended draft regulation was shelved in 1978 and new proposals submitted to the Council in 1981. Despite a number of further amendments, the draft remains before the Council (for fuller details, see Merkin and Williams, 1984 pp. 289–93). Mergers, because of their power to transform industrial structures very rapidly, remain a very sensitive issue. It is significant, for example, that in the UK, although the Director General of Fair Trading has had the power since 1973 to refer dominant firms to the MMC, sole responsibility for referring mergers remains with the Minister. Similarly, it very quickly became clear that, despite modifications and safeguards, proposals to regulate sizable European mergers are unacceptable to individual member governments jealous of their sovereignty. Market structures that in some member states may have already been transformed by mergers, in others may have so far remained untouched. The introduction of EEC regulations were seen by some as possibly conflicting with their national policies. In the meantime the draft regulations continue to be modified and gain a little more dust while the Commission does what it can on an informal basis.

For all their limitations the regulatory policies of the UK, the US, and (more ambiguously) the EEC act directly and indirectly to moderate and reduce those horizontal mergers which are likely to have the more adverse consequences for competition and allocative performance. The odds must now be fairly firmly against the eventual consummation of any sizable horizontal merger in these countries. More controversially the odds on successful completion of conglomerate mergers, which may have little direct competitive effect but which may cause considerable x-inefficiency, seem recently to have improved in the UK and the US.

V CONCLUSIONS

The regulatory problems posed by dominant positions in the private sector can be brought into focus by considering the distinction between technical efficiency (broadly interpreted) and allocative efficiency. In many markets the need of technical efficiency may threaten allocative efficiency by allowing firms that attain dominance due to economies of large size to bolster their position by restrictive or exclusionary practices. Success in this respect may then also create x-inefficiency and thus reduce welfare still further.

The important part of antitrust policy that deals with dominant positions has, therefore, been very much concerned with the analysis of market conduct – the wide range of activities covering the terms and conditions of trading – in order to sort the competitive wheat from the exclusionary chaff. As the discussions of tie-ins, refusal to supply and, especially, predatory pricing showed this seemingly straightforward exercise is, in practice, exceedingly complex. After almost a century of antitrust in the US there is still very wide disagreement, at least amongst economists if not lawyers, about what constitutes a predatory price.

As in many areas of regulation policy a wide variety of proposals to improve the performance of dominant firms have been made. At one extreme are those who advocate the minimum of intervention or control in their affairs on the grounds that market forces are swift and sure enough to see them dislodged should they become internally slack or too greedy. At the other are those who point to the long-standing pre-eminence of enterprises whose original excellence has been replaced by atrophy or privilege and that only the inertia of the market sustains. They therefore recommend a dramatic programme of dismemberment. For the most part regulatory policy has taken a path somewhere between these two extremes. In the UK the MMC has been ready to condemn a wide variety of practices that they regard as restrictive or exclusionary, but have not recommended the break-up of an enterprise, however dominant and however gross has been its abuse. Similarly, despite the recent, massive example of AT and T, the major impact of US antitrust policy has been on market conduct rather than directly on market structure. The exception to this conclusion is in the area of mergers. The intractability of the problem of dominance in some markets places a greater significance on merger regulation and, as we noted in section IV, although effective policy was somewhat late to develop it now constitutes a formidable obstacle to any firm wishing to regain or enhance its dominant position in a particular market. The ambiguity of the economic analysis and, to a degree, the empirical evidence has so far, however, allowed a much freer hand for conglomerate mergers.

APPENDIX 7.1
BRIEF OUTLINE OF THE REGULATION OF DOMINANCE,
MERGERS AND CARTELS IN THE UK, THE US AND THE EEC

I Dominant Positions

A. UK

1. The Monopolies and Mergers Commission (MMC), originally established in 1948, can be asked by the Minister for Industry or the Director General (DG) of Fair Trading to investigate markets where one quarter or more of the supply is controlled by one enterprise and determine whether or not conditions in the market operate or are likely to operate against the public interest. In their deliberations the MMC are asked to pay particular attention to the competitive effects of the 'dominant' position, and can make recommendations to the Minister.

2. Since 1980 the MMC can also be asked to investigate a specific 'anti-competitive' practice (following a preliminary enquiry by the DG) and decide whether it is likely to operate against the public interest, and make recommendations.

3. Since 1980 the MMC can also be asked to assess the efficiency, costs, standards of service and possible abuses of market position of public bodies (such as nationalized enterprises, local transport and water undertakings) and make recommendations.

B. US

Under section 2 of the Sherman Act (1890) 'Every person who shall monopolise or attempt to monopolise or combine or conspire with any other person or persons, to monopolise any part of the trade or commerce among the several States, or with foreign nations, shall be guilty of a misdemeanor. . . .' Subsequent legislation has extended this general provision in a number of ways, e.g. the Federal Trade Commission Act (1914) contained a provision making unfair methods of competition in commerce illegal; the Clayton Act (1914) made illegal specific types of conduct – price discrimination (subsequently strengthened by the Robinson–Patman Act, (1936)) exclusive and tying contracts, and inter-locking directorates.

C. EEC

Article 86 of the Treaty of Rome prohibits the abuse of a dominant position within the Common Market or in a substantial part of it, in so far as it may affect trade between member states. Abuse may involve, for example, imposing unfair purchase or selling prices or other unfair trading practices; limiting production or technical development; applying dissimilar conditions to equivalent transactions.

Following a complaint or on its own initiative the European Commission can investigate and proceed against suspected infringements.

II Mergers

A. UK

Since 1965 the MMC can be asked by the Minister for Industry to decide (normally within six months) whether a proposed merger, meeting one or both of two criteria, is likely to operate against the public interest, and make recommendations. The criteria are (i) the merger involves or will create a market share of one quarter or more and/or (ii) the merger involves net assets of £30 million or more.

B. US

Section 7 of the Clayton Act forbade any enterprise to acquire the shares of a competing enterprise where the effect may be substantially to lessen competition or tend to create a monopoly.

Judicial interpretation of this clause made it largely ineffective until an amendment was made in the Celler-Kefauver Act (1950).

C. EEC

The Treaty of Rome contained no specific provision for control of mergers. Control depends on future judicial interpretation, especially of Article 86, concerning dominant positions.

A draft regulation produced by the Commission awaits ratification.

III Cartels

A. UK

Under a series of Acts (commencing with the Restrictive Trade Practices Act, 1956) restrictive agreements between firms covering a wide range of terms and conditions of trading (such as prices, discounts, production processes, areas to be served) have to be registered with the DG. Agreements covering information exchanges (1968) and services (1973) have been included. All registered agreements are presumed *contrary* to the public interest. Agreements are referred by the DG to the Restrictive Practices Court where the defendant can seek to rebut the presumption on one or more of seven grounds (or 'gateways'), i.e. the agreement is necessary (i) to protect the public from injury, (ii) because its removal would deny consumers specific and substantial benefits, (iii) to counteract measures that would restrict competition, (iv) to balance the countervailing power of another cartel or monopoly, (v) because its abolition would cause serious and persistent unemployment in an area, (vi) its abolition would cause a substantial fall in exports, (vii) to sustain another acceptable agreement. In 1968 another provision was added whereby an agreement could continue if it was judged not to restrict competition to any material degree. If the Court is satisfied of a benefit on one or more of these grounds it then has to determine whether, taking everything into account, the agreement is on balance of benefit to the public.

B. US

Under section 1 of the Sherman Act 'Every contract, combination in the form of a trust or otherwise, or conspiracy, in restraint of trade or commerce among the several States, or with foreign nations, is hereby declared to be illegal. . . .'

An amendment under the Miller–Tydings Act (1937) allowed exemption for resale price agreements between manufacturers of products identified by brand name or trademark and suppliers in states that allowed resale price agreements.

C. EEC

Under Article 85 of the Treaty of Rome agreements amongst enterprises that have the object or effect of preventing, restricting or distorting trade between members are prohibited.

The scope of agreements may cover, for example, price fixing and other trading conditions, limitations of production or technical development, and market sharing. The Commission may grant exemptions if a series of conditions are fulfilled (in particular, the agreement contributes towards the improvement of the production or distribution of goods or promotes technical progress, and if it allows consumers a fair share of the resulting benefits).

8

Collusion and Regulation

I INTRODUCTION

Our discussion of the behaviour of dominant firms and their regulation, where the effect was likely to be exclusionary, revealed considerable disagreement. While disagreement was probably greatest on the issue of predatory pricing, there is also a wide spectrum of views on the correct analysis of such practices as exclusive dealing, refusal to sell and tie-in sales. Given the disagreement among analysts it is hardly surprising that regulatory policy has sometimes appeared inconsistent or to be hitting the wrong target.

There is much greater agreement on the subject of the present chapter, collusion on terms and conditions amongst groups of firms and the need for regulation. Ever since Adam Smith warned of the dangers that lay in meetings of businessmen ostensibly gathered to enjoy themselves but invariably ending in conspiracies against the public, there has been a strong emphasis in economic analysis that freedom to collude would have many adverse consequences which would almost certainly outweigh any incidental benefits. As we shall see in section II all three efficiencies distinguished in chapter 7 are likely to be affected by the operation of cartels.[1] Allocative efficiency will be adversely affected to the extent that the cartel succeeds in maintaining a monopoly price by restricting joint output. Depending on the method used for allocating output amongst members, technical efficiency is likely to suffer because, for example, high-cost-low-output firms will remain in the industry as the price of their cooperation with the cartel. Finally, the restrictions on market shares imposed by membership of the cartel are likely to deaden incentives amongst at least some firms, resulting in internal slackness and x-inefficiency. Furthermore cartels depend for their success on the elimination of non-members and the exclusion of new entrants. So the effect on competition will be clearly adverse, as compared with, say, a tying agreement which may exclude only under certain circumstances.

As in most, if not all, areas of economics the unanimity is not complete. Some observers are still prepared to argue that market forces can take care of the restrictive elements while the social benefits of cooperation amongst firms that can arise in some cases will only be achieved in a less hostile regulatory environment. Both sides of the issue, as well as the form that cartel regulation has taken in the UK, the US and the EEC, are discussed in section II.

The problem, however, that Smith foresaw and that has become more acute with the progressive increase in the concentration of sales in many markets, is that proscribing overt collusion may not be enough to maintain a competitive performance. If the majority of sales in a market are made by a handful of firms it may not be necessary for them ever to meet or collaborate directly. The monopolistic outcome that a cartel can achieve may be attained by tacit collusion and parallel pricing. Within a short space of time the prices and related terms of all leading brands may change by the same percentage without any formal undertaking or agreement, or, indeed, without any discernible contact between the firms at all.[2] The regulation of tacit collusion is thus much more difficult than that of overt collusion and has created serious problems, some of which we discuss in section III.

II CARTELS AND THEIR REGULATION

It may seem superfluous to a generation that has observed probably the most successful of cartels in history to explain why they are generally considered to lead to inefficiency and to damage the competitive process. However, as has often been remarked all cartels are unique and therefore progress in different ways. The OPEC cartel is no exception. The geographic, political and demographic diversity of OPEC members, not to mention the fundamental nature of its product, all make the cartel like no other.[3] Nevertheless there are certain key characteristics derived from economic analysis that apply to all cartels. The speed with which these characteristics come into play and their relative importance will vary according to circumstances. Thus the fact that members of the OPEC cartel are sovereign states rather than individual firms meant that they were beyond regulatory control and as a result in the 1970s had (in their terms) very great success with the real price of oil rising eightfold between 1973 and 1980. On the other hand what initially was a source of strength has, in the 1980s and with depressed demand, turned into a very severe weakness. In a 'normal' cartel consisting of a number of firms, the main group may be able to bring quite severe sanctions against recalcitrant members attempting to gain an individual short-run advantage at the expense of everyone else; but where the maverick is a foreign state this course of action may be extremely difficult, and the cartel is that much more vulnerable.

The central point made about a cartel is that it will seek a common, monopoly price and to the extent that it is successful will cause allocative inefficiency in the same way as a single-firm monopoly. In effect the individual firms are prepared to give up their autonomy on pricing decisions for their own products in exchange for a share in the anticipated joint monopoly profits. The prize is an attractive one: without losing their independence which they would in a merger and without winning a monopoly market share by ability or good fortune, individual firms may nevertheless get their hands on at least part of a monopoly profit.

Many of the advantages and problems of cartels can be illustrated with the simple diagrams shown in figure 8.1. Panels (*a*) and (*b*) represent the cost conditions of two firms who wish to form a cartel (the number is kept to two for the sake of diagrammatic simplicity but the principles remain the same if more firms are included, as has usually been the case in practice). We have also assumed that the cost conditions for the two firms are different. The firm represented in panel (*a*) has relatively low marginal and average cost (shown as MC_L and AC_L respectively) while the firm in (*b*) has relatively high costs (MC_H and AC_H). Panel (*c*) shows the demand (average revenue, AR) and related marginal revenue curves for the firms together and the combined marginal cost curve, MC_T. The profit-maximizing price and output for the two firms together is P_K and Q_T, where combined marginal cost and marginal revenue are equal. Given the prevailing cost

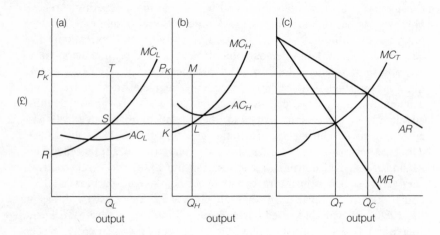

Figure 8.1 Pricing in a cartel

structure the total output should be allocated between the firms so that $MC_L = MC_H = MR$, and this implies that the low-cost firm would produce Q_L and the high-cost firms Q_H. At the cartel price, P_K and with this allocation of output the low-cost firm would earn an abnormal return shown by $RSTP_K$ (the difference between revenue and cost) and the high-cost firm $KLMP_K$.

We can now observe the efficiency effects of the cartel. As we have already noted the cartel price is the equivalent of the simple monopoly price which is in excess of marginal cost. An increase in output to Q_C (panel (c)), even with unchanged costs, would bring a net gain in consumer surplus. As long as the cartel price is maintained, allocative inefficiency will persist. In the case shown in figure 8.1 there is also considerable technical inefficiency. The low-cost firm in panel (a) is producing beyond the point where its average costs are at a minimum, while the high-cost firm is producing on an inefficiently small scale. Clearly if the average cost curves had been drawn differently we could have shown both firms operating at minimum unit cost. Although such a result is possible especially where all the firms in the market have approximately similar costs, for the reasons given below, concerning the instability of cartels, the occasions when all the members are able to operate at technically optimum levels of output are likely to be comparatively rare. In addition, under the umbrella of the cartel price there is no mechanism for weeding out or reforming high-cost firms, such as that shown in panel (b). Without the cartel the low-cost firm would eventually supersede (or acquire) the high-cost firm and reduce costs for the combined output. With the cartel in existence this possibility is eliminated. In many cases, therefore, at least some members are likely to be technically inefficient.

Figure 8.1 assumes that the two firms achieve the marginal or unit costs shown, and these are based on the respective production functions. For any specified level of output the firms can achieve the level of costs shown. However, if the cartel is a success and both firms earn abnormal profits without having to be bothered with making independent price decisions they may become complacent and internally slack. In other words the incentive to keep costs to a minimum for the output specified under the cartel may be weakened and x-inefficiency become widespread. As we shall see below the UK experience in the 1950s strongly suggests that this was the case. Observed profits may then be quite modest because member firms were in effect using them up in a different way; a quiet life, a leisurely work environment, gastronomic rather than managerial excellence.

In view of these likely results the conclusion may readily be that regulation should take the form of a complete ban on overt collusion. Essentially this has been the position in US antitrust law where horizontal agreements on prices and terms of trading are *per se* illegal; it has been the *outcome* of the much more recent policy in the UK[4] and it is the policy of the EEC under article 85. Defenders of cartels are thus likely to have a hard time convincing policy makers of their use. Those arguing in favour of a change in policy have taken two quite distinct positions. Firstly, cartels have so many internal and external sources of instability that any adverse consequences are short-lived; consequently the resources used in policing breaches of the law (under a *per se* rule) could be better used elsewhere. The sources of instability can be illustrated from figure 8.1. Although both firms in the example shown have the ability to earn abnormal returns from the cartel price, both may also be tempted to increase their sales and profits by making additional output available at a price slightly less than P_K. Both firms apparently could expand sales considerably and still cover marginal cost. The appearance, of course, is deceptive. The cartel price will only persist as long as that output is restricted to Q_T. A greater output will command a lower price. Price shading by one firm will be felt by the other as it loses market share. It will thus retaliate in order to recover its position and so make the price cutting worse. The example of only two firms is extreme: detection of the source and extent of any price cut will be rapid and this reduces the risk of it occurring. Where a larger number is involved the risk of detection will be smaller since the effects of any price cut will be more widely dispersed and the source more difficult to pin down. Consequently the danger of one firm initiating a secret price cut or attempting to cheat the cartel is greater. Beyond a certain number of members maintaining an effective cartel price for any length of time becomes impossible, although as we mention below some former cartels in the UK were remarkably effective even with a large number of members. A key to the prolonged success of a cartel is likely to be the thoroughness of its own policing system and the sanctions it can impose on offenders. If the probability of detection is high enough and the fines imposed sufficiently severe, clearly the costs of cheating could be greater than the benefits and members will remain 'loyal'.

Their discipline will come to nothing, however, unless the cartel is effective against external as well as internal stresses. The cartel price is, by definition, in excess of marginal costs and therefore attracts new firms to the market. Unless the cartel can erect barriers against such entry its position will be undermined. Successful entry either means an erosion of price or an attempt to reach an understanding with the newcomer by allowing them to join the cartel. In both cases profits for the original members will be reduced. The inability of OPEC to control new sources of supply of crude oil, for example, has meant the erosion of its members' share of the world market[5] from 67 per cent in 1973 to 44 per cent by 1983.

Recognition of these internal and external pressures may lead to the conclusion that strict regulation of cartels is not necessary because the market will eventually reach an efficient solution. The problem is that in many cases 'eventually' may be a very long time and meanwhile consumers have to suffer the consequences.

The second argument favouring a less hostile attitude to cartels is more positive. There are a number of variants of the view but they generally focus on the improvement in industry performance that may flow from increased cooperation between firms. Thus, for example, by allowing agreement on price, a greater exchange of technical information will take place and this may lead to a faster rate of innovation. Broadly speaking this was why the Restrictive Practices Court (which we discuss further below) allowed a cartel run by the *Permanent Magnet Association* to continue, although it is difficult to square this conclusion with the point frequently made that a number of *independent* centres of research are required to ensure a satisfactory rate of technical progress.[6]

Again it is argued that particularly in capital intensive industries where investment tends to be very lumpy, agreement on prices and to exchange information on investment plans will help to minimize the recurring problem of excess capacity.[7] It is not clear, however, why the presence of a cartel should ameliorate the danger. Not only will the high cartel price attract new entrants, as we have already mentioned, but unless existing producers can agree on market shares, coordination of investment is likely to fail. Indeed *within* a cartel leading firms may deliberately maintain excess capacity as a weapon in the bargaining over output quotas. If their wishes are not met they can threaten to increase output and so depress prices (Scherer, 1980).

In practice policy makers have on the whole resisted these arguments and taken a clear stand against cartels. In many ways the UK approach to this regulatory problem is the most interesting. In principle it recognizes that in some cases the net benefits to the public may be positive and thus should continue. In practice the policy has led to an almost complete abandonment of formal cartels. Compared with the investigation of dominance by a permanent advisory commission (the Monopolies and Mergers Commission, discussed in chapter 7 above) cartels or restrictive practices are examined by the specially established Restrictive Practices Court, a branch of the High Court. Some details of the relevant legislation and procedure of the Court are given in the appendix to chapter 7. The central point, however, is that a registrable agreement is presumed by the Court to be *contrary* to the public interest. The presumption is rebuttable on a number of grounds specified in the Act, but it is also necessary to convince the Court that any incidental detriments resulting from the restriction are outweighed by the benefits. It is thus possible to pass the first stage in the procedure by successfully arguing that, say, the removal of the restriction would deny the public an advantage, only to fail at the second stage, when the Court weighs up the advantage against all possible detriments.[8]

Instead of adopting, therefore, a *per se* approach (i.e. cartels are in themselves illegal), which confines the regulating procedure to establishing the existence of a restrictive agreement and which is essentially the situation in the US, the UK policy recognized that in some circumstances they could be beneficial. At the time the policy was initiated, following the Restrictive Trade Practices Act in 1956, it was difficult to predict what the effect of the policy was going to be. The report of MMC in the previous year into Collective Discrimination (MMC, 1955) had shown that restrictions were widespread throughout many sectors of British industry and furthermore, as a distinguished member of the Commission subsequently wrote, a large body of official and industrial opinion, accustomed in the 1930s and 1940s to collaboration rather than competition, was opposed to the widespread abolition of cartels (Allen, 1968).

In the event, seven out of the first eight cases went against the maintenance of restrictive agreements and there followed a wave of voluntary abolitions by the trade associations whose members decided that it was not worth the expense of fighting a case that they now seemed likely to lose. As table 8.1 shows, more than 3500 agreements have been abandoned or altered so as to fall outside the scope of the Act.

Table 8.1 Cumulative number of agreements registered under the Restrictive Practices Acts

Year	Goods		Services	
	Registered	Terminated	Registered	Terminated
1957	1200	—		
1959	2240	723		
1961	2350	1203		
1963	2430	1620		
1966	2550	2110		
1969	2660	2370		
1972	2875	2620		
1975	3100	2788		
1978	3678	3089	321	40
1983	4132	3269	846	272

Source: A Review of Restrictive Trades Practices Policy, HMSO, 1979 (p.19) and Annual Reports of the Director General of Fair Trading.

The 1956 Act referred only to agreements relating to goods. Under the provisions of the Fair Trading Act of 1973 agreements dealing with the provision of services were brought within the same procedure and were called up for registration in 1976. By 1983 a total of 846 service agreements had been registered.

Two other important developments in the regulation of collusion do not, however, show up in the table. First, after the impact of the initial decisions of the Court had been felt, it rapidly became apparent that in many instances firms were able to achieve the same result and yet escape the provisions of the 1956 Act by completing 'information agreements'. Firms would agree to circulate, through their trade associations, information on prices, discounts and other terms of trading which, because there was no commitment necessarily to follow it, was beyond the reach of the Act. Nevertheless the circulation of the information frequently allowed firms to proceed as though the formal cartel was still effective (O'Brien and Swann, 1968). The loophole was closed by a subsequent Restrictive Practices Act (1968) which made such information agreements subject to the same procedure as those on prices.[9]

Secondly, the 1968 Act also contained a provision that a number of observers regarded as retrograde. It became possible for the Minister to exempt from registration, and hence from subsequent hearing before the Court, agreements judged to be of national importance. Although most of the grounds given for exemption noted in the Act refer to promoting the efficiency of substantial projects of importance to the national economy, the last one effectively gives the Minister *carte blanche*. Exemption may be granted if 'the agreement is on balance expedient in the national interest'[10] (Swann *et al.* 1974). An area of regulation that had deliberately been placed in the hands of an official (the Registrar of Restrictive Agreements and, after 1973, the Director General of Fair Trading) and the High Court was now also subject to the discretion of a minister and was thus likely to be much more controversial.[11]

Subsequent Restrictive Practices Acts (in 1976 and 1977) codified previous legislation and provided for minor exemptions for certain loan-financing agreements. Overall, however, the position in the UK is that nearly all restrictive agreements are subject to registration and the High Court procedure. On the surface the results of the policy were dramatic. A total of 3541 agreements have been abandoned or modified and a total of only 12 have been upheld by the Court. Only a minority of these are now of any real economic importance.[12] In retrospect, therefore, it could be argued that the introduction of a *per se* rule along US lines would have been more efficient (expensive Court procedure for those cases heard would have been avoided) and the regulation would have taken the form of detecting the restrictions and, if necessary, proceeding against them.

However, as we said earlier, the outcome of the 1956 Act could not have been forecast in advance and although a majority of the MMC in the Collective Discrimination report (1955) had recommended a *per se* approach, at the time there was a considerable body of opinion that was either in favour of allowing cartels to continue, except in rare instances, or of giving those who wished to defend a cartel the opportunity to do so. The fact remains, however, that regulation of cartels in the UK now effectively means that *new* registrable agreements covering goods are unlikely to be formed, while those concerned with services, if the previous experience is repeated, will shortly be abandoned or modified.

Unfortunately it is not possible to conclude that the matter of cartel regulation can now rest. Two issues in particular have received growing attention in the wake of the Restrictive Practices legislation: the need for an effective follow-up or monitoring procedure for those agreements declared void (or allegedly made non-registrable) and secondly the possibility of firms operating secret, non-registered agreements despite their illegality. For the pro-competitive impetus of the abandonment of cartels to be maintained, it is clearly important that the Director General of Fair Trading has adequate sanctions at his disposal against firms that do not keep to undertakings previously given or deliberately flout the law.[13]

In the first case it is now part of the duty of the Director General to ensure that any undertaking given to the Court is being followed. If he considers that firms are ignoring or avoiding an undertaking (by having an agreement 'to the like effect') then he can institute contempt proceedings. The danger that firms run in trying to avoid the procedure established by the legislation can be illustrated by the case involving the Tyre Mileage Conference in 1966. In common with many other cartel members, firms in the Conference abandoned a price agreement (relating to tendering for the maintenance of local authority bus tyres) and gave an undertaking that no other arrangement would be pursued having the same effect. Before the registrable agreement was ended, however, an information agreement was arranged that meant that members notified the Conference secretary of the price they intended to submit for a particular contract. The information was then circulated to all members. Clearly as long as all firms abided by the rules they would all know precisely the lowest price they would have to match. As a result the tenders were usually remarkably similar (Swann *et al.*, 1974). The Court decided that the information agreement had the same effect as the abandoned price agreement, that members had therefore violated their undertaking and were therefore guilty of contempt. Each member was fined £10,000. Since 1968, of course, such an agreement is registrable. However, the outcome of the case demonstrated that firms attempting to avoid the cartel regulations by a more informal arrangement are likely to be fined for contempt *as long as they have given an undertaking in the first place.*

The emphasis highlights a weakness of the current machinery for controlling cartels, and brings us to the second point. What sanctions can be applied to firms that simply ignore the registration procedure and operate a secret price agreement? The answer, unfortunately, is that they are surprisingly weak. Firms that have obeyed the law, registered their agreement but then abandoned or modified it, give an undertaking to the Court. Subsequent joint action then renders them liable for contempt. However, firms that ignore the law and operate an unregistered agreement have given no undertaking and therefore cannot be found guilty of contempt. The worst that can happen if a secret agreement has been operated is that the court declares it automatically void and can *then* get an undertaking from the firms about their future conduct. The problem was graphically illustrated in 1978, when in the course of the MMC enquiry into the supply of electric cables, an unregistered market sharing agreement for the supply of telecommunications cable was discovered (MMC, 1978). Since restrictive agreements are no longer within the scope of an MMC enquiry they could make no further comment. Subsequently, however, the Director General secured an undertaking from members party to the illegal agreement and, in addition, the customer responsible for nearly all purchases of the cable, the Post Office, eventually negotiated a repayment of £9 millions from the cartel in recompense for the amount it had been overcharged for a period of several years. The repayment, however, was due to the exceptional circumstances of the case. A state-owned near-monopsony does not occur in many markets. Buyers of less consequence would probably have had great difficulty recovering anything. Although they can sue members of the illicit agreement for damages, as the authors of the review of restrictive practices policy remarked 'it may be . . . difficult for an aggrieved party to demonstrate to the satisfaction of the Court that loss has arisen' (*Review*, 1979, p. 48). The problem was regarded as potentially serious since, although it was not possible to make a precise estimate of how widespread the practice was, unregistered agreements had recently come to light 'in cables, road surfacing materials, Diazo copying materials, ready-mixed concrete, baking, animal feed stuffs and the supply of house-coal' (ibid). As the authors somewhat ruefully remark, most other countries operate penalties against those who ignore the provisions of their legislation, but in the UK there are no effective remedies against those operating an unregistered agreement.

The recommendations in *The Review* therefore included two specific proposals to help improve the regulation of collusion. Firstly, it was suggested that the Director General should have the discretion to ask the

Restrictive Practices Court to impose fines in serious cases of non-registration, and that the Court should be given the appropriate powers. The discretionary element was included so that smaller firms that may have acted out of ignorance and lack of readily accessible legal advice would not necessarily be penalized.

Secondly, there was a recommendation that collusive tendering should be *per se* illegal and that provision should be made for prohibiting any further practice or types of agreement following investigation by the MMC (*Review*, 1979).[14] In fact some of the strongest words in *The Review* were reserved for the practice of collusive tendering, whereby tenders for a particular contract, frequently to supply the public sector, 'enter into an agreement that prevents or distorts the true operation of competition in this method of purchasing' (*Review*, 1979, p. 50). The most frequent practice is for suppliers to arrange beforehand who should receive a contract and subsequently to fix their tender prices accordingly. The review concludes: 'Collusive tendering is clearly a registrable agreement under the present legislation. However, it is obvious that a form of collusion which is designed to eliminate competition when such competition is precisely the object of the tendering procedure is almost certain not to pass through any of the gateways of legislation. Since the parties will wish to conceal their collusion, they have no reason to register their agreement. Because of the growing evidence of evasion of the law in respect of collusive tendering and because of the fraudulent nature of the practice we recommend that more stringent action should be taken against this particular practice' (ibid., p. 50). Not only was it therefore recommended that it should be made illegal (thereby removing it from the scope of the Restrictive Practices Act) but that criminal penalties should apply if the prohibition was infringed.

Implementation of these proposals would undoubtedly have put more teeth into what is the weakest part of UK cartel policy and would have brought it closer to the system operated in the US which we discuss below. In the event, although the two reviews of competition policy[15] led directly to the 1980 Competition Act, neither of the above recommendations was implemented. Collusive tendering thus remains registrable, but for the cogent reasons given by *The Review*, is in fact unregistered, while the DG is still unable to bring effective financial sanctions to bear on offenders through the Court. His diligence in seeking out unregistered agreements receives only the unsatisfactory reward of preventing the members from continuing with their illegal activities.

The contrast with recent US practice is probably greatest in this respect. We have already noted that under Section 1 of the Sherman Act (1890) 'every contract, combination . . . or conspiracy, in restraint of trade or commerce among the several states or with foreign nations is hereby declared illegal'. It is thus only necessary to demonstrate that such a restriction exists for it to be declared illegal and struck down by the Courts. The uncompromising language of the Act has given little room for manoeuvre in the Courts which have followed a strict *per se* interpretation.[16] For a long period, however, the penalties for violation of this section of the antitrust laws were so low that, as in the British case, it was probably more profitable to maintain an illegal restriction and risk the consequences. Until 1955 the consequences were fairly negligible: a maximum fine of $5,000 on each count (although this excludes the costs of preparing for the case and any lost sales that might result from adverse publicity). Since 1955 the maximum fine has been raised to $100,000 for individuals and $1 million for companies, neither of which, as Scherer drily remarks, is tax deductible. These figures are the maximum possible, and frequently the actual fines imposed have been considerably less. Since conspiracy under the Act constitutes a crime it is also possible for offenders to be sent to gaol, again providing a sharp contrast with UK law.[17] However, for the most part sentences have been very light or non-existent; 'judges have traditionally been reluctant to treat white-collar antitrust violations as harshly as, say, forgers, burglars and other non violent garden variety criminals' (Scherer, 1980, p. 503). The fine alone, even at current levels, may not provide a sufficient deterrent and even when the possibility of a prison sentence is present, it may have to be considerable to be really effective. The position was summed up by an executive who had been fixing prices with others, as follows: 'When you are doing $30 million a year and stand to gain $3 million by fixing prices, a $30,000 fine does not mean much. Face it, most of us would be willing to spend 30 days in jail to make a few extra million dollars. May be if I were facing a year or more, I would think twice' (Greer, 1983, p. 286). In response to this attitude the US Justice Department since the mid-1970s has been pressing for tougher fines and prison sentences for antitrust violators. If a similar law had been in existence in the UK when the unregistered market sharing agreement in telecommunications cable was uncovered in 1978 the leading executives of the following highly respected companies which were members of the agreement would have faced a possible prison sentence, BICC, Telephone Cables, Pirelli General and Standard Telephones and Cables. The example is given not as a recommendation for the path UK regulatory policy should take, but to highlight the considerable gulf between UK and US attitudes to these matters. However, it is also clear that despite the much longer and more robust tradition of cartel regulation in the US it has not been able to eliminate the widespread inclination to collude.

Another development, which has relatively recently come to prominence in the US and which may provide some guide to the improvement of enforcing UK policy, is the right that parties injured by an illegal agreement have to sue the violators for triple the damages suffered.

Although the right has been available since 1914[18] it has only become significant since some Supreme Court decisions after the Second World War simplified the procedure for individuals or groups to prove actual damage. As a result the number of private suits has grown dramatically. Compared with the 1950s when the rate was about 200 per year, by the 1970s they were running at about 1500 per year and the sums awarded were considerable. The widely reported Laker case was brought under this procedure, although it eventually ended in an out-of-court settlement.

We have seen that at present in the UK although the individual injured party can sue members of an unregistered and therefore void agreement for damages, the likelihood of success is remote enough to deter all but the foolhardy or the extremely wealthy. Courts are quite familiar with awarding damages in other (probably more complex) cases and it should not be difficult to devise a method of applying such judgement to cases of non-compliance with the Restrictive Practices Act. We have already noted that the cable-makers paid back £9 million to the Post Office. Clearly they had not expected that they would have to do this when they decided *not* to register their collusive agreement. However, if they had been aware at the time that they ran the risk of having to re-pay not £9 million but £27 million should they be discovered, they would have been much more likely to have abandoned the whole collusive enterprise. Unless the growth of non-registration is to continue some effective sanction along these lines will have to be introduced.

By not incorporating the recommendations made in the official *Review*, for strengthening the enforcement of anti-cartel policy in the 1980 Competition Act, the government missed an important opportunity for reform. However, *The Review* itself also stopped short of making a recommendation that would have made much easier the DG's task of uncovering non-registered agreements. The list of products mentioned above was compiled from a variety of sources – enquiries by the MMC, by the Price Commission, from reports in the trade press and from information supplied by discontented parties, competitors and employees (*Review*, 1979, p. 48). In short, information becomes available in a rather random and haphazard fashion. The authors of the Review considered the advantages of giving the DG powers similar to those enjoyed by his counterparts in the EEC: 'Regulations of the EEC provide that Officials of the Commission may examine the books and other business records of undertakings and ask for oral explanations of them on the spot. There is authority to enter premises for this purpose' (ibid., p. 49). As we saw in the last chapter it was the discovery of damaging cost information on the premises of AZKO that led to their prosecution for predatory pricing under article 86. Furthermore, at the end of the most comprehensive study of the effects of the Restrictive Practices Act so far available, the authors make one of their main recommendations an extension to the powers of the DG and the Office of Fair Trading so that they could appear unannounced at a firm's premises and go through the relevant records. Firms that are aware that they are evading the law by non-registration are not likely to keep a book of rules about how to fix their prices and therefore the presence of collusion has to be inferred indirectly. Unfortunately although the authors of *The Review* seem at one point to favour an extension of the DG's powers of entry and search, they shy away from making any proposals. The reason for their reluctance seems dubious: 'because registration of restrictive trading agreements depends upon the form of such agreements and not their object or effect it may be argued that the Office of Fair Trading does not need sweeping powers to enter and search the premises of those who are suspected of having covertly entered into such agreements' (ibid). The growing evidence of non-registration that the Review itself presents appears to contradict this optimistic view. In the event, the authors simply noted the Government's intention of increasing the DG's powers to obtain information about unregistered agreements, without making any detailed recommendations of what form this should take to make it as effective as possible. The 1980 Act contained no provisions for the extension of the DG's powers in this respect and therefore the haphazard discovery of non-registered agreements is likely to continue.

We have deliberately emphasized the current weaknesses in UK cartel regulation because initially the policy was a great success and it is a pity that the momentum has not been maintained by providing adequate machinery for enforcement. Most commentators are agreed that the sweeping away of many overt and then information agreements had an important positive effect on the performance of many UK industries.[19] The results of a very detailed enquiry into 40 industries[20] suggested that in both the short- and long-term there were competitive gains from the policy (Swann *et al.*, 1974). Although experience differed somewhat across industries, the authors estimated that something like 50 to 60 per cent of the sample experienced intensified competition when the policy was introduced. This took the form in the short-run of renewed price competition (with prices sometimes falling by as much as 25 per cent) and, as we have already anticipated, attempts to avoid the worst effects of abandonment. In fact a large part of the explanation of why the proportion of industries with re-invigorated competition was not higher stems from the initial success of information agreements. In many cases these achieved the same results as their more formal predecessors; therefore 'it is a great mistake to see the abandonment of the post-1959 period as marking the general onset of competition. In a significant number of cases that did not come until ten years after the 1956 Act had been passed' (ibid. p. 163).[21]

Nevertheless a considerable improvement in resource allocation was thought to have occurred as the policy developed. After a detailed review of the long-run changes that had occurred in their sample of industries the authors concluded: 'Taking both major and minor case studies together it seems clear that the 1956 Act has had a significant effect on resource allocation and that this effect has been almot entirely for the better. In the case of very few industries, mainly those with an agreement upheld by the Court, can it be said that the Act has been far outweighed by the achievements in relation to all three kinds of efficiency . . . the removal of barriers to entry and the stimulation of rivlary and competition in other industries' (ibid. p. 193). Furthermore, subsequent research gave no support to the hypothesis that the abolition of cartels had led to the depression and greater instability of profits (O'Brien *et al.*, 1979).

The fundamental change in cartel policy from toleration and even encouragement, to registration and abolition, thus produced an important once-for-all gain in efficiency, plus the continuing advantage of a commitment to open competition rather than collusion. However, it rapidly became apparent, especially in the late 1960s and 1970s, that while some firms may have sought to avoid the consequences of the 1956 Act by information agreements and others by merger, amongst many other firms there was a growing acceptance of a more subtle and intangible form of cooperation, in the form of 'parallel pricing' or 'conscious parallelism'. In the next section, therefore, we discuss the policy issues that it raises.

III THE PROBLEM OF PARALLEL PRICING

Only five years after the introduction of the 1968 Restrictive Practices Act making information agreements registrable, the MMC reported that 'parallel pricing is a fairly widespread phenomenon over industry as a whole' (MMC, 1973a, p. 15). Firms operating in oligopolistic markets, and accustomed to the collusive environment that prevailed in the UK until well into the 1960s, were almost bound to seek a substitute for a formal cartel. Where sellers are few and more or less evenly matched, independent price action is likely to create such great instability that all firms end up worse off. Some means of maintaining price discipline in such markets is therefore inevitable. The vehicle most frequently used for this purpose has been price leadership.

In the theoretical literature three main forms of price leadership have been distinguished: dominant firm, collusive and 'barometric'. As its name implies the dominant firm type refers to a market where one seller has a sufficiently large market share to determine the price. The presence of a number of smaller, 'fringe' suppliers, however, means that the leading firm will adjust its price according to their expected supply curve. Price will therefore be below the short-run monopoly level but sufficient to allow the dominant firms to earn an abnormal profit.[22] Thus the model deals with dominance rather than inter-dependence which in this section is our main concern. We therefore concentrate on the second and third types of price leadership. In a somewhat neglected part of the theory of Monopolistic Competition, Chamberlin argues that the Cournot theory of oligopolistic pricing in which firms never learn from previous market conduct is not only counter-intuitive but does not accord with the facts. For him a much more convincing case was where firms realized that if they acted together their joint returns would be higher than if they continued to attempt to act independently. One means of achieving this, where overt collusion was illegal, was for the major firms to accept the pricing policy of a leader. Industry-wide demand or cost changes were likely to affect them all more or less equally. The appropriate price adjustments could be made by the leader and then imitated by the other firms. No direct communication need take place, although with modern methods of information transfer it may take place surreptitiously despite the law. The price leader may be the lowest-cost firm or the largest overall or, again, the one first established in the market. What is important is that all firms retain such confidence in the leader as effectively to give up their independence in price determination. The reward, just as in the case of a formal cartel, will be a share in the monopoly return earned by the group as a whole.

Indeed, as Markham points out, the probability of successful collusive price leadership will be highest when a number of important conditions are met. They bear a very close resemblance to those necessary for a successful cartel. Firstly, the number of firms must be relatively small and each of sufficient size to recognize the inter-dependent nature of their market decisions. Secondly, entry barriers must be considerable if the price leadership strategy is to continue to yield a monopoly return in the long-run. Thirdly, unit cost variations between firms in the group must be unimportant. Significant cost differences will make it impossible for any leader to maintain price discipline. Fourthly, although collusive price leadership may be compatible with a degree of product differentiation, where the products of the different firms are not close substitutes it will clearly be impossible to attempt meaningful price leadership. Markham concludes: 'In such industries price leadership may conceivably be so effective as to serve all the ends . . . of a closely knit domestic cartel and hence, in a political environment where overt collusion is illegal, may be the only feasible means of assuming parallel action amongst sellers' (Markham, 1958, p. 186).

In their report on parallel pricing the MMC (1973a) appears to rely closely on Markham's analysis of collusive price leadership and concludes that the efficiency effects are likely to be serious. Although using slightly different terminology they suggest in effect that technical, allocative and x-efficiency are all likely to suffer as a result of collusive price leadership. To retain the allegiance of higher-cost firms the price leader may set prices at a level that ensures that even they can make profits that they regard as satisfactory. However, more importantly, as individual firms have surrendered their power to set prices, the mechanism for weeding out technically inefficient firms may be severely weakened. To the extent that the price set approaches the monopoly level there will be an adverse effect on allocative efficiency. Consumers will be charged prices out of line with production costs. In addition, firms protected by barriers from new entry and sheltered from active competition amongst existing producers by the tacit collusion may well become x-inefficient. The MMC were even prepared to suggest tentatively that a regime of parallel pricing may weaken the incentives to innovate by making it difficult for a firm to exploit, independently, new products that it had developed.

If these conclusions are correct and if price leadership is widespread the implications for the performance of industry are very serious because as we have already mentioned (and as the MMC report confirmed) it may be extremely difficult to regulate conduct that grows out of the very structure of the market and for which there may be little tangible evidence.

Before accepting this line of reasoning, however, we must first examine the other relevant form of price leadership christened by Stigler (1947) 'barometric'. As its name implies a price leader of this kind acts as a barometer for the leading firms in the market. The barometric leader will thus only retain its position so long as it remains sensitive to the requirements of others. It will therefore have to assess what response is necessary following, say, an increase in costs. Whereas a collusive price leader may have undertaken that role for a considerable length of time, a barometric leader is likely to change relatively frequently, as one firm or another feels that a particular response is 'wrong' and therefore, for example, refuses to follow a price increase. By not responding to the initiative of the current barometric leader, the firm is in effect signalling to others that it is assuming the mantle of leadership. In an oligopolistic market structure such a move will not be taken lightly because there is always the risk that it may be misunderstood by other competitors who respond aggressively with the result that all suffer.

The discipline envisaged under barometric leadership is thus much less rigid than under collusive price leadership. Stigler has argued that, in effect, the barometric leader simply responds to the underlying conditions in the market but in a manner that allows the oligopolists to avoid a short-lived but destructive period of price competition. Given the structure of the market, continuous and direct price competition is infeasible. Barometric price leadership may, therefore, be the least damaging form of price determination. The adverse consequences for efficiency are likely to be far less than under collusive price leadership. Not only are prices likely to be lower since the lowest-cost producer has an incentive to assume the leadership role and thus determine the timing and level of any price changes, but also, since the leadership does change rather than remain unquestioningly in established hands, there is a greater pressure on firms to remain technically and x-efficient. If they do not then they run the risk of being caught in a weak position should a new price leader become established following a significant industry-wide increase in costs. An x-inefficient firm expecting, say, a 25 per cent increase in prices but confronted by a new leader content with a 5 per cent increase will clearly be vulnerable.

Price leadership of the barometric type is, on this view, much less detrimental to efficiency broadly interpreted. The significance of 'parallel pricing' therefore, as an issue in regulation policy, depends on the relative incidence of the two kinds of price leadership. Judging from the tenor of the conclusions of the MMC, they considered collusive price leadership to be the more frequent type. While recognizing that it may take various forms some of which were less harmful than others they nevertheless concluded that 'parallel pricing may have certain particular detriments commonly associated with the exercise of market power, namely excessive prices and profits and excessive costs at least of some sellers in the industry. There may also be more general detriments namely, a weakening of the incentives to innovate and an exacerbation of the inflationary process' (MMC, 1973a, p. 37). Similarly following their empirical study of the effects of the 1956 Restrictive Practices Act, Swann *et al.* recommended that 'price leadership should quite explicitly be brought within the ambit of the 1956 Act' (1974, p. 207). We consider below the problems that might arise if price leadership were to be registrable.

For the moment we will consider a number of points made by observers who see price leadership as a much less serious problem. The first point is that while it may be analytically convenient to consider collusive and barometric price leadership as quite distinct types, in practice the distinction may be much more difficult to draw. Simply because a price leader changes does not automatically mean, for example, that an oligopoly has switched from collusive to barometric leadership. On the other hand, the conditions necessary for collusive leadership are substantial and comprehensive. There may be some markets were *all* conditions are met but they may be far fewer than indicated by the MMC. If only one of the conditions is not met then it seems quite likely that the extreme form of collusive price leadership will not be sustainable.

This point was convincingly argued in a critique of the MMC's conclusions (Polanyi and Polanyi, 1974). Part of the MMC report consisted of brief case studies of five markets where price leadership was thought to prevail: bread, electric lamps, gramophone records, petrol and tyres. Polanyi shows that in each case the absence of one or more of the conditions necessary for successful collusive price leadership had effectively frustrated its emergence. In bread, there were no important entry barriers and countervailing power by large retailers was a growing problem for sellers. Similarly in electric lamps leading market shares had been changing considerably and there was evidence of widespread discount and import competition. The gramophone record market had undergone very rapid growth and the lack of significant entry barriers had led to the erosion of the leader's market share. This had also been the experience in petrol retailing where the oil majors had suffered a considerable decline in their market shares at the hands of 'fringe' sellers who, in this case, were usually subsidiaries of large international groups. A number of factors in the tyre market made it very difficult to classify it in the collusive price leadership category: several significant innovations had occurred (contrary to one of the necessary conditions for successful collusive price leadership according to the MMC); there was significant price discounting at the retail level, growing competition from imports and significant countervailing power from car manufacturers in the initial equipment market.

While price leadership in such markets may thus be attempted, and for a time may succeed, according to Polanyi and Polanyi, it is likely to be of the less damaging 'barometric' kind. In the same way that cartels may come under increasing pressure both from internal and external sources, so a collusive price leader may find that, like a general whose army has decided to desert and finds no one to obey his orders, his market response produces no reaction or a perverse reaction amongst his competitors. The regulatory question then becomes one of determining which cases of price leadership should be condemned and which allowed.

In the US the pinnacle of achievement as far as parallel pricing is concerned was in the 1946 Supreme Court judgement against the leading three tobacco firms whose pricing policies had shown a remarkable degree of parallelism for about 20 years, although no direct evidence of meetings or communications was presented.[23] The Court concluded that 'No formal agreement is necessary to constitute an unlawful conspiracy.... The essential combination or conspiracy in violation of the Sherman Act may be found in a course of dealing or other circumstances as well as in an exchange of words' (quoted in Scherer, 1980, p. 515). If this approach had been systematically followed in subsequent cases, it would not only have embraced all uniform behaviour by firms where this could be demonstrated from the facts, but would undoubtedly have posed a policy dilemma. Once parallel behaviour *in itself* becomes illegal, or in the UK context, registrable, oligopolistic firms would be placed in an impossible position. In the face of an industry-wide increase in labour costs, for example, not to increase prices may squeeze profit margins unduly, but if all firms respond in a more or less identical fashion they would run the risk of an antitrust action. Even if initially firms attempted an independent response to the cost increase the degree of uncertainty and instability that this would probably generate would be great enough to ensure that sooner rather than later some form of tacit understanding would once more be reached. In other words the interdependent nature of firms' decisions is inherent in the oligopolsitic structure of the market. To prevent effective collusive price leadership and the adverse consequences for efficiency, it is necessary to alter the structure of the market.

Perhaps fortunately for the subsequent development of US antitrust policy, the apparently clear view expressed in the American Tobacco (1946) case that an illegal agreement could be inferred from evidence of parallel action was not treated as a precedent. In the decades that followed, the courts appeared to move further and further away from this interpretation of the law, to one that has been characterized as 'parallelism plus'. Firms are unlikely to be found guilty of an offence merely because their market conduct is uniform with that of their major rivals. However, if there is sufficient additional evidence to infer that some form of covert communication or information exchange had taken place, then an offence might well be found. Precisely what form the 'plus' has to take, therefore, for an adverse findings is still not entirely clear. For a similar reason it is difficult to see how Swann *et al.'s* proposal for the registration and trial of price leadership in the Restrictive Practices Court would work in practice. What degree of conscious parallelism would the Director General of Fair Trading have to have evidence of before he could act? If the accused firms denied any form of tacit collusion how could they be expected to argue their case in terms of the net benefits that the public derived from it?

The MMC recognized the problem in their conclusions when they stressed the additional importance that the growth of parallel pricing places on merger regulation. If parallel pricing has harmful consequences for efficiency[24] but is also inherent in some types of market structure, then since altering structure by the break-up of firms is generally not feasible it is important to ensure that such structures are not allowed to develop unnecessarily. They therefore recommend that when mergers were being screened by the Department of Trade and Industry, it should be remembered that high seller concentration was a necessary condition for parallel pricing. Mergers that would lead to a substantial increase in concentration or possibly trigger others having this effect should be assessed for their likely effect on market conduct. Given the current attitude in the UK towards important horizontal mergers that we discuss in chapter 7 it seems unlikely that mergers having this effect would now be allowed to proceed. Furthermore, the MMC may have been unduly pessimistic in its view that the most frequent form of price leadership was of the collusive kind. By ensuring that other structural characteristics necessary for price leadership, such as high entry barriers, are removed or modified it may thus be possible to minimize the dangers of parallel pricing.

IV CONCLUSION

Compared with the varied market behaviour of dominant enterprises, where there is great scope for disagreement, most observers accept that overt collusion leads to inefficiencies and should therefore be heavily regulated. On the surface this has led to considerable achievements for regulatory policy. In the US, restrictive agreements governing terms of trading amongst groups of firms have for a long time been *per se* illegal, while in the UK despite a quite different tradition and a business environment, which had tended to favour collusion over competition, the early decisions of the Restrictive Practices Court ensured the wholesale abandonment of registrable agreements during the 1960s and 1970s. Similarly article 85 of the Treaty of Rome, making inter-state restrictions illegal, has, for the most part, prevented the spread of overt collusion in the European Community.

Despite these clear-cut gains, however, there are a number of areas where the policies have been less successful. The most important is the detection and effective prosecution of covert agreements where firms are prepared to infringe the law for the gains that successful collusion can bring. In the US the threat of *criminal* proceedings and triple-damage suits now probably makes many firms think more than once before entering any arrangement that might be interpreted as an infringement of the Sherman Act. In contrast, UK policy is possibly at its weakest in this respect. There are negligible sanctions against firms that deliberately and illegally fail to register as a restrictive agreement. Proposals made in the 1978 official *Review of Restrictive Practices*, which would have gone some way towards closing the loophole, were not taken up in the 1980 Competition Act and an opportunity for important reform was missed.

For all regulatory agencies the problem of parallel pricing in concentrated oligopolistic markets remains. Even in the US the apparently unequivocal view expressed by the Supreme Court in 1946 that collusion could be inferred from parallel behaviour has since been progressively attenuated, so now much more indirect evidence is probably required. In the UK there is effectively *no* policy towards parallel pricing or its ally price leadership, despite the suggestions of some observers that the latter practice should be registrable. In practice, to the extent that entry conditions, broadly interpreted, can be kept relatively open, there is a strong possibility that price leadership will take the less serious 'barometric' form.

PART IV
Regulating Natural Monopoly

9
Regulating Natural Monopoly and Dominant Enterprises in the Public Sector

The regulation of dominant firms or groups of firms in the private sector by means of antitrust or competition policy is an attempt to restore market forces, especially competition, in industries where they had been weakened and were not, therefore, producing a satisfactory economic performance. The previous two chapters have analysed how effective these restoration attempts have been. As we indicated in the introductory chapter, however, it had long been recognized that for a group of industries usually known as natural monopolies, the maintenance or re-creation of competition may not be feasible, however imaginative the director of antitrust policy happens to be. Where unit production costs for any relevant level of output are lower for a single firm than for a number of individual firms, a monopoly will result and resist any challenge from new entrants. The policy dilemma is then to derive the benefits that large-scale production can bring in the form of low costs while simultaneously ensuring that suppliers do not exploit their monopoly by overcharging customers.

If the industries were small and peripheral the problems would not be serious. Unfortunately most of them lie at the centre of the economy. Indeed earlier writers on natural monopolies such as gas, electricity, water, post and telecommunications emphasized this characteristic – that practically everyone purchased their services and also that their installations usually required a direct physical supply link to all customers.

Although different countries have attempted to tackle the dilemma in different ways, broadly speaking whatever form of regulation is adopted there are a common set of problems that are likely to arise. Some of these are discussed in section II. This is followed in section III by a brief review of the attempts to regulate the conduct and performance of these enterprises in Britain. Some evidence on the performance of the nationalized enterprises is then discussed in section IV. Dissatisfaction with their performance has not only led to renewed theoretical interest in the exact nature of 'natural monopoly' but has also resulted in some major policy changes, characterized as 'privatization' in Britain and 'deregulation' in the US. Many ideas previously regarded as settled have been challenged and there is now a much longer menu of regulatory options that can be used in such industries. These issues are taken up in the next chapter.

II PRICING AND INVESTMENT PRINCIPLES FOR PUBLIC ENTERPRISE

If competition cannot be relied upon to 'regulate' the prices charged by natural monopolies the question immediately arises as to how their prices should be determined. For them to pursue profit-maximization strategies would result in output restriction and monopoly prices. Not only would resulting allocative performance be unsatisfactory but the restricted output would also imply a poor level of technical efficiency given that they operated under conditions of increasing returns to scale. The pricing principles that such enterprises should adopt in order to avoid these problems has spawned a literature large enough to warrant a separate book. We will have to content ourselves with selecting some of the central issues.

Unlike much of antitrust policy, which does not try to apply theorems derived from static welfare analysis to the pricing problems created by private sector monopolies, most of the discussion of the pricing principles appropriate to natural monopolies has centred around the application and suitability of marginal cost pricing rules. It is a well-known result from standard welfare analysis that in a perfectly competitive economy, with no externalities, price equal to marginal cost is a necessary condition for an efficient allocation of resources.[1] Consumers' evaluation of the marginal unit produced and sold, as expressed by their willingness to pay, is just equal to the alternatives foregone, as shown by the marginal resource cost. The principle of marginal cost pricing is then carried over into the realm of the natural monopolies. Competition will not drive price down to marginal cost but the managers of the public or regulated enterprises can be instructed to use marginal cost pricing and to the extent they are successful, the resulting resource allocation will be efficient.

Leaving aside for the moment the problem of 'second best', theorists were still able to have a field-day drawing out the full implications of this deceptively simple-looking conclusion. For the most part these have centred around four issues: whether short- or long-run marginal costs were the relevant concept to use; how peak-load demand problems should be incorporated into the marginal cost pricing scheme; the most suitable investment criteria to adopt, especially when much of the capital is in large indivisible units; and the best methods for financing the losses that would occur where marginal cost pricing was used in decreasing cost enterprises. With the exception of the last point we may note that the other problems arise in modified form for enterprises in the private sector pursuing not the maximization of social welfare but the maximization of their own profit. To be sure, in many cases indivisibilities may not be very significant and peak demand on existing capacity more predictable; but the strict dichotomy between the problems of public and private enterprises is not really so sharp as much of the literature suggests. (It is also significant that contributions to the marginal cost literature have been largely from European, especially British, economists, where natural monopolies have tended to be nationalized until recently, whereas in the US much more attention has been paid to the distortions that may arise from attempting to regulate enterprises that have largely remained in private hands.)

As long as the short period is defined correctly it can then be argued that short-run marginal costs can in many circumstances form the starting point for an optimal pricing policy. The simplest case can be taken from conventional cost theory where it is assumed that capacity is perfectly divisible and is to be based on perfect technical knowledge. Any plant built, therefore, will be optimal for its designed output. Under these assumptions it is a standard result that for the optimal output from the plant where short- and long-average costs are equal, it is also true that short-run marginal cost will be equal to long-run marginal cost. In other words at the optimal short-run capacity the question of which marginal cost is relevant for pricing purposes does not arise because they are equal. Price at the optimal output will thus be equal to both short- and long-run marginal cost. Whether or not the enterprise in this model makes losses or profits depends on whether it is producing in an output range where there are increasing or decreasing returns to scale. With a conventionally drawn U-shaped long-run average cost curve, production to the left of the minimum unit cost output will mean losses while production to the right of this output will lead to profits.

The result depends on the *optimal* level of capacity having been built. Yet part of the problem of public enterprises pursuing a policy of marginal cost pricing is which criteria to use to ensure that investment is optimal (issue three mentioned above). In the case of perfectly divisible capacity the answer to this question follows from the above analysis. As long as the cost of an additional unit of output from the existing capacity is less than the cost of producing that unit by adding new capacity, then existing capacity is adequate. In the reverse case capacity should be extended. If demand is such that existing capacity is used to the point where short-run and long-run marginal cost are equal then capacity is optimal (as we argued in the previous paragraph).

Although the case is slightly more complex where capacity is not perfectly divisible but has to be made in discrete lumps, the same principles can be applied. The case where a piece of equipment can be operated at constant cost up to designed capacity but beyond this costs effectively become infinite is shown in figure 9.1. Each piece of equipment has a capacity output of Q_1. The short-run marginal costs for one such piece of equipment installed are shown by ABE. Long-run marginal costs (*LMC*) exceed short-run marginal costs (except at capacity) by an amount reflecting capital charges per period. If demand is initially at D_1 then the public enterprise can install two pieces of equipment to supply a total output of OQ_2 (where $OQ_1 = Q_1Q_2$). At this output short-run and long-run marginal costs are equal and a price of P_2 will ensure an optimal use of the capacity. This result is exactly the same as that derived in the perfectly divisible case but depends on the precise coincidence of demand and full capacity output Q_2, at the point F. Suppose demand now rises to D_2 and the enterprise has to decide whether to install further equipment that would raise its output capacity to Q_3. The incremental benefit of the change is shown by the area Q_2Q_3GH whereas the incremental cost is Q_2Q_3KF. Thus as long as the area FJH is greater than GKJ the investment in the third piece of equipment can be justified. In this case, however, the optimal price, P_1, is where short-run marginal cost is less than long-run marginal cost. Clearly given that the decision to expand capacity has been taken, to price at P_2 where short- and long-run marginal costs are equal would result in less than full capacity output, Q_3, being demanded. The result is thus different from both the perfectly divisible plant case and where demand coincided exactly with previous capacity (at Q_2). In the case shown in the diagram, because price is below long-run marginal cost the enterprise would run at a loss. It is quite possible to envisage other cases where the enterprise would charge a price equal to short-run marginal cost but where this exceeded long-run marginal cost, resulting in a surplus.[2]

Further refinements of this analysis are required where the industry is characterized by demand cycles showing peaks in any time period[3] but two important points emerge from the brief discussion of pricing and investment problems when plant is indivisible. The first has already been referred to and is that under certain supply conditions the optimal pricing strategy may be where short-run and long-run marginal cost diverge. Secondly, by pursuing an optimal pricing strategy with indivisible capacity, the enterprise may run at a loss, even though it is not operating under conditions of decreasing cost. The more familiar case of the loss-making public enterprise is where marginal cost pricing is pursued but where decreasing costs throughout the entire output range means that simple

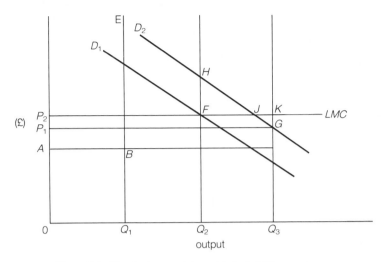

Figure 9.1 Marginal cost pricing with indivisible capacity

pricing will lead to losses. These cases bring us to the fourth problem raised at the beginning of this section, namely how best to finance the deficits that they are likely to incur for either of the above reasons.

A wide variety of potential solutions have been discussed in the literature, depending on the different characteristics of the industries concerned. Some solutions, such as two-part tariffs and price discrimination are operated by the enterprises themselves while others, such as special taxation, would depend on the government. Where feasible the two-part tariff may provide the most satisfactory solution to the problem. Consumers are charged a uniform price per unit, based on marginal operating costs, and also a lump sum quarterly or annually designed to cover the difference between short- and long-run marginal costs. The theoretical objection to such a pricing scheme is that some consumers who would be prepared to pay the per unit price equivalent to short-run marginal cost may be deterred from consumption by the fixed charge. In effect, some consumers have insufficient consumers' surplus out of which to 'pay' the fixed charged. To this extent, therefore, the optimal conditions are violated.

A pioneer in the field of public enterprise or natural monopoly pricing favoured special taxes as the means of financing deficits. Hotelling (1938) proposed, for example, taxing in such a way that the price of no commodity was changed and the optimal conditions were not violated. He therefore proposed taxes on land, inheritance and items in fixed supply (where the effect would be simply to reduce economic rents) as well as income taxes, although if these were of the usual graduated variety rather than lump sums they would affect the individual's choice between work and leisure. As a matter of practical policy, deficits are most likely to be financed by the usual forms of indirect and income taxes. There are very few recorded instances of poll taxes being used, however desirable their economic properties.[4]

In cases where the cause of the deficit is due to indivisible capacity and a price below long-run marginal cost, the deficit may not be very large. It will depend upon the size of the increment in capacity to the existing capital stock. If this is small then the future losses will be small and vice versa. The intractable nature of the problem when the deficit is likely to be large (where there are strong increasing returns to scale or significant indivisibilities) has led some observers to recommend average cost rather than marginal cost pricing (Coase, 1970; Wiseman, 1957). The case is strengthened by the argument that it may be extremely difficult to maintain the internal or x-efficiency of a large public undertaking if it is all-along known that its pricing plans are *designed* to ensure that losses are made. On this view, whatever desirable effect for resource allocation may be achieved by the marginal cost pricing policy is likely to be nullified by the resource misallocation that results from the internal failure to keep costs for any level of output to a minimum. This point is taken up again in section IV.

So far we have avoided the most serious objection that may be raised to marginal cost pricing policies. When discussing theories of economic regulation in chapter 2 we pointed out that the theory of second best has rather devasting conclusions for policy makers. In the present context it means that if the marginal conditions for an optimal resource allocation do not prevail throughout the rest of the economy, then it may well *not* be second-best policy for the public enterprise or utility sector to use marginal cost pricing. Indeed it is quite possible that marginal cost pricing in such circumstances may lead the economy away from its constrained optimum resource allocation rather than towards it. Thus if monopoly or collusive oligopoly of the kind discussed in the previous two chapters is present amongst prominent private sector enterprises it is likely to be counter-productive for the natural monopolies to pursue independent marginal cost pricing. If the private sector monopolies were insignificant or peripheral, or, again, if the public enterprises supplied only a narrow group of customers who operated, by and large, in competitive markets, marginal cost pricing may be second best as well as first best policy. However, neither of these conditions is likely to be met in practice. Monopolistic industries may frequently have a central role in the economy, supplying to or purchasing from many other markets, while the public enterprises and utilities occupy, by definition, a position embedded in the heart of the economy. While it is possible in principle to devise rules that would give the 'optimal departure from marginal cost pricing' (Baumol and Bradford, 1970) or more informally to suggest ways of relating public enterprise prices to those in the private sector supplying a competing good or service (Turvey, 1969) the very formidable data problems that implementation of such policies would require has effectively prevented their use.

Our discussion so far in this section has been largely theoretical: on what principles should public enterprises be instructed to base their price and investment policies. As is usual in such discussions we assumed that the relevant variables could be measured. A criticism often made of marginal cost pricing on a more practical level, however, is that in many circumstances it may either be extremely difficult to measure, or depend largely on the particular assumptions underlying the evaluation of future demand and cost conditions.[5] It may be particularly difficult, for example, for a railway network to allocate the many joint costs involved in the system between the multitude of diffrent services (or 'products') that it supplies in a particular time period. Similarly when making crucial decisions about whether capacity should be expanded or not an estimate of long-run marginal cost would be required. In practice this will depend very much on the length of time horizon used and the assessment of future input costs. Different assumptions will yield different results. Instead of the unique price structure, therefore, that would yield an optimal result, in practice there will be a number of different price structures that would apparently give this result. The monitoring of marginal cost pricing will thus be extremely difficult. Given the problems of cost measurement, management will tend to choose those time horizons and demand forecasts that provide the price structure most favourable to their own objectives. It may thus be almost impossible for any outside regulatory body to determine whether the enterprise has in any objective sense been pursuing a policy of marginal cost pricing.

Nevertheless it is now necessary to ask how far the pricing and investment principles discussed in this section have been carried into the practice of the public enterprises administering the natural monopolies that in the UK have, since just after the Second World War, been nationalized.

III PRICING AND INVESTMENT POLICIES IN PRACTICE

An observer fresh to the study of UK natural monopolies since the War cannot fail to be struck first by the gradual introduction of the principles discussed above but then by the disillusionment and rather more rapid movement in the opposite direction. Government policy in the late 1980s is designed to complete the circle begun in the late 1940s: from private (albeit regulated) ownership, through nationalization, to renewed private ownership. In the remaining sections of this chapter we consider the policies and performance of the nationalized enterprises, leaving until the next chapter an assessment of the most recent developments.

In view of the considerable body of literature on pricing and investment policies of public enterprises already contributed by economists by the 1940s, it is remarkable how little was its impact on the legislation nationalizing key industries. To some extent this is more easily understood against the background of the times. The postwar Labour government had been overwhelmingly elected on a platform of widespread social and economic reform. An important part of this programme was the nationalization of the 'commanding heights of the economy' which would not only allow for greater efficiency by the achievement of economies of scale but would also ensure an improvement in working conditions for employees in the industries and facilitate the introduction of wide-scale planning which was seen as the necessary accompaniment to postwar recovery.

With hindsight the guidance given in the legislation for running the nationalized industries has been condemned as extraordinarily vague and ambiguous. The industries were charged with providing a 'comprehensive', 'co-ordinated' and efficient service without discriminating between, say, urban and rural areas. While it was evident, therefore, that as *public* enterprises they had wider responsibilities than those in the private sector it was not made clear under what circumstances, if any, some services could be discontinued. From the outset there was thus likely to be a conflict between efficiency and comprehensiveness of service, leading to a misallocation of resources.

The financial guidance was equally vague. The enterprises were expected in effect to break even 'taking one year with another'. Guidance to Area Boards in the Gas Industry was typical of the legislation: they were 'so to exercise and perform their functions under this Act so as to secure that the revenues of the Board are not less than sufficient to meet their outgoings, properly chargeable to revenue account taking one year with another'.[6] Since it was nowhere explained how many years might be included in such calculations, the criterion, if that is a suitable way to describe such a vague description, could become highly elastic. Mr Micawber would almost certainly have applauded such a generously worded objective.

As we have already indicated, despite the quite highly developed analysis of pricing questions for public enterprises, there was no explanation or guidance given in the legislation of what criteria should govern their price structure. Apart from some references to the avoidance of 'excessive' prices and the need to keep prices 'reasonable' in the transport sector there was no indication of how prices should be set. Similarly they were exhorted to run efficient and up-to-date industries without receiving any guidance or rules on how this could be achieved through their investment policies. The conclusion of one observer of this early period of the nationalized industries' history was that they 'followed a policy that was akin to sales maximisation. Evidence of this comes from the fact that they operated unremunerative services that could have been closed down on profit maximisation criteria yet, at the same time, could not make out a specific case for their retention on social cost–benefit grounds' (Tyson, 1979, p. 409).

The position remained largely unchanged until the White Paper of 1961 (Financial and Economic Objectives, 1961) which was specifically concerned with the financial objectives of the nationalized industries. It was intended that a set financial target, expressed, for example, as an overall rate of return on assets and depending on the circumstances of the particular industry, should replace the general and open-ended principle of breaking even, 'taking one year with another'. In this way it was hoped that in future it would be easier to determine whether or not the nationalized industries were achieving their objectives. The financial targets were to be sufficiently flexible to encompass explicitly those parts of the industry that were accepted as being commercially non-viable. By endorsing the financial targets the government was, at least implicitly, making a policy decision about the allocation of resources to the nationalized industries and about their position in relation to the private sector. In a subsequent White Paper, six years later, these considerations were made much more explicit.

Although the 1961 White Paper marked something of an advance over previous policy, in that it became easier to monitor the performance of the nationalized industries, it was nevertheless very limited. There was still no guidance on pricing or what criteria should be used in investment appraisal. By now the theoretical discussion of marginal cost pricing for public enterprises had probably reached its apotheosis but, perhaps more importantly, the French electricity industry had, since 1956, been using a pricing tariff for industrial users that was largely based on marginal cost principles. The tariff depended on a detailed analysis of the pattern of demand throughout the day and at different times of the year. Since different demands impose quite distinct costs on the electricity supply system these were reflected, as far as possible, in the tariff structure.[7] The introduction of a similar structure in the UK industry had to wait another 11 years, and it was not until the 1967 White Paper that the possible advantages of marginal cost pricing were officially recognized. Furthermore, although the establishment of financial targets influenced in a general way the allocation of resources to the nationalized sector in relation to the private sector, there was no more detailed indication of how resources were to be allocated *within* the sector between the different industries.

In theory this shortcoming, along with several others, was remedied by the subsequent White Paper, published in 1967. The principles on which the nationalized industries were expected to base their pricing and investment decisions were set out in some detail. At the same time there was clear recognition that in some of their operations there were substantial divergences between social and private costs and benefits where the normal procedures would not apply.

Thus on pricing it was recognized that their special position in the economy meant that social objectives could not be achieved simply by profit maximizing and that insistence on an overall financial target was likely to lead to resource misallocation. While the financial targets for the industries were retained and they would normally be expected to earn sufficient revenue to cover full accounting costs, including the service of capital and provision for its replacement, it was nevertheless important that prices 'if they are to contribute towards a more efficient distribution of resources, must also attract resources to places where they can make the most effective contribution to meeting the demands of users' (Nationalised Industries, 1967, paragraph 17). The general pricing principle that the industries were to use to achieve this objective was to align prices with long-run marginal costs. However it was also recognized that in certain circumstances short-run marginal costs might be used (where for example, there was excess capacity) or again, a price above long-run marginal cost (where excess demand was pushing against the limit of existing capacity). Thus the advantages and also the possible complexity of marginal cost pricing were both accepted in the White Paper.

Given the diversity of the industries involved and the varying conditions under which they have to operate, it would have been remarkable had the guidelines proposed in the White Paper been uniformly adopted and successful. In some industries, notably electricity supply, where there was the French experience to draw on, considerable advances were made in the application of marginal cost pricing through the Bulk Supply Tariff. In others, where management was more sceptical of the rationale of marginal cost pricing, little or no progress in this direction was made. The National Coal Board, for example, continued to use average cost pricing.

The same recognition of their wider social objectives was given in the guidance on investment decisions set out in the White Paper. The main innovation in this respect was the recommendation of the use of discounted cash flow techniques for ranking investment projects, employing a test discount rate of eight per cent for all industries.[8] The suggested test rate was chosen to reflect the prevailing average real rate of return on low-risk projects in the private sector. In principle, therefore, the prospective merit of projects in different industries could be compared although it was explicitly recognized that the use of a test discount rate did not rule out investment in projects that were considered justified on social grounds. Where there were strong grounds for believing that there were significant divergences between social and private costs and benefits a detailed analysis was to be undertaken, although in this case by the relevant ministry, not the industry.

At the same time, therefore, as the private sector of industry was being urged to use more systematic methods of investment appraisal (apparently with somewhat limited success[9]) the nationalized industries, with wider responsibilities, were being encouraged to do likewise. Just as the recommendation on marginal cost pricing, however, met with a mixed reception from managements, so also the investment appraisal suggestions had a muted response, as became clear in the subsequent White Paper (The Nationalised Industries, 1978).

When it was published in 1978 the White Paper formed the first official review of the nationalized sector for eleven years. One of its central comments was the very limited use that had been made of the test discount rate in the assessment of investment proposals. For the most part, where they had attempted to use present value techniques at all, the industries had confined them to expansion plans and not to those investments aimed at maintaining the existing system which were regarded as 'essential' and therefore not requiring any formal justification or analysis. Rather than continue arguing the case set out in the earlier White Paper, that a proper allocation of investment resources within and between industries requires a full present value analysis of alternatives, the authors of the 1978 White Paper threw in the towel. Use of the test discount rate was downgraded in favour of an overall real rate of return on capital. Although, of course, present value analysis in no way precludes the achievement of an externally set target rate of return (in fact properly applied it should lead to its achievement) its deliberate downgrading in the White Paper, in effect, endorses the unsystematic policies that most industries had continued to use. If the recommendations on the use of a test discount rate made in the 1967 Paper were basically sound, it seems to establish a very bad precedent subsequently to abandon them on the ground that they had been ignored by the industries concerned.

In view, however, of the government's own treatment of the nationalized industries in the early 1970s, the effective abandonment of the use of the test discount rate is perhaps more understandable. At a time of rapidly rising prices the industries were deliberately used as an arm of the government's anti-inflation policy by having to hold down their prices. Largely as a result, even the hitherto very profitable electricity, gas and Post Office (then including telecommunications) were driven into large losses. Subsequently from about 1974 onwards a major aim of the government's policy towards nationalized industries was to restore them to profitability or surplus. Thus the emphasis in the 1978 White Paper on the overall rate of return objective might be seen as a reflection of this chastened mood, even though as the Monopolies and Mergers Commission later pointed out, it may be uncomfortably easy for a natural monopoly to make profits.[10]

At the same time, however, while it was generally recognized that the size and character of many investment projects undertaken by the nationalized enterprises were such as often to generate considerable external costs and benefits,[11] no guidance was given in the White Paper on how these were to be incorporated into their investment appraisal. Clearly attempts to achieve a correct balance of investment between public and private sectors as well as within different industries in the public sector may be nullified if no systematic analysis of spillovers is undertaken. The lack of guidance in this respect was more difficult to understand when set beside the quite unequivocal statement made about non-commercial or social objectives for particular industries. It was made quite clear that in setting the financial target for an industry social objectives would be recognized and published. In other words in future explicit recognition of the additional obligations that the industries carried would be incorporated in their objectives as well, presumably, as in the assessment of their performance.

This aspect of the White Paper can also be linked to the pricing recommendations. Marginal cost principles that had been the main focus of attention in the 1967 Paper while not abandoned were, rather like the test discount rate, given much less prominence. It was recognized that the complexity of the industries frequently made such pricing unrealistic. While the industries were urged, therefore, to relate prices as far as possible to the costs of supplying a particular service and to avoid arbitrary cross-subsidization, pricing decisions were left up to the management of the individual enterprise and their judgement of the market.

There has also been a charge of emphasis in the general discussion of public enterprises in recent years. The various pricing and investment rules discussed in the series of White Papers were essentially concerned with static and dynamic aspects of what we referred to above in chapter 7 as allocative efficiency. In particular how should prices be set in such industries to ensure an optimal level and distribution of output across their different services, as well as an optimal current and future allocation of resources to investment? More recently much more attention has been given to the equally important issue of x-efficiency. Gains in allocative efficiency achieved, for example, by a more precise application of marginal cost principles, may be dissipated by the growth of internal slack and the failure to minimize cost for a specified output. Marginal cost pricing rules for public enterprises are derived from the principles of welfare economics and the theory of market failure. Thus where natural monopoly occurs enforcement of marginal cost pricing, in effect, simulates what would prevail under perfectly competitive conditions. The lack of competition is replaced, at least in principle, by application of the marginal cost rules. However, competition is also supposed to ensure the internal efficiency of firms. Failure to maintain internal efficiency at least comparable with that of other firms will result eventually in bankruptcy and withdrawal from the market. In contrast public enterprise monopolies may not only have no competition for many of their services[12] but also know (perhaps only implicitly) that in the last resort the Treasury will come to their rescue. If marginal cost pricing simulates the market in order to ensure allocative efficiency what alternative mechanism should be employed to maintain x-efficiency?

In retrospect it is again extraordinary that the problems of internal efficiency were given so little attention in the literature compared with that devoted to the refinement of marginal cost principles. The problem may be severe in a private sector monopoly but in a public enterprise producing under conditions of decreasing cost and where, therefore, marginal cost pricing implies losses, they are likely to be acute and pervasive.

Recent analyses of the ownership and control structures of public compared with private enterprises have, however, served to highlight the difficulties.[13] A private sector firm sheltered from strong competitive pressures is likely to suffer from x-inefficiency. Furthermore, if the firm is large the divorce of ownership from control is likely to be considerable and it may therefore be difficult for individual shareholders to bring pressure to bear on the management to mend its ways and improve internal efficiency. Despite this, there are a number of grounds for believing that such pressures will be stronger in an enterprise in the private sector than one in the public sector. Shareholders (and, to a lesser extent, management) in private sector enterprises have a direct pecuniary interest in the size of the residual income. They therefore have an incentive to monitor the performance of the enterprise and respond if they are dissatisfied. Although attempts to reprimand or even unseat directors at a shareholders meeting are unlikely to be successful, a disgruntled shareholder always has available the option of selling the shares. Sales in a sufficient number may make the company vulnerable to a takeover bid and the new owners may well be in a position to replace the incumbent management. Thus even if product market pressures are relatively weak, capital market pressures for all but the very largest private sector enterprises, although attenuated, may nevertheless be real.

In contrast the owners of a public enterprise may have very little inclination or incentive to monitor their performance or take an active part in forcing through a change of policy. For individual owner-voters of public enterprises, who unlike their private sector counterparts have no direct pecuniary interest in residual profits, the costs of monitoring performance are likely to be out of all proportion to any eventual benefit. There is no counterpart for public enterprise ownership of selling out individual 'share-holdings'. It is possible to register disapproval of the way public enter-prises perform by supporting a political party that aims to 'denationalize' or 'privatize' but in practice the issue is unlikely to be at the forefront of any political agenda.[14] As a last resort an individual owner-voter might emigrate, as Milward and Parker (1983) suggest, but there can be few people roused to such a pitch of indignation by the performance of the railways, telephone or postal services as to contemplate such a drastic step on this ground alone. In short, most owners of public enterprises are likely to regard the performance of public enterprises as part of the natural order of affairs, rather like the weather, over which they have little control.

Those to whom in principle authority for supervising and running the public enterprises has been delegated by the owners, namely ministers and civil servants on the one hand, and chairmen and managers on the other, clearly have an interest in the performance of the enterprises but these may not coincide with those of the owners. Neither group has a direct pecuniary interest in the size of the residual or profit of the enterprise but ministers will be interested in re-election and therefore votes. They may therefore attempt to keep prices as low as possible and employment in the enterprises as high as possible. Similarly chairmen and managers may be more concerned with the size of the enterprise and its rate of growth than with either the size of the profit or technical efficiency. The sectional interest groups – ministers, civil servants, managers – are thus likely to prevail over the general interest group – the owner-voters – who as consumers have a direct interest in the price and quality of services and as taxpayers also have an interest in cost minimization and technical efficiency. The ownership and incentive structures of public enterprises are thus likely to accentuate the problem of x-inefficiency.

The question remaining, therefore, concerns the performance of public enterprises. In particular how well have they fared in view of the initially vague and then consistently changing guidelines proposed by the government and what has been their performance relative to enterprises in the private sector? These issues are discussed in the next section.

IV THE PERFORMANCE OF PUBLIC ENTERPRISES

Since one reason for nationalizing the enterprises was their natural monopoly characteristics, performance measurement is especially difficult: once nationalized there are no other comparable domestic enterprises against which their performance may be measured. In the UK at least, therefore, investigators have had to devise special indicators to compare the relative performance of public and private enterprises. In addition in the UK since 1980 the Monopolies and Mergers Commission has been able to receive references covering many aspects of the behaviour and performance of the nationalized industries and these form a growing and authoritative independent source of analysis. In other countries the presence in some industries of both private and public enterprises allows more direct comparisons to be made.

It is as well to recall from the discussion in the previous section that where no very clear guidelines had been given to the industries of their objectives (as in the decade or so immediately following nationalization) it may be especially difficult to determine whether their performance has been satisfactory or not because of the lack of appropriate benchmarks. Furthermore attempts to measure technical efficiency by looking at cost levels may have to make allowances for the social obligations placed upon the industries and the requirement to buy inputs that may not be at lowest available cost. Hence comparisons with, say, private industry may be especially difficult. Similarly the profitability of public enterprises may be a very poor indicator of their contribution to allocative efficiency. Not only have their profitability guidelines been changed periodically, but on occasions governments have intervened directly to depress profit levels.

One observer who has been well aware of these problems has been Richard Pryke. His two substantial books on the nationalized industries (Pryke, 1971, 1981) form a useful starting point for our review of their performance. What is particularly striking about his work is the dramatic change he records in the performance of the industries after 1968. The first book, published in 1971, gives a detailed account of their technical and allocative performance, and on the basis of the results Pryke concludes with a vigorous defence of public ownership and centralized control in the face of those critics who already saw the nationalization experiment as a failure and were even then calling for the re-introduction of private ownership and competition. He places particular emphasis on technical efficiency (at a time when most attention was being given to allocative efficiency and the problems of marginal cost pricing) on the ground that this is likely to be quantitatively much more significant. Technical inefficiency in an enterprise, for example, will affect the whole of its operation whereas allocative efficiency will be impaired only to the extent that prices diverge from the optimal level.[15]

In the first decade after nationalization Pryke concluded that due largely to reorganization and administrative teething problems the performance of the nationalized industries was inferior to that of the private sector. The rate of growth of their labour productivity, for example, was about 1.5 per cent per annum compared with manufacturing industry's 1.9 per cent. In contrast, during the second decade (i.e. from 1958 onwards) Pryke provides a considerable amount of evidence to support his contention that the performance of the nationalized industries more than fulfilled the expectations of those who believed public ownership was a more efficient method of organization. Firstly, using labour productivity as a partial measure of technical performance he compares the nationalized industries with the private sector, with the interwar performance of the same industries and with the contemporary performance of similar enterprises abroad. In all three respects the nationalized industries' performance, 1958–68, was, according to Pryke, impressive. The rate of growth of labour productivity in the nationalized industries was 5.3 per cent per annum compared with 3.5 per cent for manufacturing industry. In fact the only manufacturing industry to have a faster rate of productivity growth than the public enterprise sector in this period was chemicals. Similarly 'the productivity of the coal, gas, rail and electricity industries has increased at a faster rate since the war, and especially since 1958, than it did in the inter-war period' (Pryke, 1971, p. 434). In comparison with foreign industries the coal, rail and electricity industries' productivity growth was exceeded by only one other country, while that for the combined air corporations[16] was better than seven out of ten major international airlines (ibid.). Thus while the productivity record of the private sector in this period was poor by international standards, in the public sector it was very good.

Secondly, when allowance is made for capital inputs as well as labour inputs the overall conclusion is confirmed, although the details differ. Since the nationalized industries are capital intensive it can be argued that labour productivity comparisons with the less capital intensive private sector are bound to show the former in a favourable light. In fact in the first post-nationalization decade (1948–58) this view tends to be confirmed: the nationalized industries' performance was even worse than that shown by labour productivity. However, for the second decade the original conclusion stands, with the airways, gas and electricity having larger increases in total productivity than manufacturing industry and the railways a similar rate. It was also true that total productivity increased at a faster rate after the war than in the interwar period.

Pryke suggests a number of reasons for these improvements in technical performance. He points, for example, to the rapid introduction of new methods (such as power-loading and self-advancing pit-props in coal, and oil-based processes in gas), positive attempts to secure the available economies of scale, and the conclusion of productivity deals over a large part of the nationalized sector.[17] He therefore ends his first volume on a note of high optimism: 'After reviewing the evidence the conclusion seems irresistible that the technical efficiency of the public enterprise sector has been rising more rapidly than that of the private sector, and that this must in part have been due to the way in which it is organized and managed' (ibid., p. 436). The hazards of economic forecasting are highlighted when set beside the conclusions of his subsequent book which reviews the experience of the sector from 1968 to 1978: 'As yet the difference [between the level of efficiency in the public and private sectors] does not appear to be very great but it seems likely that the nationalized industries will rapidly pull ahead because their productivity will go on increasing more rapidly than that of the private sector' (ibid., p. 437).

Unfotunately, as he rather sadly demonstrates in his later work, the progress shown in the 1960s was not maintained and by the end of the 1970s the movement for the denationalization or privatization of most of the industries in the sector was in the ascendant. Although the statistical data in his second study were less comprehensive than in the first, there were sufficient for him to conclude that 'the productivity performance of gas, telecommunications and the airways seems excellent while that of most of the other nationalized undertakings looks dismal' (Pryke, 1981, p. 242). Over the decade 1968–78, for example, the growth of total factor productivity in manufacturing was 16 per cent compared with 66 per cent in telecommunications and 71 per cent in British Airways. Although no figure is given for British Gas, productivity growth was thought to have been large. On the other hand, industries like coal, buses and steel had substantial *declines* in total factor productivity in the period, while even electricity which showed a two-thirds growth in labour productivity, could only manage 7 per cent when capital was taken into account.

Part of the explanation for the deterioration in performance lies, especially in the second half of the decade, with the general economic difficulties experienced by the UK and many other economies following the dramatic rise in oil prices. Pryke also concedes that slow growth in demand and output in some industries contributed further to their poor performance. However, even when due allowance for such factors has been made the overall technical performance of most of the industries was very poor and certainly did not live up to the promise expected after their successes during 1958–68. A combination of trade union obstruction and bad management, according to Pryke, played a major role in the process. He cites in particular the obstruction by the postal workers of almost every change attempted by management, the policy of the National Union of

Mineworkers to agree to closing collieries only on grounds of geological exhaustion and the resistance in the steel industry to changes in manning levels and work practices. In part management is blamed for not attempting early enough, or in a more determined fashion, the reduction in manning necessary to improve productivity. However, an equally important criticism was their failure in the areas of planning and capital expenditure. It is perhaps at this point where the contrast between Pryke's earlier and later analyses are most sharply drawn. In the earlier report although recognizing that their planning and investment appraisal were far from perfect, he nevertheless makes a very favourable comparison between their perform-ance and that of the private sector. In the later work, however, he is dismissive: 'Estimates of future sales which, even at the time, were manifestly unrealistic have been used for planning purposes by BSC, BL and British Rail. Moreover capital expenditure has been misdirected and mishandled' (Pryke, 1981 p. 246).

Pryke's work was completed before the operation of the 1980 Competition Act became fully effective.[18] However, many of the conclusions that he was able to pinpoint have since been underlined by the Monopolies and Mergers (Commission (MMC) reports into the perform-ance of the nationalized industries that have been published. Under the Act, the Secretary of State for Industry can ask the MMC to examine the costs, efficiency and standards of service, as well as possible abuses of monopoly power, of nationalized industries or indeed other enterprises operating in markets where competition is limited by statute or for some other reason (for example, bus operators, water authorities and agricultural marketing boards).[19] The references may also ask for an assessment of whether or not specific practices by an enterprise operate or may be expected to operate against the public interest. For example, the references on the Central Electricity Generating Board (CEGB) and the Civil Aviation Authority (CAA) contained such a request whereas that on the National Coal Board was confined to a consideration of whether and how efficiency could be improved. Specifically excluded from the scope of these enquiries is an assessment of any financial guidelines or obligations placed on the enterprises by the Central Government. The reports have been noteworthy for their comprehensiveness, their speed of completion (between six and nine months) and the number and scope of their conclusions and recommendations. The present government sees this role of the MMC as essentially performing efficiency audits on the enterprises concerned and has indicated that the major industries will be referred approximately every four years. As the programme unfolds, therefore, it will provide a continuing assessment of many aspects of their performance.

Some of the earlier reports were particularly interesting for the comparisons that could be made with the work of others (notably Pryke) and for the fresh light they were able to throw on managerial and labour practices.[20] Their conclusions on labour productivity were as gloomy as those of Pryke. Thus, for example, productivity in the distribution of mail in London declined by between 20 and 25 per cent between 1968 and 1979. On the London commuter services of British Rail 'improvements of manpower productivity . . . proceeded at a considerably slower rate after 1970, and in the last two years has practically ceased' (MMC, 1980b). In the electricity supply industry they were concerned that recent productivity improvements had been lower than formerly (MMC, 1981a). The poor performance in the Post Office and British Rail could be explained, at least in part, by a variety of restrictive labour practices such as shifts ending before their scheduled time; insistence on agreed manning levels whether or not the traffic merited; and unnecessary procedures for the revision of manning levels.

The MMC has, however, been equally critical of weak management which in the Post Office had 'no continuous procedure for monitoring productivity nor any systematic and reliable procedure for estimating traffic flows through each office or the man hours to deal with them at each stage of operations. The failure to gather this information derives from UPW [Union of Post Office Workers] opposition' (MMC, 1980a, p. 51). The management were also too ready to adopt the view that (in a phrase that conjures up visions of the early days of Wells Fargo) 'the mail must go through at almost any cost'. In its report on the Electricity Board its most damning criticism was reserved for the management's investment appraisal methods. Although sophisticated modelling techniques were used, the whole exercise tended to be undermined by the central assumptions used, in particular the forecasts about the pattern of future coal prices. The choice of generating plant was highly sensitive to variations in the forecast price of coal at the margin. A detailed consideration of the CEGB's forecasts led the MMC to conclude that they lacked plausibility and internal consistency. As a result, in their view, the investment appraisal procedures operated against the public interest. Similarly parts of the British Railways Board (BRB) investment programme were heavily criticized. The electrification of the King's Cross commuter services was singled out for special mention: 'the project seems to have been considered with a considerable degree of "appraisal optimism" and the provision of rolling stock was decidedly generous' (MMC, 1980b, p. 165).

It would be wrong, however, to give the impression that the MMC has only been critical. Where it is specifically asked to pinpoint ways in which costs may be reduced or efficiency improved, a long list of recommendations may give the appearance of general condemnation of the performance of the industry; but it can be extremely complimentary. A good example was the report on the Civil Aviation Authority where it was impressed 'by the evident dedication of the staff at every level to the maintenance of a safe and expeditious service; and by their pride in the reputation that the Authority has for providing one of the best Air Traffic Control services in the world' (MMC 1983a, p. 200).

The MMC reports are also important, however, at a different level of analysis, for the insight they show into the general problems besetting a public enterprise sector. Although they are precluded by the 1980 Competition Act from discussing the appropriateness of any financial obligations imposed on the enterprises by the government, they have been able to make a number of pertinent references to them. For example, they have warned that the faith a number of writers show in the operation of financial targets as an internal control mechanism is misplaced. Where the public enterprise is a monopoly (such as the Post Office) providing services that apparently have a low price elasticity of demand, a government-established target rate of return on turnover can be more than achieved simply by raising prices. They cited the two substantial price increases in 1979 and 1980 made by the Post Office to meet a target in the face of wage settlements greater than originally expected. They concluded that 'in so far as the financial target applies strictly on an annual basis it can be used to justify tariff increases which would be positively *discouraging* to efficiency' (MMC, 1980a, p. 99, my italics). In other words a regime of externally imposed targets on a natural monopoly may lead not only to a deterioration in allocative efficiency through raised prices but this may be made worse by the growth of x-inefficiency. One function, therefore, of their four-year cycle of reports (if it is maintained) will be to assess whether the enterprises have avoided these effects by carrying out their recommendations.

Secondly, while the internal efficiency of the individual enterprises is clearly significant it can be linked to another issue of the greatest importance for the sector as a whole. We have already referred to the central place the natural monopolies have in the economy. What is also true is the considerable interdependence between the different enterprises. Having demonstrated such an interdependence between the CEGB, British Rail and the National Coal Board, the MMC makes the following comment: 'Where nationalized industries, each having a virtual monopoly, deal with each other as these industries do, the purchaser may not resist the seller's demands as vigorously as it ought, since it can pass on its costs to its customers. Also there can be no certainty that the bargains which they strike will lead to the most efficient use of resources. In its purchase of coal, the CEGB cannot be at all confident that the charges which it pays are related to the costs incurred in providing the fuel and transport which it requires. It knows no more about the National Coal Board's costs than it can glean from the NCB's Annual Report and Accounts; while as to the carriage of coal by rail, British Rail admit that they do not themselves know the costs of carrying coal over various distances, and therefore the rates charged are not systematically related to costs incurred' (MMC, 1981a, p. 200). Quite apart from the alarming information this conveys about the cost system of British Rail, it demonstrates the way in which allocative inefficiency in one part of the public enterprise sector may be spread to that of another, and since the enterprises deal with customers in practically every part of the economy, the distortions in resource allocation will clearly be magnified.

The position is made worse by direct interventions in the sector by the central government. Here the criticisms of the MMC again reinforce those of Pryke. In his first book he was, in the Tawney tradition, an enthusiastic supporter of public enterprise, pouring scorn on those critics who wished to see them returned to the private sector. By the end of his second book, however, he himself was questioning the viability of their public status and was convinced that what he had judged to be their 'third rate' performance in the 1970s was in part due to the fact of public ownership (Pryke, 1981, p. 266). Pryke catalogues a series of interventions by government that upset the industries finances and impaired not only their efficiency but ultimately management morale. Similarly the MMC concluded that the CEGB's costs could have been substantially lower if it had been free, firstly, to time power station orders in line with forecast demand instead of at the behest of government and, secondly, to seek low-cost fuel supplies. However, 'mainly for reasons of government policy the CEGB has been unable to take full advantage of such opportunities as were available' (MMC, 1981a, p. 184), which would have meant imported coal.

Thirdly, the MMC highlighted a problem in its report on the London and South East Commuter Rail Service that has bedevilled nationalized industry performance and to which we referred in the previous section, namely the precise distinction between objectives and funding of the *social* parts of the industries' services and those that can be run on purely commercial lines. According to Pryke the failure to clarify these distinctions early on in the experience of the public enterprises contributed greatly to the confusion and financial chaos of the middle 1970s when their call on public funds was estimated to be £2.75 billions in one year (1974–5) alone. Clearly in such an environment their affairs are a highly sensitive political issue. Thus in comparison with the 1960s when, by and large, they were told to operate as efficiently as possible and behave commercially, in the 1970s they had to pursue a variety of policies that were not always consistent and where it became clear that they were 'instruments of economic and social policy and . . . not commercial undertakings' (Pryke, 1981, p. 262).

The issue of the social versus the private or commercial obligations of these enterprises will not disappear if some of them are privatized. What it may mean, however, is that the justification and extent of the social provisions will be more clearly identified since it may involve direct payments from the government to the private sector. For those that remain in the public sector we may expect the MMC to continue to press the point that the social parts of a service should receive special treatment only as long as the case is properly made.[21]

The performance of the nationalized industries in the 1970s was poor enough to make even previously sympathetic observers doubtful of whether their public status was compatible with a sustained, first-rate performance. Pryke's final assessment was, however, suitably cautious: 'I do not believe that public enterprise always tends to perform worse than private industry. I suspect that nationalized undertakings function efficiently when economic conditions are generally favourable but particularly badly when the economy is in difficulties' (Pryke, 1981, p. 266).

An intriguing and highly topical question, therefore, is whether the services of the natural monopolies would have been more efficiently provided had they been in the hands of private enterprises. For the UK the question is difficult, if not impossible, to answer, because when the industries were nationalized no operations were left in the private sector and indeed the legislation made it impossible for private firms to enter any of the markets they served. Few direct comparisons between public and private enterprises supplying the same market were therefore possible. In other countries, however, some markets have been supplied by both types of enterprise and a number of comparative studies have been possible. We are fortunate in having available a recent comprehensive survey of these studies by Millward (1982) and the following remarks are based on his analysis.[22] The supply of electricity in the USA is made by a variety of public (including municipal) and private undertakings and for this reason has been the most extensively studied. In answer to the question of whether public enterprises have lower costs than private enterprises in supplying markets with similar characteristics the weight of the American evidence suggests that they do. Furthermore Millward was unconvinced by the argument that the significant differences revealed by the statistical analysis could be attributed to the regulations placed on the private sector firms. In the case of Canadian railways where comparisons were possible between the publically owned Canadian National and the private Canadian Pacific for the period 1956–75, there was no overall difference in total factor productivity. On the other hand, studies of water utilities and Australian airlines suggested a better performance by the privately owned enterprises. Particularly striking was the airline case where the firms operated their inter-state services in an environment where practically every aspect of their operations was regulated by the government. Although the productivity gap between the firms narrowed considerably between 1958–9 and

1973–4, the private firm outperformed its public rival in volume of freight, number of passengers and revenue. Without explaining the difference the author nevertheless notes that the industry has been overshadowed for more than 25 years by political influences of both right and left anxious to press the cause of the respective forms of ownership.

Thus overall the international evidence is neatly split and Millward concludes that 'there seems no general grounds for believing managerial efficiency is less in public firms' (Millward, 1982). In another recent study, however, Pryke was able to compare the performance of privately- and publically-owned enterprises competing in the same UK markets. His sample consisted of the following paired companies, showing the privately-owned enterprises first: civil aviation (British Caledonian with British Airways); cross channel ferries (European Ferries with Sealink, UK); hovercraft (Hoverlloyd with BR Hovercraft); and retailing of gas and electricity appliances (Currys and Comet with British Gas and the Electricity Boards). The date for comparisons were not always the same across markets but almost without exception the public enterprise performed worse than its privately-owned competitor, whether measured in terms of market share (as in ferries and appliance retailing), labour and capital productivity (in aviation, ferries, appliance retailing) or profitability (in all four markets). Even allowing for the special responsibilities of the public concerns (and the fact that the privately-owned enterprises were probably the best in the field, others having failed), their performance was poor. Pryke concluded that a major part of the explanation was bad management resulting from a weakening of incentives under public ownership (Pryke, 1982).

There is certainly as yet insufficient evidence, however, to draw any strong conclusions about the relationship between market structure and the pattern of enterprise ownership. As we shall see in the next chapter, at the beginning of the debate in the UK about the possible benefits of privatization many argued that a crucial part of the policy should be the introduction of a substantial amount of competition into the markets. However, in the event this was judged politically inexpedient.

V CONCLUSIONS

Despite the attention theorists had paid to the pricing and investment problems of public enterprises, their conclusions were largely ignored in the legislation which delivered the natural monopolies into public ownership. The objectives and responsibilities of the nationalized indust-ries were drawn in such general terms as to leave scope for practically any policy. Thus in the crucial areas of pricing and investment there was initially no guidance as to what criteria should be employed to ensure the correct distribution of current services amongst existing customers or of the growth and form of future services. As long as the enterprises continued to break even 'taking one year with another' they were fulfilling their legal obligations. The belief was widespread that, the revolution in ownership having taken place, the public enterprises could be left quietly to perform their duties and this would inevitably produce a performance 'in the public interest' without any need for close and continuing regulation. Even when steps are taken to tighten up their procedures and introduce guidelines designed to improve their allocative performance (by marginal cost pricing) and investment decisions (by discounted cash flow methods) they met with only limited success, and were subsequently played down.

For a time the problems did not necessarily seem very important because the relative performance of the public sector enterprises, especially during the 1960s, was impressive. Productivity comparisons with similar industries in other countries and with the private sector in the UK showed them in a very favourable light and there seemed no reason for which their performance should not continue to improve. When the economy ran into difficulties at the beginning of the 1970s, however, the unresolved problems were exposed, and since 1980 have been closely analysed by the MMC. Although their role is only advisory, the intention to ensure that each major industry is examined approximately every four years may go a long way to fill the gap in monitoring their performance to which we referred above.

In its earliest reports under this procedure the MMC highlighted four problems concerning both the performance of the public enterprises in particular and the overall allocation of resources in general. First, it reiterated a well-known but often neglected point that a public (just like a private) monopoly can maintain or increase its profits simply by raising prices. To impose a rate of return standard on a public enterprise, therefore, as did the 1978 White Paper, may have little effect on the technical and x-efficiency of the enterprise or on protecting consumers from monopoly abuse. Secondly, the interdependence of a number of the enterprises – coal, rail, electricity and steel – and their place at the heart of the economy, makes it particularly important that their pricing and investment decisions should be soundly based and, a point on which the MMC laid particular stress, that as much information as possible about these decisions should be published. The increased information should help to minimize the distortion in pricing and thence resource allocation that results from inaccurately priced inputs passing from one stage of production or industry to another. Thirdly, despite forty years of nationalization and recognition of the *social* obligations of the public enterprises, the problem of precisely how they should be handled is unresolved. Over the years a combination of arbitrary cross-subsidization and political expediency has been used, until in the 1970s it seemed as though any existing service provided by the public enterprises was sacrosanct whatever the demonstrable costs compared with the benefits and regardless of the alternatives that might be available. In common with a long list of previous observers the MMC has urged that any social obligations should be clearly distinguished from the remainder of those provided by the public enterprises and their costs and benefits clearly understood. Finally, it has drawn attention to the damage that can be done to the performance of the public enterprises by *ad hoc* government intervention for reasons not directly related to their efficient operation. The electricity industry has had both the timing and direction of some of its investment decisions affected in this way while nearly all public enterprises suffered in the early 1970s by becoming, for a time, a major instrument of counter-inflation policy. While the former type of intervention may be built into whatever criteria are used for monitoring public enterprise performance, the latter makes it extremely difficult, if not impossible.

The last two points strongly suggest that although the industries were originally nationalized to foster the public interest, more recently this admirable objective has been subverted by the sectional interest of politicians seeking re-election. Indeed one reason offered for the need to privatize the public enterprises has been to guard against this happening in the future. Whether or not the form that privatization has taken will have this and other desirable effects is discussed in the next chapter.

10

Privatization
and De-regulation

I INTRODUCTION

The instrument used to control the natural monopolies in the UK has
been nationalization. The ownership of all assets in the industries was
placed in the hands of public corporations responsible to the relevant
ministry for running their affairs 'in the public interest'. Nationalization
thus involved unified control, a statutory prohibition on entry to and exit
from the industry, guidelines on price and investment decisions and,
latterly, externally imposed rates of return. Except for the decade of
buoyant aggregate demand in the 1960s the performance of many of the
industries has been widely criticized even by those previously sympathetic
to the idea of public ownership. By the end of the 1970s, therefore, the
diminished ranks of those who had always opposed this method of dealing
with the natural monopoly problem were reinforced by many (including the
new leaders of the Conservative Party) who were newly convinced that a
better alternative was available. Initially the proposal contained two major
conditions: a change of ownership, involving a return of the public
enterprises to the private sector, and, secondly, a removal of the restrictions
on competition, often referred to as 'liberalization'.

As we shall see below, between the rhetoric and the practice there has
been a large gulf. The government settled for the first condition, de-
nationalization or privatization, but largely sacrificed the second, liberalization of the market. The issue has raised considerable controversy in the
UK with many arguing that both conditions were necessary for an
improved performance, while others regarded ownership as irrelevant and
liberalization alone as sufficient. Judged from the way the policy has so far
developed, the natural monopolies in the UK will in future be in private
hands but subject to regulation by a specially created bureau.[1] Although
the similarity is not exact, this general framework is close to that used for
many years in the US. The irony of the British move, however, is that at a

time when the US has been abandoning this model of regulation as unsatisfactory, it is being embraced by the British government. To consider the likely consequences of this policy, therefore, it is useful (see section II below) to consider briefly the way this form of regulation has worked in the US and why it was so heavily criticized. We may also at this stage refer again to those theoretical developments that have already formed and are likely to continue to form an important element in the regulation debate, namely the theory of contestable markets (cf. chapter 6). In section III we can then consider the implications of the present policy of privatization in the light of these developments.

II THE REGULATION OF NATURAL MONOPOLY IN THE US

Although the oldest federal regulatory agency, the Interstate Commerce Commission, was founded one hundred years ago (1887) it has only effectively been since 1934 that the Courts accepted that the executive arm of government could regulate any industry that it pleased. Since then, and especially in the 1960s and early 1970s, the scope of regulation increased dramatically despite a mounting chorus of criticism claiming that inefficiency and waste were the results.

The federal regulatory machinery has generally taken the form of a special commission for the industry concerned, staffed usually by a selection of lawyers, businessmen and politicians who frequently may not have the specialized knowledge that the detailed investigations may require and who may, on the whole, be sympathetic to the industry rather to the objective and dispassionate pursuit of 'the public interest'. Each Commission has a back-up staff of civil servants trained as accountants, engineers and economists but it has been a frequent complaint that the asymmetry in resources between the regulators and the regulated has meant that the former cannot perform their allotted tasks efficiently. This imbalance led one critic to conclude that the regulatory machinery was like 'herding elephants with flyswatters' (quoted in Greer, 1983).

The range of variables for which the Commission may have direct responsibility is considerable and in principle gives them the power to control the performance of the firm or firms in their industry. Thus they may have authority for agreeing the level and structure (i.e. between regions or customers) of prices, the quality of the product and the entry and exit conditions, although not necessarily all of these to the same degree. Since the guiding principle in setting prices has been to allow a 'fair' rate of return on the assets employed, it is evident that profits are determined as well. McGee's 'tar-baby' effect, to which we referred in chapter 2, is thus more easily understood. If the Commission wishes to establish a maximum price in a particular market this could be adhered to by the supplier diluting the quality of the product or service. Inevitably, therefore, price regulation leads to quality supervision with all the scope for disagreement that it may entail. Again, a 'fair' rate of return may be earned on an inflated cost base unless the regulators take steps to monitor costs. In short, what may start out as the seemingly simple and commendable task of protecting the public from abuse by a natural monopolist may develop into a quagmire of intervention.

There is now a good deal of agreement amongst students of recent US regulation that it is likely to generate a number of distinctive costs. Amongst the most important of these is likely to be x-inefficiency and for similar reasons to those mentioned in the previous chapter when discussing the performance of UK nationalized industries. The regulatory Commission usually grants exclusive authority for an existing firm or group of firms to supply the market. No further competitors can thus enter and where there is more than one firm (such as in the transport industries) all have to abide by the stipulated terms and conditions of service. Prices will then be set high enough to ensure not only a 'fair' rate of return but also to allow regulated firms to raise additional funds on the capital market. Under these circumstances firms that have not kept their costs to a minimum may be reasonably confident that, at the next hearing, prices will be adjusted upwards to guarantee that they can meet these targets. The problem will be most acute where the market is served by only one sizable firm and where, therefore, no comparisons of performance are feasible. Where a group of firms are involved, individual firms may retain an incentive to do better than the anticipated cost levels in order to earn a higher than normal profit, as long as they are confident that their performance will not lead to a subsequent price reduction by the regulators. On the whole, however, it is accepted that the incentive structure under a regulated profit regime is likely to lead to inflated costs. Furthermore, to the extent that firms feel secure behind a guaranteed profit their incentives to innovate may be weakened, particularly if they would be unable to retain any increase in profits resulting from a breakthrough in technique.

Secondly, it has been argued that firms under a regulatory constraint will tend to over-invest in capital. To the extent that they stray from the optimal input mix, costs will again be higher than necessary. The regulatory agencies in the US usually proceed to determine the asset base of the firm and then allow a 'fair' return on this base. Quite apart from the controversy that is likely to surround the evaluation of the assets,[2] Averch and Johnson (1962) have shown that where the allowed rate of return is set below what could have been earned in a free market but above the cost of capital, then the regulated firm will tend to substitute capital for labour and will operate at an output where cost is not minimized. The essence of this process has

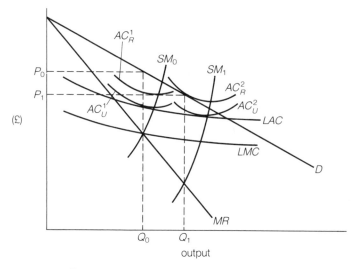

Figure 10.1 Output and costs of the regulated firm

been translated into conventional cost curve terms by Stein and Borts (1972) and it is their interpretation that is used below. In figure 10.1 the demand (D) and marginal revenue (MR) for the services of a natural monopoly are shown, together with their long-run marginal cost (*LMC*) and long-run average (*LAC*) cost. The optimal profit-maximizing position for the firm prior to regulation is shown by output Q_0 and price P_0. The output Q_0 is optimal in the sense that short- and long-run marginal costs are there equal ($SM_0 = LMC$) and consequently short-run average costs, AC_U^1, are equal to long-run average costs. There is thus no incentive for the firm to expand or contract its productive capacity and its capital stock is also optimal. A profit constraint is now imposed and if this is incorporated into the short-run average cost curve it becomes AC_R^1. However with an unchanged output the firm would make 'excessive' profits, in other words, the regulated profit is set below what the firm could earn in the free market. It therefore has an incentive to expand both output and capital stock. If the firm expands so as to produce output Q_1 the new short-run average cost curve, inclusive of allowed profits, is shown in the diagram as AC_R^2. With these costs the firm can produce an output Q_1 and clear the market at price P_1 while just earning the regulated profit, i.e. AC_R^2 is tangential to the demand curve. In addition, however, while marginal revenue is equal to the new short-run marginal cost (SM_1) the long-run marginal cost exceeds the short-run marginal cost and therefore the short-run average cost, excluding allowable profit (AC_U^2), is greater than long-run average cost. The firm is thus not optimally adjusted to the output Q_1 and in particular has over-expanded its capital base.[3]

Although there have been a number of subsequent theoretical contributions, the empirical evidence on the extent of the Averch–Johnson effect is as yet rather slender (both are reviewed in Fromm, 1981, ch 1). In this connection, however, it is worth mentioning a conclusion drawn by Pryke after his very detailed studies of the British nationalized industries: 'The poor use of capital appears to be a general feature of the public enterprise sector, and also a continuing one' (Pryke, 1981, p. 249). And again: 'That public ownership tends to be accompanied by a relaxation in control over capital expenditure and a greater willingness to invest in low yield and high risk projects seems to be borne out by the way in which nationalization was accompanied or followed by ill conceived programmes of investment at BL and BSC' (ibid.). Although he had not arrived at this conclusion by applying an Averch–Johnson type of analysis it is suggestive of the way regulated enterprises may approach their capital investment decisions.[4]

The implication of the analysis, emphasized by critics of regulation, is the effect on technical efficiency of the over-emphasis on capital. However, it has been pointed out, notably by Kahn (1968), that a worsening of technical efficiency may be more than outweighed by an improvement in allocative efficiency. It is clear, for example, from figure 10.1 that the output of the monopoly is greater when it is regulated (and the price is consequently lower) than when it is left unregulated. In other words profit regulation may tend to counteract the output-restricting tendencies of a natural monopoly.

The conclusions of the Averch–Johnson analysis depend in part on the excess of the regulated rate of return over the cost of capital to the firm. It is possible, however, that instead of investing their funds in an excessive amount of capital, firms that are regulated in some of their markets may seek out similar but unregulated markets and use their surplus funds to finance a campaign of marginal cost pricing. By this means, it is argued, they may obtain a dominant position as an indirect result of the regulation of their original markets. We concluded in chapter 7 that predatory pricing by a dominant firm may be comparatively rare, but in some circumstances it is particularly damaging to competition. This additional gloss on the potential for unfair competition by partially regulated enterprises is especially interesting in view of the British policy of privatizing the natural monopolies which no longer have to confine themselves to their primary markets. The issue is mentioned further in the next section.

A third source of added costs identified as resulting from regulation occurs in those markets, such as transportation, where a number of firms operate rather than a single natural monopolist. If the price structure is regulated but other forms of competition are not, in those markets where price–cost margins are more generous (e.g. long-distance air routes meeting less competition from surface transport) non-price competition amongst regulated firms may escalate and thus reduce or even eliminate supernormal profits. On US domestic routes this process apparently led to over lavish (and half-full) services on long hauls and minimal services (and queues) on the less lucrative shorter routes (Scherer, 1980). To the distortions in resource allocation that thus occur must be added the unintended income transfer from shareholders to some customers that such a process of non-price competition implies. Although formally no outright loss occurs – what would have been surplus profits are taken up by efforts to entice away customers from competitors – lower profitability will strengthen the case of those who see a need for an upward revision of prices. It can hardly have been the purpose of regulation, in any case, to cause simultaneously an over-elaborate provision of some services and under-provision of others.

Fourthly, the complexity of many regulated industries and the great diversity of their services places a very great burden on the regulatory agency. If the established price structure is wrong, as is almost bound to be the case, given administrative delays, complexity of service and changing economic conditions, then distortions in input combinations are likely to follow, with a consequent effect on technical efficiency. Firms will make their production decisions according to the regulated price structure even though changed circumstances may mean that these no longer conform with the underlying economic reality. The primary effect will be on the regulated industry itself, but clearly there will be further distortions as customers adjust to the services provided.

Finally, there are the administrative and enforcement costs of the regulation which must be weighed against any benefits derived from the system. The increasing criticism that regulation has been receiving throughout the 1970s and 1980s in the US has been backed up by estimates of the size of these direct costs. For example one study estimated that the Federal government's expenditure on regulatory activity increased from $2.2 billions in 1974 to $4.8 billions by 1979 (DeFina and Weidenbaum, 1978). An estimate from the Chase Manhattan Bank put the costs incurred by firms attempting to comply with government regulations at $85 billions in 1977 (quoted in Koch, 1980).[5] Putting these costs of administration and compliance together to arrive at a global estimate suggests that the equivalent of about 5 per cent of GNP in the US was taken up in this way. Even allowing for the wide margins of error that estimates of this type are subject to, the direct costs are evidently very considerable and, when added to the other costs to the economy previously enumerated, may amount in total to as much as seven per cent of GNP (ibid., p. 466). The order of magnitude of this cost is very similar to the (upper end of) estimates made recently of the welfare losses that may result from the exercise of market power in the private sector (see for example, Cowling and Mueller, 1978). A major difference between the two types of estimate, however, is that a sizable proportion of the direct regulatory costs are, at least in principle, supposed to generate a greater benefit to the economy, whereas the welfare loss estimates are dead-weight losses, with no compensating benefits.

Recent moves in the US to dismantle regulation either partially or completely are evidence of the widespread conviction that the industries' performance can be improved without exploitation of consumers despite their special characteristics. The impetus for these changes came mainly from a considerable body of empirical evidence demonstrating the generally adverse consequences of regulation (Fromm, 1981). However, more recently an added impetus has been given to the movement for de-regulation by the theoretical contributions of Baumol and a group at the Bell Laboratories involving the notion of 'contestable markets', to which we referred in chapter 6. The development is particularly interesting because it has not only had a considerable impact on the policy debate in academic circles on both sides of the Atlantic but some of the leading participants have been able very quickly to apply the principles to the actual process of de-regulation.[6] Before turning, therefore, to British policy it is worth summarizing the main points of contestable market theory insofar as they bear on the de-regulation of markets that had previously been classed as 'failing' either because they were natural monopolies or for some other closely related reason.

The point of central importance to regulatory problems is the emphasis that contestability theory places on entry and exit conditions. Thus if entry is free (new firms face no costs not also borne by existing firms) and exit easy (in particular, there are no sunk costs) then potential competition will force on the existing firms a performance that is efficient, in all senses in which we have been using the term. Prices straying above marginal costs will attract entry until excess profits disappear while prices lowered below marginal cost will cause some firms to exit (costlessly) from the market. Hence under these circumstances the number of firms operating in a market at any one time is irrelevant to the question of efficiency. Even a single firm operating in a perfectly contestable market 'performs in a competitive fashion' (Bailey, 1981). Although claims for the theory may have been exaggerated by some of its more audacious proponents,[7] if properly handled it can assist in the analysis of how to improve on existing systems of regulation.

A starting point is to scan those industries hitherto regulated to see how far their entry and exit conditions depart from the requirements of contestability. In some cases this might point fairly immediately to changes in the form of regulation so as to make the markets more contestable. Thus in US domestic airline and trucking industries, the severe regulation of entry has been greatly reduced after an analysis that suggested that despite superficial appearances (especially in the case of airlines) both entry and exit, although not costless, were far easier than hitherto considered. Aircraft can, after all, be leased rather than purchased outright with the sunk costs that that is likely to involve. 'The new policies are based on the theory that both trucking and aviation markets are, in the absence of regulatory intervention, naturally contestable' (Bailey, 1981).

Application of the theory can also help to highlight inconsistencies in regulatory policy and indicate possible remedies. For example, the simultaneous regulation of prices and no restriction on entry invites cream-skimming. Similarly, controlling entry but not prices is likely to lead to monopoly pricing. The lesson from contestable market theory would be that entry should be de-restricted in both cases and coupled with a relaxation of price controls, assuming that the market in other respects was 'contestable'.

It needs to be recognized, however, that the latter assumption may not hold in many important cases. Formally opening up *entry* to previously regulated markets may be comparatively easy if only because restriction was artificially imposed. Removing constraints on exit, on the other hand, may be a much more intractable problem. We have already observed that safeguards are required to protect an entrant from a predatory response by an incumbent firm. The safeguards are all the more important in the likely case of a de-regulated market that is not perfectly contestable in the sense that exit is not free, that is, sunk costs are positive. Under these circumstances unless potential entrants can be assured that their entry cannot provoke a reduction in price to a predatory level (because, for example, the sanctions against such action are effective) they will not come into the market because they would be unwilling to incur the necessary sunk costs. The incumbent firm could thus continue to charge monopoly prices free from the threat of entry. In fact the constraints may be even more serious than suggested by this example. Vickers and Yarrow (1985) have shown that, on the plausible assumption that sunk costs are positive, and that the incumbent firm can respond before the entrant is fully established at an efficient scale, then the knowledge that competition would reduce price to the level of marginal cost will prevent entry because it would be impossible for sunk costs to be recovered. Again the established firm could persistently charge a monopoly price, only in this case there is no necessity even to threaten predatory pricing.

Vickers and Yarrow emphasize that the main purpose of their example was to question the robustness of the theory of contestable markets and therefore its suitability as a basis for framing public policy. However, their analysis also serves to underline the crucial significance of sunk costs.[8] The theory forces the policy maker into a careful analysis of the nature of sunk costs in a particular industry and, if necessary, into devising alternative ways of handling the problem. It is no accident that examples of apparently successful recent US de-regulation, trucking and air transport, involve a fairly clear-cut distinction in ownership and operation of sunk cost elements, compared with operating costs. Thus in trucking, the roads and associated services, and in air transport, the airport facilities, are owned and operated by organizations separate from transport firms and airlines. Entry to the industries therefore involves incurring a minimum amount of sunk costs and as a result exit is also easy, given not only highly developed second-hand and leasing markets for equipment, but also the possibility of switching to other markets with the same equipment. In other industries the separation may not be as distinct and easy to enforce. For a variety of reasons, therefore, the de-regulation of the US air transport industry was especially interesting and its progress has been very closely watched. Although it is still too soon to conclude that all adjustments to the new competitive environment have finally been made, it is possible to highlight the main effects and to consider whether the optimism of those urging de-regulation has been justified.

Prior to 1977 the Civil Aeronautics Board (CAB) had very wide-ranging powers to regulate the US industry. Any carrier wishing to start a service (either on an existing route or a new one) had to be licensed by the CAB which needed to be sure that the proposal would be profitable and not jeopardize the viability of an existing service. Airlines were certificated by the CAB according to category of service (i.e. trunk, local, commuter, charter or cargo) and it also had to authorize any change of category. In addition to controlling entry, the CAB also prescribed the fares which airlines had to charge, according to a formula dependent solely on distance. In practice entry to the industry, or even to a particular route, was blocked or extremely difficult and the only way existing firms could compete was in such non-price forms as flight frequency and on-board services (Civil Aviation Authority, 1984b).

In 1977 the CAB began to liberalize its licensing policy by allowing multiple entry to certain routes, but this was merely an introduction to the major reorganization that resulted from the Airline Deregulation Act in 1978. The central purpose of the Act was to change the whole environment in which US air carriers operated. Competition was to replace the rigid regulation which had prevailed in the industry for forty years. The Act provided for the scaling down and then the complete abolition of the CAB within seven years. Thus from 1978 to the end of 1981 a degree of control over *entry* of carriers was retained, but from the beginning of 1982 the

CAB's domestic licensing authority expired. Thereafter the certification procedure became largely a formality (the carrier having to demonstrate that it was 'fit, willing and able' to operate, ibid., p. 6) and any carrier was then allowed to operate on any domestic route that it chose. Equally significant, in view of the anlaysis of contestable markets referred to above, exit from the market, which had been heavily circumscribed before de-regulation was now usually approved automatically on the expiry of a 90-day notice period.

As far as fares were concerned, for an initial period following the Act, the CAB assessed a standard level of fare for each route. Carriers were allowed to set their actual fares within a band around the standard level. The bands were gradually widened, allowing more and more price discretion to individual carriers until, at the end of 1982, *all* official controls on US domestic fares were removed. Finally, in January 1985, the residual authority of the CAB (e.g. over foreign air transport) was transferred to the Department of Transportation and it was wound up.

Thus in a comparatively short time, entry and exit conditions to the industry were fundamentally changed and prices were free to vary according to the state of competition. It was widely accepted prior to 1978 that regulation had led to inefficiency in the industry and an unduly rigid industrial structure which did not properly cater for the changing pattern of consumer demands. De-regulation was expected to go a long way to remove the sources of inefficiency and to promote a more adaptable industry. According to a number of analyses that have been made of the industry since de-regulation, these predictions have, to a considerable extent, been proved correct although the transition has not been without its difficulties, some of which are still unresolved. There have been a number of complicating factors which have tended to cloud the main issues (such as the near doubling of fuel prices in 1979, the sluggish growth of the US economy, and the effects of the air traffic controllers' strike in 1981) but nevertheless it is possible to point to the following effects of de-regulation. First, not surprisingly a considerable amount of new entry to the industry has taken place both by new firms (such as People's Express, Midway and Pacific Express)[9] and by existing airlines expanding their route structure. In a number of cases the entry has been accompanied by the development of secondary airports in major cities (e.g. New York Air at Newark and Midway Airlines at Midway, Chicago). Secondly, although not universally true, the operating costs of the new entrants were often considerably below those of their more established rivals, as a result of less complex route structures, lower labour costs and simpler services. In some respects this reflected a reduction in product quality but the ability of the new airlines to offer lower fares was in large measure thought to be due to their greater technical efficiency (Forsyth, 1983). Part of the adjustment that the established airlines have had to make to the new competitive environment has been to slim down their operating costs which had become inflated during the long period of regulation. There are also likely to have been sizeable improvements in x-efficiency. Thirdly, the period immediately after the de-regulation of fares was one of intense price competition but not precisely in the form anticipated. Established carriers adopted a policy of selective rather than across the board price cuts and this had the effect of making their fare structure exceedingly complex. The new entrants adopted simplified but substantially lower fare structures. The fuel price increase of 1979 favoured the new entrants with their smaller, twin jet aircraft and as the US economy moved further into recession in 1981-2, thus halting the growth in demand, price competition became especially fierce with widespread, steep discounts. In this environment not only the established airlines but also the new entrants were feeling the pressure, and the spectre of predatory pricing which we have now encountered in several different contexts, was allegedly seen in a number of markets (Eads, 1983, pp. 163-71).

Given the comprehensiveness of the de-regulation, however, some violent short-term reactions were bound to occur in the industry. Summing up the CAB's own interim assessment of the effect on prices the CAA concluded that 'the travelling public in general has benefited, since average fares paid have fallen in real terms and there is now a greater number and variety of services than before. Within this broad picture individual routes have lost services or now have a lower standard and there are routes where passengers, particularly business passengers, are paying significantly higher fares. In the context of the total US industry, however, these specific disbenefits may be small' (CAA, 1984b, p. 40).

Against these benefits of increased efficiency and lower average fares, however, must be set two possible restraints on the continued vigour of competition in the industry, namely access to computer controlled reservation systems and to landing slots at key airports. Increasingly, booking agents for air tickets use a computerized system to display seat availabilities on any specified route. (In fact the enormous growth in complexity of services and fares since de-regulation necessitated the kind of system that only a computer can provide.) Almost inevitably the agent will tend to make bookings from amongst the first half dozen or so flights shown on the display. If an airline can ensure that its services are always shown in the first group of available flights it will help to bolster its market share. The corollary is clearly that entrants to the market may have their growth severely curtailed unless they can, by some means or other, ensure a 'reasonable' chance of display for their services amongst the first shown. By the early 1980s the systems provided by three airlines (American, United and TWA) included more than 90 per cent of all computerized travel agents, although a number of others were being developed. The specific complaint made against the market leaders in this field was that their systems were deliberately biased in favour of their own services, although other carriers could receive the same treatment as the 'host' in return for appropriate payments. But it was also claimed that new entrants had been denied access altogether to the system. Before its abolition the CAB, in collaboration with the Department of Justice, had presented a report to Congress on the issue and also approved rules designed to minimize any bias in reservation systems. Together with the development of new reservation programmes – based, for example, on fares rather than flight times (Eads, 1983) – these should ensure that this particular impediment to competition is eventually removed, but clearly it may take some time to persuade travel agents to switch systems.

The second difficulty may be more problematical. The special importance of key take-off and landing 'slots' at over-crowded, central airports was highlighted at the time of the air traffic controllers' strike in 1981. In the wake of the widespread sacking of controllers, the number of flights had to be drastically reduced. As the system gradually returned to normal a major problem was the re-allocation of key slots, especially at airports like Washington National and Chicago O'Hare, where flight movements are restricted on environmental grounds. An allocation to airlines based on historic flight patterns would have favoured incumbent firms at the expense of new entrants, while simply allowing the price mechanism to determine the allocation would have favoured the financially strongest firms and thus have the same effect (CAA, 1984b). For a short period in 1982 lotteries were used to try to resolve the problem, with new entrants given priority for a limited number of slots in each draw. It was also possible for airlines to trade slots and their individual importance is illustrated by the huge sums paid, e.g. People's Express was prepared to pay $1.75 million for five slots at National Airport and three at Boston (Eads, 1983). In the face of strong opposition from smaller airlines, however, sale of slots was ended in June, 1982. The system eventually used was for a once-for-all draw to determine the order in which airlines could receive those slots suspended during the air traffic controllers' strike. Subsequent draws then allocated the slots according to this ordering.

While the lottery system provided a more or less acceptable solution to the short-term re-allocation problem caused by the strike, the underlying capacity constraint at key airports remains. New airlines were not able to enter markets at the times they wanted and from the airports they favoured. A partial solution may be that adopted by People's Express and Midway of developing previously underused airports in the same cities, but it still does not overcome the central problem. It is worth noting that in the UK the constraints imposed by the pre-eminence of London's Heathrow airport make for an even more intractable problem. It is favoured by most passengers and therefore airlines, because of easy access to London and other cities. Flights, however, are limited on environmental grounds and there is considerable suppressed demand for access. As part of government policy British Airways is the only British airline allowed to operate internationally from Heathrow and is also the major domestic carrier. As the CAA concludes 'the conflict between encouraging a policy of competition and the need to find some mechanism for rationing scarce resources is far more acute than in the USA, where only a relatively small proportion of the industry has been affected' (CAA, 1984b, p. 42).

The results of the first years of de-regulation of air transport in the US have been broadly as predicted. Fares have, on average, been reduced and there have probably been gains in all three forms of efficiency. Some smaller, new entrants have had considerable success and route structures have changed markedly. The claim by Bailey and others that the market can remain contestable in the longer term may depend very much on the response to new technological and capacity barriers that the process of de-regulation itself has accentuated.

Thus dissatisfaction with the traditional form that regulation had taken in the US based on considerable evidence both of inefficiences of the industries involved and of the high administrative costs has led to a major change in the direction of policy. The main emphasis of the de-regulation that has so far taken place has been on relaxing restrictions on entry and abolishing price controls. An important influence on these developments has been the theoretical analysis of contestable markets. Whether the theory has as much direct applicability to industries such as telecommunications, gas, and electricity where sunk costs are likely to be problematical as to the transport industries where they may be more tractable, remains at present an open question. It is also debatable whether the ideas can be applied in a much smaller economy like the UK with a different regulatory tradition.

III PRIVATIZATION AND DE-REGULATION IN THE UK

By the late 1970s a similar discussion on the unsatisfactory performance of the natural monopolies was taking place in the UK. However one highly significant element in the discussion was different. In Britain the natural monopolies (and over the years a number of miscellaneous enterprises from manufacturing industry) had not remained in private hands but had been nationalized, so they were owned by the public but run by a board of directors responsible to the government. As a result, in the UK, the issue of de-regulation has become inextricably bound up with the question of ownership. Indeed the government's policy in the 1980s was characterized by the specially invented term 'privatization'. Little confusion arose in the US when the subject of de-regulation was discussed because although views might differ as to the form and extent of the policy, everyone understood that it referred to measures designed to increase competition in the industry, remove administrative interventions and so (it was hoped) improve performance. No such clarity of understanding has unfortunately attended the UK debate.

The benefits claimed to flow from opening up the market to competition (in the UK context often referred to as liberalization) are regarded by many observers as independent of the ownership of the existing firm. Reductions in x-inefficiency and prices together with a greater incentive to innovate and responsiveness to consumer demands are thus seen to depend on increased competition and to have nothing to do with the status of the predominant enterprise as a nationalized rather than a private entity. Proponents of this view might add that the theory of contestable markets strengthens their position. There is nothing in the theory that suggests that it is inapplicable to cases where a leading player is nationalized. Free entry and exit will have the same chastening influence on performance regardless of ownership. The complicated and economically sensitive process of selling a large nationalized undertaking back to the private sector is thus seen as a time-wasting and irrelevant exercise in political dogma.[10]

The alternative view is that market liberalization is a necessary but by no means sufficient condition for improving the long-run performance of the nationalized industries. The ownership status of the industries is seen as of central importance for a number of reasons. Despite the good intentions of future governments, experience over the last two decades demonstrates clearly that under pressure they find the temptation to interfere with the running of the nationalized industries irresistible. Depending on the circumstances, therefore, they may institute price and profit controls, specify input purchases or insist on a re-timing of investment. Attempts to open up these markets to additional competition would not alter this propensity to intervene except that to be even-handed they would have to treat all firms (nationalized and private) in the same fashion. However, it is argued that effective entry is unlikely to occur while the incumbent firm remains nationalized, precisely because potential competitors will not be prepared to risk competition with an enterprise which in the last resort can be rescued by the Treasury. The prospect of any government being prepared to stand aside while the market share and profitability of a public enterprise are eroded by new private sector firms is very difficult to imagine. Even in less dramatic cases where the nationalized enterprise is apparently responding to the aggressive pricing of a private sector entrant – because of cream-skimming for example – it is likely to be very difficult to enforce curbs on their market conduct. If the nationalized enterprise is accused, for example, of predatory behaviour a regulatory agency (responsible to one branch of government) will have a difficult task applying sanctions against a nationalized enterprise (answerable to another branch of the same government). The position was neatly summed up by Brittan (1984) as follows: 'Competitive behaviour is not produced simply by removing restraints on new entrants in enterprises whose losses are made by the state and where profits disappear into the Treasury coffers. You do not make a mule into a zebra by painting stripes on its back' (p. 120). In common with a number of economic observers he thus regards it as vital that liberalization of the market is accompanied by privatization. Both conditions are necessary if the desired improvements in performance are to take place.

At the same time, however, it is recognized that apart from the logistics of the capital market absorbing the enormous flotations that privatization involves, there is the extremely difficult issue of the *terms* on which the enterprises are offered to the public. The flotation of any company on the Stock Exchange involves, on the one hand, an assessment by the promoters of what value to place on the shares and, on the other hand, conjecture by buyers of the shares about the future profit prospects. In fact once the flotation has taken place the value of the company will depend on the assessment in present value terms of its future profit prospects. In large measure this will depend on the firm's performance in the recent past.

For the privatization of what has hitherto been a protected nationalized enterprise, however, the considerations are quite different. Although a Conservative government may wish to restore enterprises to the private sector on ideological grounds the change has become part of a policy that aims also to restore a degree of competition to the markets that they serve. (At least this was the original purpose. We consider below whether it has survived in practice.) Because it is accepted that the markets contain strong elements of natural monopoly it is also agreed that they will have to be regulated in some way after privatization has occurred. Hence both the structure of the market and the form of regulation after privatization has a direct effect on the valuation placed by the market when the enterprises are floated. A British Telecom (BT) divided into a number of separate enterprises performing different functions and serving different markets, all of which were open to new entry under a liberal licensing arrangement, is clearly likely to be worth considerably less than a monolithic and essentially unchanged enterprise operating in markets where entry is very strictly limited. Similarly the sale of British Airways with its route structure largely intact (and inherited from a system whereby routes were awarded to the airline by the government rather than won by competition) is worth more than if some lucrative routes were reallocated to rivals. The British

Airports Authority which is at present responsible for both of the main London airports (Heathrow and Gatwick) has a higher valuation because of the market power they impart than the combined value of the two airports sold separately. In short, there is basic dilemma at the heart of the UK privatization and de-regulation policy that does not arise in the US. The more effective the liberalization measures are expected to be, the lower the valuation placed by the market on the enterprises to be sold. The more protected the newly privatized firm is, naturally the higher the selling price will be.

If the prime concern was to improve the performance of the natural monopolies then the post-privatization regulatory framework could be devised with this in mind, drawing on the recent US experience and, possibly, on the theory of contestable markets. However, as we have just indicated this implies that the amount of money raised by the sale will be much reduced. It never seemed possible on political grounds, however, that the government could keep future industry performance in the forefront of its objectives. Already under attack from the Opposition[11] on the very principle of privatization, the government could not be seen to be selling off state-owned assets at what would have been interpreted as 'knock-down' prices based on fully liberalized markets. What was not foreseen at the start of the policy, however, was that it might be forced to the other extreme and provide the minimum of constraints on the privatized enterprises in order to maximize the amount raised by the sale, thus both easing pressure on the public sector borrowing requirement and assisting another part of its policy (reducing taxes).

An interesting change of attitudes by chairmen of the nationalized industry board took place in the course of the growing debate on the privatization issue. Initially when a variety of proposals for increasing competition in their markets were being aired, they were known to be hostile to the idea of a change of ownership. When it became clear, however, that if they handled the situation properly they may end up not as chairmen of truncated companies vulnerable to substantial new entry but instead as heads of unified private sector monopolies, subject to fairly token competition and supervision, their views changed. They became enthusiastic supporters of the principle of privatization.

If the long-term performance of the natural monopolies is to be assured the time to liberalize their markets is at the time of privatization. Investors can then make their assessment of the future profit prospects of the enterprises and value them accordingly. Once the privatization has occurred within a specified regulatory framework it then becomes very difficult, if not impossible, to envisage fundamental changes taking place, because if those changes directly aim to intensify competition, the valuation of the assets and thence the shares will be correspondingly reduced. Since another objective of the whole privatization policy has been to create as wide a share ownership as possible, especially amongst small savers, purchasing shares for the first time, the partial destruction of those share values would be politically unthinkable.

Most of these problems associated with the valuation of the enterprise could have been avoided, while the twin objectives of private ownership and liberalized markets were still attained, if the imaginative proposal of Brittan (1984) had been adopted. He urged that a government seriously interested in improving the performance of the industries would focus squarely on measures designed to open them up to fresh competition. At the same time shares in each privatized enterprise could be issued free to all adult citizens of the UK who, after all, had been their owners since nationalization.[12] Thereafter a market in the shares could be made and exchanged at a price reflecting their future prospects. Apart from the great advantage this has of allowing the government to devise a suitably liberal market structure and regulatory framework, it would also make re-nationalization, following a change of government, extremely difficult. From the government's point of view, however, it is totally unacceptable because it raises no money. The extent to which this short-run political imperative led to the sacrifice of market liberalization can be judged by a closer examination of the case of British Telecom.

Although the first Conservative administration in the 1980s had sold off holdings in a number of state-owned enterprises (notably 51 per cent of British Aerospace for £43 millions, 75 per cent of Cable and Wireless for £442 millions and 51 per cent of Britoil for £627 millions,[13] the sale of fractionally more than one half of the shares in British Telecom plc (BT) for £3.9 billions was both quantitatively and qualitatively different. The sum raised, in three tranches, dwarfed all other sales and indeed all previous flotations on the London market, but also the industry lay at the heart of the public enterprise sector and raised nearly all of the issues surrounding the control of natural monopoly. It is therefore useful to consider it in some detail.

In most of the discussion that has attended the privatization of BT, the operations of the industry have been divided into three main areas: the supply of terminal apparatus (used by final customers), the development, maintenance and operation of the telecommunications network, and the provision of services (including both conventional voice transmission and, for example, the transmission of data). Although the scope for liberalization differs between one part of the industry and another, it is important to remember that the rate and direction of technological innovation is so rapid in the industry that an analysis relevant to the mid-1980s would probably require substantial revision by 1990. In these circumstances it is clearly important to avoid imposing an inflexible regulatory procedure that cannot be adapted easily to the changing circumstances.

Until 1981 the Post Office (which had responsibility for telecommunications until the formation that year of British Telecom as a public corporation) had a statutory monopoly over all parts of the industry. The 1981 British Telecommunications Act, however, broke the monopoly over terminal equipment by substantially relaxing the constraints on entry. Although a number of firms are now making their equipment available in competition with that from BT, the latter's dominant position in the remaining sections of the market clearly gives them an advantage. The strongest elements of natural monopoly occur in running the networks, especially those serving local areas. Consumers will wish to subscribe to networks with the greatest number of links. The firm with the most subscribers will therefore tend to drive out lesser rivals and, in any case, supply by more than one network is likely to be inefficient. Local communications networks are usually the most dense and these factors will be at their strongest. For long-distance and international communications they are likely to be less strong and the scope for competition can be widened if the provision of the network link can be separated by regulation from the supply of the services using the network (Vickers and Yarrow, 1985). In principle, therefore, the supply of services such as voice and data transmission over an existing network can be opened up to competition (see also the dismantling of AT and T in the US referred to in chapter 7).

Thus although parts of the industry do have strong forces making for natural monopoly, in other parts there may be considerable scope for liberalizing the market. Indeed the government made a point of finding out about the possibilities by commissioning an independent report on the matter soon after making the announcement that BT was to be privatized. A central recommendation of the Beesley Report (1981) was that it would be desirable to allow the unrestricted leasing of BT's telecommunications capacity to firms that could, if they wished, sell it to their customers. If, for example, a leasing firm saw the opportunity of providing a trunk service between two cities, it should be able to lease the capacity from BT and then sell the service on a retail basis. Such firms would clearly be in competition with BT. The main advantage of such a system was reckoned to be the incentives it would provide both for BT and others to ensure that the most efficient use was made of BT's telecommunications capacity. As Vickers and Yarrow argue, even if actual competition was slow to develop, the threat of entry would provide a salutary competitive restraint on BT. The problem would be over the negotiation of a 'fair' price for the lease. Beesley recommended that this could be left to negotiations between BT and competitor firms, although it is clear that this would leave the dominant supplier in a very strong position. It could deliberately ask what amounted to a monopoly price in order to stifle the competition. Only if the bidding company felt it could *still* earn a favourable return, despite the very high price, would the deal proceed. The alternative would be to have some independent agency attempting to arrive at 'reasonable' terms for the lease and this would also raise many problems. On balance, prices determined between the parties would probably provide the most efficient solution, especially if BT's profits were to be the subject of review.

In the event, although BT's profits were to be watched, the government decided to reject the important recommendation of the Beesley report and prohibit any resale of BT's capacity, at least until 1989. This conclusion was announced in mid-1984 by which time it had been decided that BT and Mercury[14] were to be the sole recipients of licences under the Telecommunications Act. It had been clear for some time that BT would be very much the dominant supplier for the foreseeable future, and the main reason given for refusing to allow the competitive resale of capacity was the protection of the new company, Mercury, while it was establishing its network. Since BT was expected to retain about 95 per cent of the market some form of price or profit regulation was necessary. For the reasons discussed in section II above, a straight profit regulation may have a number of undesirable effects. To inform itself of the relative efficiency of different kinds of control, the government commissioned a second report, from Professor Littlechild. His recommendations fared rather better than those of the Beesley report. A variation on one of the possibilities that he considered was finally adopted for the regulation of BT's prices. The system, which has become known as the (*RPI-X*) scheme, provides for the prices of a representative sample of BT's services (trunk and local) to fall in real terms. The extent of the fall (the X of the formula) was subsequently fixed at 3 per cent after negotiations between BT and the government.

Several observers have commented adversely on the likely impact of this regulatory system (Sharpe, 1984; Vickers and Yarrow, 1985). First, given the rate of technical change in the electronics and telecommunications industries, the 3 per cent does not seem to be particularly onerous, an impression strengthened by the fact that BT was party to the negotiations rather than having the level of cost savings imposed by an independent body. The level is thus likely to represent what BT thinks it can accomplish rather than what it *ought* to achieve. It is also significant that the Littlechild report concluded that this system of price regulation would have no effect on the flotation value of BT shares; in other words, its impact on future profit prospects was likely to be zero. The Littlechild report envisaged price regulation as an intermediate measure (lasting five years) while competition was established. However, the report was prepared before the government's intentions for the industry were fully known. For a number of reasons that we mention below, it now seems highly unlikely that Professor Littlechild's optimism will prove to have been well founded. The price regulation will have to continue well beyond 1989. In these circumstances as Vickers and Yarrow (1985) point out, if the regulatory formula is based on BT's costs actually achieved, it becomes indistinguishable from profit regulation and is likely to have a similar deadening effect on x-efficiency.

The conclusion is based not the pricing system itself but on the way it is likely to work within the overall regulatory framework determined by the government and largely embodied in the 1984 Telecommunications Act. The Act formally abolished BT's monopoly over telecommunications systems but required every operator to be licensed by the Secretary of State. It also established the Office of Telecommunications (OFTel) headed by a Director General, to ensure that the provisions of the licences were complied with and to monitor competition in the industry. In many ways, therefore, OFTel is akin to the Office of Fair Trading, but with a more specialized brief. Under certain circumstances licences may be modified either with the consent of the licensees or after reference to the MMC. By the time OFTel was actually established the government had announced, as we have seen, that apart from BT and Mercury no further licences were to be issued until November 1990. In the meantime any other operators have to use the fixed links of one or another of these two companies.

The licence granted to BT contains provisions for it to supply certain 'social' services (e.g. emergency services and those for the disabled) but the most interesting feature for present purposes is the attempt to protect competitors or customers against discrimination. It has, for example, to publish standard terms for a range of its services, including maintenance; it must not give favourable terms to its subsidiaries and cannot impose exclusive dealing conditions. In addition, it has to connect any other licensed system to its own equipment on terms that allow it to cover costs and make a return high enough to finance its social service obligations. Mercury's licence does not contain any social obligations or price control (the *RPI-X* terms are contained in BT's licence) but is similar in other respects.

With this regulatory framework in mind we can ask three questions. Firstly, how 'liberalized' are the telecommunications markets likely to be in the aftermath of this major piece of privatization? Secondly, how well does the framework stand up to what we might call the Bailey–Baumol test of creating contestable markets? And thirdly, what are the prospects for other enterprises if they are privatized according to broadly similar terms?

On the first question it is difficult not to agree with Vickers and Yarrow

(1985) that the framework is a highly restrictive one, likely to slow considerably the development of competition in the industry. Firstly, there is no satisfactory explanation of why only two basic telecommunications operators should be licensed. The main reason offered by the government was that this would protect Mercury while it was becoming established. It is difficult to accept this argument given that a major motive for the whole privatization policy originally was to enhance competition and so improve performance. Licence restriction protects both BT and Mercury from the threat of new entry, and if the argument was good in 1984 for Mercury why should it not be used again in 1989 to protect any additional entrant? There is, then, the danger that licence restriction will continue a good deal longer than the original five years. In the meantime the knowledge that no further licences will be issued removes any threat of entry with its positive impact on internal efficiency. Secondly, the restriction on the resale of BT's capacity effectively prevents entry by firms attempting to compete while avoiding the considerable sunk costs that fixed-link communications normally involve. The opportunity for increasing competition in parts of the industry where it is probably most difficult has thus, at least for the time being, been lost. Thirdly, the obligation on firms using related technologies (such as cable television) to offer telephone services only in conjunction with BT or Mercury is a further restriction on the development of alternative and independent sources of competition. It is clear, therefore, that the whole industry will continue to be dominated by BT for the foreseeable future.[15]

The combination of BT's size and the deliberately restricted competitive environment in which it will be working raises a number of doubts about its likely market conduct. Despite the licence provisions, for example, there was a long-running dispute between BT and Mercury over the terms on which Mercury can link in to BT's capacity. In the field of terminal equipment where competition has been possible since 1981, entrants have to contend not only with BT's own products but also with the fact that the equipment has to be linked to BT's system. Many customers may thus feel confident in buying what they might regard as compatible equipment (i.e. from BT) rather than from another supplier. The experience in the US suggests that a dominant firm in such a position may be able to employ a number of devices for limiting competition. Furthermore, although the licence contains provisions to safeguard competitors and customers against discriminatory pricing, the US experience again indicates that however hard-working and tenacious the staff of OFTel are, they are unlikely to be able to monitor every aspect of BT's operations so as to eliminate all possible abuse. The point is underlined when we remember that OFTel will be dependent on BT itself for details of its operations. Finally, the price control formula includes a number of BT's services but not all. Since privatization the prices of some services outside the scope of the price control have risen considerably. (In contrast, shortly after the announcement that Mercury was to be licensed and was likely to be particularly concerned with long-distance commercial services, BT reduced its prices by 35 per cent.[16])

In view of our answer to the first question it is hardly surprising that our conclusion on the second is that the market established post-privatization is far from being contestable, not primarily for technological reasons but because the regulations imposed make entry either impossible (the licence restriction, and no resale of capacity) or very difficult (the requirement on other operators to use BT or Mercury fixed links). If entry is largely blockaded a consideration of the conditions of exit is not required (although we have indicated above an important sector of the market that could be made contestable if the restriction on resale was lifted).

The first really ambitious part of the privatization policy, therefore, must be regarded as a missed opportunity. Ownership of a majority of the new private sector company was transferred from the government to shareholders but the markets it serves have been opened to a minimal amount of competition. The hard lessons that were learnt during the protracted antitrust action in the US which ended with the restructuring of AT and T were not absorbed by those responsible for UK policy. AT and T had to divest itself of its local telephone operations, retaining (in this industry) responsibility for long-distance services and equipment supplies. In principle there was no reason for which a similar separation in the UK industry should not have taken place. However, as we argued above, the time for restructuring in this as well as other industries was before privatization not afterwards. The sectional interest groups that were already well organized before the change of ownership are reinforced once the new pattern of operations is established. The advantages of restructuring are unlikely to be realized in future and yet, according to Vickers and Yarrow, these could have been considerable. While the separation of local services (organized, for example, through a series of regional companies) from long-distance and other services would not have generated direct competition between the new independents, they would have been able to compete in other sectors of the market. Reducing the scale of each separate company's operations would probably also have reduced the scope for anti-competitive conduct which is present with a single monolithic enterprise with its capacity for cross-subsidization. Finally the existence of a number of similar enterprises supplying a comparable range of services would have provided a very useful basis for comparing and monitoring relative performance.

The characteristics of the enterprises to be privatized differ but the fundamental questions of regulation are common to them all. Given that the government has adopted a highly restrictive regulatory framework for telecommunications, we can now address the third question raised above, namely the prospects for further privatization if it proceeds along similar lines. For a number of reasons, not least the government's anxiety to maximize the sales proceeds and the determined opposition of senior management, it seems likely that the BT model will be replicated in the privatization of other public enterprises involving the gas, electricity, airline and airport industries. In particular the sale of the British Gas Corporation (BGC) late in 1986 retained the enterprise intact and with a minimum of opportunities for increased competition or of regulatory restraint. Although the natural monopoly elements in the gas industry are stronger even than in telecommunications, most of the advantages of restructuring mentioned above could also be attained by, for example, creating a series of independent companies, based on the previous structure of area boards. They would be able to buy their gas supplies from a separate company responsible for the purchase of gas from the producers (mainly oil companies) and for the pipeline transmission system. Divorcing the gas showrooms from the gas industry had already been recommended in an earlier MMC report (MMC, 1980c) but rejected by the government. Recognition that scope for competition in some phases of the industry did exist was given in the Oil and Gas (Enterprise) Act (1982). In principle this provided for gas producers to supply large industrial consumers directly by using the pipelines owned by British Gas. In fact experience since then has indicated that the pricing policy of British Gas has kept competition of even this limited kind to the minimum (Hammond *et al.* 1985). Most of the doubts expressed about the capacity of OFTel to oversee adequately the whole of BT's operations also apply to the comparable body in the gas industry, the Office of Gas Supply (OFGas). If anything these doubts are even greater in this case where OFGas has direct authority only over domestic gas prices (based on a similar rule to that for telecommunications) while industrial users negotiate their own terms. Any disputes can be taken up by OFGas which can also refer cases to the OFT or the MMC.

When the conditions under which British Gas was to be privatized became known, late in 1985, there was general agreement amongst observers that the regulatory constraints had been deliberately kept to a minimum. The size of the problem was put in market share terms by *The Economist* (21 December 1985) which pointed out that British Gas was responsible for 60 per cent of the domestic energy market, 80 per cent of all appliances, 40 per cent of all heating, 36 per cent of energy used by industry and 30 per cent of that used by commerce. The scope for cross-subsidization is thus considerable (a point that the electricity industry fearing unfair competition was quick to point out). *The Economist* concluded that 'those are the kinds of market share which make predatory pricing to repel competition tempting and easy' (ibid.) especially when it may be perfectly possible to disguise the true situation in individual markets in the accounts. Again, this danger would have been much reduced if regional companies had been established and the vertical divisions of the industry, mentioned previously, had also been implemented.

We referred earlier to the rejection by the government of proposals by the Civil Aviation Authority to reallocate some routes to airlines other than British Airways, despite the enormous disparity in size of firm that in any case would exist in the industry. The scope for substantial de-regulation of Europe's air transport industry along the lines of what has recently taken place in the US is, however, greatly limited by the attitude of the different governments. The designation of airlines to particular European routes has hitherto been negotiated by government representatives. Any substantial moves toward de-regulation will therefore also require their agreement. At the moment, with some minor exceptions in Belgium and Holland, enthusiasm for de-regulation amongst other members of the EEC has been noticeable by its absence.[17]

In the related industry of airport services, however, where the British Government has complete discretion over the form that privatization and de-regulation can take, the most likely prospect is that all of the assets owned by the British Airports Authority (including the two major London airports, Heathrow and Gatwick) will be sold as one enterprise rather than as a number of separate enterprises which, subject to regulation, could offer competitive services.

A central conclusion from the UK experience of privatizing natural monopolies so far is that the change of ownership need not be accompanied to any significant extent by an increase in competition. Even where some of the markets could quite clearly be opened up to more competition by relaxing entry conditions and making exit easier, these have been largely passed over in favour of an option that maximizes the valuation of the enterprise at the time of sale.

IV CONCLUSION

Where natural monopolies have remained in private hands (as in the US) a regulatory framework has usually been established to try to ensure that consumers are protected from exploitation. The regulatory commissions that had primary responsibility for achieving this objective frequently attempted to control prices, profit rates and service quality, although not necessarily at the same time. In fact a central problem they had encountered was the tendency for the regulation of one variable, say profits, to lead irresistibly to the regulation of others, as the firms concerned sought to minimize the impact of the constraints. What the US experience has also shown is that the regulatory process imposes considerable costs on the economy not merely in the form of the direct costs of compliance and monitoring, although these appear to have been considerable, but because of the resulting distortions in the regulated firms' behaviour and performance. The regulation of rates of return, for example, are thought likely to encourage the growth of x-inefficiency, lead to over-capitalization and, in some cases, to excessive non-price competition.

The growing claims of distortion and excessive cost encouraged the de-regulation movement in the US in the late 1970s and early 1980s. It was further bolstered by the development of the theory of contestable markets, which was thought to have special relevance to the problems of natural monopoly. Concurrently in the UK the problems of improving the conduct and performance of the nationalized industries were made unnecessarily complex by mixing two related but distinct issues: ownership and de-regulation. The Conservative government initially appears to have envisaged the simultaneous achievement of its political objective of returning the natural monopolies to the private sector (the ownership issue) with the economic objective of improving their performance by increasing competition (the de-regulation issue). Although many highly imaginative and seemingly feasible proposals were made for increasing competition in markets hitherto considered impregnable, in the event nearly all of these were ignored. A major example was BT where no attempt at restructuring was made, entry was heavily circumscribed and the regulatory agency (OFTel) likely to suffer from the same difficulties that had hampered its US counterparts.

The government's central concern with ways of reducing the PSBR was allowed to influence its privatization policies. The result was that the ownership issue dominated questions of de-regulation. Thus while ministers argued that privatization would prevent in future the arbitrary intervention by government in the affairs of the natural monopolies, the future structure of their markets was being largely determined by precisely the same kind of short-term consideration. It is generally agreed that the most favourable time to liberalize the markets previously restricted by legislation would have been immediately prior to privatization. If this is the case then an important opportunity, with implications for the long-run performance of the industries, has been lost.

11

Conclusion

I INTRODUCTION

There has probably never been a period when industry could operate free from government regulations of one kind or another although clearly their incidence and direction has varied. Most observers are agreed that the UK, in common with other industrialized economies, has undergone a substantial increase in many forms of regulation since the end of the Second World War. Some of the many reasons for this were explored in earlier chapters and it was apparent that no single theory was sufficient to explain all of the regulatory response. Thus growing real incomes, complexity of products, together with the increased concentration of industry all played a part in promoting the move for consumer protection which has resulted in dramatic extensions of laws originally passed to guard against the charlatan and the quack. In the case of competition policy, which in the UK reversed completely the interwar tradition of cartelization and control, an explanation for its initial introduction can be found in the wartime White Paper on employment policy. It was recognized that if postwar governments were successful in maintaining full employment then an essential micro-economic accompaniment was competitive markets. In contrast, those industries where the underlying technology meant the incompatibility of technical efficiency and competition would have to be run on principles different from those of other sectors of the economy. The method originally chosen for these cases was nationalization although, as we suggested in chapter 9, it was not always very clear what these alternative principles should be.

In all three areas – consumer protection, competition, and natural monopoly – the need for regulation results from different kinds of market failure. Furthermore the main reason, at least initially, behind the types of regulation introduced was to protect or further the 'public interest'. Many measures regulating the production and distribution conditions of food and drugs clearly have this purpose. The investigation of dominant market positions and the prevention of large mergers are designed to maintain competition and contribute to an efficient industrial performance. The attempt to introduce marginal cost pricing in nationalized public utilities was also seen as a means of improving resource allocation. In other words at the introduction stage the types of regulation we have examined can be viewed as a 'public interest' response to market failure.

In some cases, notably competition policies, subsequent developments have done nothing to change this position. The MMC and the DGFT have not been 'captured' by either industrial, commercial or political groups. Extensions to the authority of the Director General have not been forced upon him by sectional interests. On the other hand, there are a number of indications from other areas considered that later developments were more in accordance with the alternative economic theories of regulation discussed in chapter 2. The most obvious examples of this process can be drawn from the nationalized industries. Because they are under the direct control of government, they have been used by successive administrations as a means of strengthening their position, either by protecting a particular group (trade unionists in the industries themselves, customers for uneconomic services in marginal seats) or more generally by assisting other objectives (containing inflation, reducing pressure on the PSBR). Such policies forced periodically on the industries have thus much more to do with promoting the sectional interest of the ruling administration than the 'public interest', however generously that term is interpreted. Furthermore the most recent developments in UK policy towards these industries – privatization – suggests that the sectional interest group itself has become the prisoner of its own policy. The over-riding objective has been turned from one of ensuring the proper regulation of the newly privatized industries, to one of maximizing the amount raised by the sale. In this situation the industries themselves are likely to have a large influence on the form that regulation takes. Although this is not the 'capture' that was discussed in chapter 2, the effect is likely to be very similar. In any case judging from the US experience, the new regulatory agencies are, in time, likely to become closely identified with the interests of the firms they are supposed to oversee.

Although there are a number of similarities between the OFT and the newer agencies, such as the Office of Telecommunications (OFTel) and the Office of Gas Supply (OFGas), there is an important difference which in the long-run is likely to have a very significant effect on their respective behaviours. As we saw, especially in chapters 5 and 8, the OFT has *general* responsibilities in the fields of consumer protection, restrictive agreements, and the behaviour of dominant firms[1]. In contrast, the other agencies are concerned only with the behaviour and performance of firms in *one* industry. Moreover, for the foreseeable future these industries will be dominated by a monolithic concern. The danger of 'capture' or at least impotence is thus much greater in their case than for the OFT. In one respect, however, all three organizations are likely to suffer the same disadvantage. To perform their function properly they require a great deal of information and data on the conduct and performance of the firms concerned. In the previous chapters we have mentioned a number of instances that suggest firstly that such information may be incomplete or haphazard, and secondly that the kinds of regulatory framework established do very little to improve this situation. Thus, for example, the DGFT has essentially to rely on individual complaints from consumers before investigating infringements of the Trade Descriptions Act, or from traders and other bodes (such as the MMC) on the existence of unregistered price fixing agreements. Unless a specific undertaking has been given at the time of a merger enquiry by the MMC, there is no formal mechanism for discovering whether claims for, say, cost savings, have subsequently been achieved. As a final example we can mention the widely expressed apprehension that the imbalance in resources between the privatized monopolies and their regulatory agencies will also mean an inadequate or even misleading information flow between them. Again the US experience in this respect is not encouraging. In short, a major function of regulation, the *monitoring* of firm's conduct and performance, is impaired by the problems of providing adequate information to the regulatory bodies. It is ironic that the unique economic characteristics of information (which has resulted in a number of the measures for consumer protection), which we discussed at length in chapter 4, should also be the source of many problems for the regulatory process itself.

However, it is on this issue that two recent developments in the US are particularly instructive and ideally could help to guide future policy in the UK. First, as we saw in chapter 10, part of the case made *against* regulation in the US was the increasing burden placed both on industry and other institutions[2] by the demands of regulatory policy. Monitoring conduct and performance may require detailed information but the provision of that information is costly and in some instances it may not be clear that the additional benefits derived from improved monitoring are greater than the additional costs imposed on industry, a point to which we return below. As we have just seen, to an extent, the information problem grows out of the regulatory process itself especially if that involves price and product quality control. It is made worse, as McKie (1970) explained, because of the almost inevitable tendency, once regulation has been introduced into an industry, for the scope of the regulation itself to grow. What may start as an apparently simple price regulation may develop into a dense network of price, profit, cost and product control, with greatly increased information demands. The information problem thus gets worse as regulation proceeds rather than better. Part of the explanation for de-regulating US industries has, therefore, been to reduce costs of this kind. Before the UK moves too far along a road that the US is attempting to leave it should perhaps learn more about their mistakes.

The second development is the theory of contestable markets and its careful application to regulatory questions, especially to natural monopolies but also to other markets where dominance appears to create problems. If regulation is flawed as a means of promoting the public interest in improvements in industrial behaviour and performance, alternative methods should be sought. The most useful service the theory may be able to provide is therefore as a general framework that policy makers can use to determine, firstly, whether any immediate action is required (i.e. is the market already contestable?) and if it is, secondly, what measures of de-regulation may increase contestability. Thirdly, in cases where contestability is not currently feasible, which regulatory measures are likely to be most efficient? In this connection 'efficiency' should take account not only of the cost distortions discussed in the previous chapter, together with compliance and monitoring costs, but also the need for flexibility. Non-contestable markets in the mid-1980s requiring some degree of regulation may, by the early 1990s, be potentially contestable because the rapid pace of technical change has obliterated previous market boundaries and produced many new alternative sources of supply. Telecommunications and electronics are the most obvious examples. We should now know enough about the ways that certain regulatory controls may create vested, sectional interests to avoid a recurrence of the problem. Unfortunately, as we argued in chapter 10, the restraints within which UK regulatory policy has been formulated are likely to make future de-regulation especially difficult. An important lesson that contestable theory can teach may therefore have been ignored. The lesson is simply that nearly all markets may be or become contestable and should therefore be reviewed on a more or less continuous basis to determine what regulatory changes are required.

In addition to flexibility, it is important that the kind of regulation used should be the most appropriate to the circumstances. Thus it was clear in chapter 5 that the *reason* for a number of regulatory measures in consumer markets was the inadequate or unequal distribution of unbiased information. In contrast, the *remedy* chosen to correct the failure did not always aim to increase information. In some cases the response was to maintain the quality of products by stipulating the ingredients they have to contain. In this way what may begin as an information problem ends with the regulation of product quality with all of the additional costs that this implies. Another example of the inappropriateness of a regulatory measure is the licensing system established for entry to the UK telecommunications industry. If the purpose of regulation is to improve industry performance then a highly restrictive licensing policy is not the way to achieve it. More generally, although restoring nationalized industries to the private sector may change the motivation of management (for reasons considered in chapter 9), the change of ownership alone is insufficient to improve their performance in ways that will benefit consumers.

Writing in 1981, Peltzman argued that despite the advances that had been made in estimating the magnitude of the effects of regulation in some industries, there were still very large gaps in our knowledge (Fromm, 1981). Thus although we can suggest that the licensing policy in the UK telecommunications industry is too restrictive we do not know the size of the potential welfare loss that may result from that restriction. Nor do we know whether there has been a net gain in consumer surplus as a result of regulating the quality of certain food products. Peltzman does not claim that such research would be easy but indicates that further major regulatory activity should not proceed until at least some quantitative estimate of its likely direct and indirect effects has been made. In view of the criticisms that have been levelled against the new regulatory agencies in the UK it is perhaps inappropriate to suggest the creation of yet another one. However, in the light of the past and likely future growth of regulation in areas discussed in previous chapters, as well as in others that were not, it may be salutary to establish an Office of Regulatory Review (OFER). Its tasks could be twofold: to undertake and sponsor research into the direct and indirect costs and benefits of proposed increases in regulation, and to monitor the suitability of existing forms of regulation. It would not solve the ancient problem of *quis custodiet ipsos custodes*, but at least it might help to minimize it.

Notes

CHAPTER 1 MARKET FAILURE AND THE CASE FOR REGULATION

1 The neo-Austrian school, which is inspired particularly by the work of von Mises. A leading exponent of these ideas is Kirzner (1974).
2 Schultze (1977).
3 Perhaps the definitive treatment appears in Arrow and Hahn (1971).
4 See for example, Demsetz (1968) and Williamson (1976).
5 For recent critical surveys see Schmalensee (1979) and Joskow and Noll, in Fromm (1981).
6 See chapter 9.
7 Cf. Breyer (1978–9). As we have already indicated other considerations seem, for the most part, to dominate the policies of the nationalized industries in the UK.
8 There may also be external benefits that work in the opposite direction, but it is generally recognized that in *production* external diseconomies are probably of greater significance.
9 It may also, of course, ensure my annihilation.
10 At times of peak demand my use may impose additional costs on other users which should be accounted for in order to correct the externality.

CHAPTER 2 DEVELOPMENTS IN THE ECONOMIC THEORY OF REGULATION

1 The analysis also provides the basis for the private interest theory of regulation to which we refer below.
2 The original formulation can be found in Lipsey and Lancaster (1956–7). A proof of the central result can also be found in Scherer (1980)
3 When still part of the Chrysler Corporation, Chrysler UK had received assistance from the government. It was subsequently sold to Talbot–Citröen.
4 Whether they have actually succeeded is still an open question which we discuss in chapters 7 and 8. Some commentators on US antitrust policy have argued that at times it has been interpreted to mean the survival of small businesses rather than the improvement of efficiency through the maintenance of competition.

5 The harshest was probably Allen (1968): 'the guidance [of what constituted the public interest] given in the Act consisted of a string of platitudes which the Commission found valueless' (p. 66).

6 It was possible to argue, for example, that a cartel should be maintained because its abandonment would cause either local unemployment or a reduction in export earnings (see the appendix to chapter 7).

7 The conventional analysis of entry barriers suggests, for example, that scale economies, product differentiation or absolute cost differences may make entry difficult in concentrated industries.

8 Although it has been observed both in the US and the UK recently that a number of influential officials do subsequently take up lucrative appointments in the industries they have previously regulated.

9 Prior to the proposed de-nationalization British Airways had 85 per cent of the authorized routes (Civil Aviation Authority, 1984a).

10 The problems surrounding a de-nationalization programme are dealt with more fully in chapter 10.

11 For a review and critique see Needham (1983) and Scherer (1980).

12 No competition in the sense, for example, that the tasks performed by, say, the Ministry of Agriculture. Fisheries and Food cannot be competed away by, say, the Department of Industry. Given the temper of the times, however, there is no reason in principle for which one ministry should not tender for the functions of another and so diversify its activities.

13 See, for example, *The Guardian*, 3 February 1984, and *The Observer*, 1 April 1984.

CHAPTER 4   INFORMATION AND CONSUMER PROTECTION

1 For example in the late 1970s both the *Quarterly Journal of Economics* (1978) and the *Review of Economic Studies* (1979) published collections of articles on the economics of information.

2 In a remarkable (but unduly neglected) series of articles published in the 1940s, Hayek attempted to demonstrate how a market economy can make the best use of the myriad pieces of information and knowledge possessed by all its inhabitants. He emphasized that a major function of markets was to find out, act upon and respond to changes in information (Hayek, 1948).

3 The papers we have in mind are by the Nobel Laureate, K.J. Arrow, and H. Demsetz, which are reproduced as chapters 7 and 8 in Lamberton (1971).

4 In practice costs of disclosure would eventually put a halt to this process, so disclosure would never be complete. However, in the theoretical limiting case where there are no disclosure costs, it would be complete (cf. Grossman, 1981).

5 A series of advertisements by one car manufacturer (Volkswagen) showing the product of a major rival (Ford) that it wished to ridicule apparently misfired completely. Ford was delighted that a competitor had paid to show its (Ford's) product in the national press.

6 An interesting and unusual insight into the potentialities of modern selling methods was given at the 1984 Conference of the Social Democratic Party. A hitherto unknown speaker was rapturously received by the delegates and given

widespread coverage and lavish praise in the press the following day. What delegates and all but one newspaper did *not* know was that the speaker had been trained by the voice coach of the Royal Shakespeare Company, her speech had been written by a former speech-writer to Harold Wilson and an Oxford don had shown her video recordings of politicians, to teach her the tricks (and gestures) of the trade.

7 For a classic reference on moral hazard see Arrow (1971).

8 Until comparatively recently the opposite view was taken by the medical profession.

9 The 1983 Conservative Government has made it much easier for non-qualified opticians to supply spectacles. See chapter 5.

10 The difficulty with this solution is to maintain, for a long period, the absolute independence of the government research association.

11 See chapter 5.

12 The case is discussed in Borrie and Diamond (1981).

13 We exclude products such as drugs that consumers cannot usually purchase but that may be prescribed and for which much higher probabilities may be required. See chapter 5.

14 The effect was aptly caught in a cartoon in the Wall Street Journal showing an advertiser in a radio commercial who was saying: 'Remember we make no claims for Quill's pills, so if they do anything for you think what a pleasant surprise it will be'. This is quoted in Greer (1983).

CHAPTER 5   REGULATING CONSUMER MARKETS

1 In fact the Committee on Safety of Medicines, formed by the Commission.

2 Quite apart from the social and ethical arguments that can also be brought to bear on such an issue.

3 The task may require dedication and talent of a rare order. An inspector employed by the US Food and Drug Administration was featured in the Wall Street Journal. Apparently Mr Weber was employed full time to smell consignments of fish. He had been doing this demanding task for 32 years and on average smelled 4000 fish or shrimps in a day. The fish were classified into Class I (good commercial), Class II (slightly decomposed) or Class III (advanced decomposition). Some samples were apparently even beyond Class III which 'you have to smell at arm's length' (Greer, 1983).

4 The drug, developed in Germany, had been cleared for general use in a number of European countries including the UK. Women taking the drug during pregnancy gave birth to terribly malformed babies.

5 For example between 1950 and 1962 an average of 54 new chemical entities were approved in the US by the FDA each year; but from 1963 to 1975 an average of 16 new entities were cleared (Greer, 1983).

6 A rather analogous case concerns the obligatory introduction of safety features in cars, and in particular the requirement to wear seatbelts. Supporters claim that such safety features save many passenger and driver lives. Opponents argue that making drivers feel more safe causes them to drive more recklessly with the result that more pedestrians and cyclists are injured (see Peltzman, 1975).

7 Under the 1961 Act, Local Authorities were expected to comply but were under no obligation.

8 But the American CPSC has, for example, defended its standards for power mowers on the ground that they resulted in annual benefits valued at $211 millions (from reduced injuries) compared with costs of $190 millions.

9 In Scotland it apparently has the additional aim of ensuring the moral probity of solicitors.

10 Chapter 2.

11 The report makes clear that a reference to the Monopolies and Mergers Commission (MMC) would have been made in this case were it not for a legal technicality. Rules laid down by the Optical Council can only be changed by the Privy Council. Had the MMC recommended changes to the rules, the Minister would have had insufficient power under the Fair Trading Act (1973) to change them (OFT, 1982). (Note for convenience in the text we always refer to the Commission as the MMC, even though its title has changed over the years).

12 Simultaneously restrictions on advertising spectacles were lifted but, with a nice irony, only for non-qualified opticians. The body that had protected opticians from new competition for so long, the General Optical Council, had its proposals for lifting the restrictions turned down by the Privy Council, so for a time qualified opticians were not able to advertise their services.

13 For a more detailed treatment of the major provisions the reader is referred to Smith and Swann (1979, chapter 5).

14 The position of the Director General in the field of consumer protection is discussed more fully in section IV of this chapter.

15 Provisions concerning advertising are discussed in section III

16 In particular the 1965 Hire Purchase Act and the 1967 Advertisements (Hire Purchase) Acts.

17 Under the 1967 Advertisements (Hire Purchase) Act, advertisements referring to a rate of interest had to base it on a prescribed formula.

18 An example cited by Greer was the editor of a trade paper, *Food Field Reporter*: 'We suggest that the housewife . . . should be expected to take the time to divide fractionalised weight into fractionalised prices in order to determine the "best buy"' (Greer, 1983, p. 251.)

19 The same procedure governs advertising on commercial radio.

20 The rules are given in OFT (1982, Appendix 4). It is clear that they do not allow opticians to advertise in order to win more customers.

21 Similar evidence from the US Federal Trade Commission (1980) was cited in the Report.

22 Not least in a comprehensive enquiry commissioned originally by the OFT and eventually published (Cowling *et al.* 1975)

23 The Food and Drugs Act and the Medicines Act discussed in section II both make it an offence to give false or misleading information for the products covered.

24 For example: about the provision and nature of any services, accommodation or facilities; the time and manner in which any services, accommodation or facilities are provided; the examination, approval or evaluation by any person of any services, accommodation or facilities provided; the location or amenities of any accommodation provided.

25 Borrie and Diamond (1981, chapter 5).
26 *British Airways Board* v *Taylor* (1975), 1 All E.R. 65.
27 See p. 72.
28 It is significant, for example, that when the Conservative Government abolished the Prices Commission in 1980 it retained the position of Minister for Consumer Affairs.
29 References can also be made by the Minister.
30 Any Order has to be approved by both Houses of Parliament.
31 A branch of the High Court whose activities are discussed more fully in chapter 8.
32 For reasons that we discuss more fully in chapter 7 the Director cannot refer mergers to the MMC. This power rests with the Minister.

CHAPTER 6   THE ECONOMICS OF COMPETITION POLICY

1 Marginal cost can either be viewed as the aggregation of costs for all firms in the industry or those of the sole firm in the case of a monopoly.
2 We are thus suppressing, perhaps unjustifiably, second-best arguments (cf. chapter 2).
3 For a full discussion of the model see Stigler (1957).
4 The results for a 'contestable monopoly' are not as general. See Baumol *et al.* (1982).
5 The authors also show that in the special case of a perfectly contestable market with natural monopoly but where prices are unsustainable, entry could actually worsen economic performance (Baumol *et al.* 1982, p. 222–3).
6 If entry is free in the Baumol–Stigler sense the 'limit' price coincides with the 'contestable' price.
7 As Dr Bailey has been a member of the Civil Aeronautics Board in the US she has had the opportunity of putting her ideas into practice, as her 1981 article demonstrates.

CHAPTER 7   REGULATING DOMINANT FIRMS IN THE PRIVATE SECTOR

1 There is a very thorough discussion in Bork (1978).
2 We take up the case of price discrimination in section III of this chapter.
3 We assume here that there is no divergence between social and private costs.
4 The partial analysis does not take account of general effects emphasized in the theory of second best. We are also assuming that input prices are competitively determined.
5 Monopolists need not necessarily, of course, earn an excess profit. A decline in demand may mean that losses are made. However, the profit-maximizing output price will exceed marginal cost, causing some resource misallocation.
6 For a review of these results see Scherer (1980).
7 To the extent that this is true in practice dominant firms may therefore record only modest profits.
8 In the areas GFA and $P_M P_N FG$ respectively. For a recent analysis of the distinction between rent-seeking and x-inefficiency see Schap (1985).

9 Circumstances tend to vary from industry to industry, e.g. the new and replacement markets for car components; the hospital and general practice markets for tranquillizers.

10 Rather than cite all contributors separately we refer the interested reader to the authoritative work edited by Salop (1981) where full details of the discussion are given.

11 An irrational firm is doomed to oblivion in any case.

12 Similar difficulties would probably attend the adoption of Baumol's proposal of non-rescindable price cuts by a dominant firm following entry. Against a background of shifting demand, costs and inflation, the policy is likely to bring far greater disadvantages than benefits.

13 It was given one reference on the specific issue of whether uneconomic prices had been charged but concluded, after a rather sketchy enquiry, that they had not. See MMC (1966).

14 A fuller discussion of these cases can be found in Utton (1985). The full titles of the MMC reports are given in the list of references.

15 At the time of the reports, for example, British Match had a market share of 92 per cent, British Oxygen 90 per cent and Hoffmann–la Roche 99 per cent.

16 The market affected was for benzoyl peroxide for flour milling, although it was the victim's attempt to enter the plastics section of the market in Germany that triggered AKZO's response.

17 Notably Redland (MMC, 1981d) and de Mulder (MMC, 1985).

18 Unless a special exemption was granted by the Restrictive Practices Court.

19 They recommended the withdrawal of section 2(4) (MMC, 1970a), paragraph 53).

20 In 1980–1 the parent company introduced some fundamental production and managerial changes.

21 It is also obviously similar to loyalty rebates which we mentioned above.

22 An exception may be for very high-quality, high-margin and 'exclusive' (in its snobbish sense) products where distributors may find it worthwhile to restrict themselves to a limited market.

23 This case is obviously very closely related to loyalty rebates and requirement contracts referred to above.

24 For different approaches compare Bork (1978) with Scherer (1980).

25 In this case the tying arrangement was accompanied by exclusive dealing which we mentioned in the previous section.

26 Although, as we have already mentioned, this conclusion must be modified if the position of the market for B, covered by the tie, is small.

27 The losses are most likely to come not in production so much as in innovation and distribution where the fragmentation of research teams and distribution networks may cause considerable dislocation.

28 Once a precedent for break-up has been established, vulnerable firms will presumably spend considerable resources in lobbying and advertising in order to avoid a similar fate. These resources too should be counted as a dead-weight loss of the policy. This point is taken up again in chapter 10.

29 Initially it was regulated by the Interstate Commerce Commission but since 1934 by the Federal Communications Commission (FCC).

30 A consent decree is an agreement negotiated out of court between the parties and it is binding once it has been approved by a federal court.

31 For those who have followed the controversy surrounding the privatization of British Telecom and the conditions under which new entrants are to operate, much of this has a familiar ring. The British case is discussed more fully in chapter 10.

32 Under the reconstruction a shareholder with 10 AT and T shares received 10 shares of the 'new' AT and T and 7 shares in addition, one for each regional company. Shareholders with less than 10 shares received cash instead of shares in the new regional companies. The scale of the operation can be judged from the fact that there were about 3.2 million shareholders with 950 million shares in the 'old' AT and T.

33 At the time of the AT and T agreement a long-running antitrust action against IBM was dropped.

34 A summary of the legal position is given in the Appendix to this chapter.

35 See, for example, Hart and Clarke (1980).

36 It has frequently asked for estimates of expected cost savings from mergers, and on the whole these have been modest (Sutherland, 1969).

37 There is no presumption that a merger referred to the MMC is likely to operate against the public interest.

38 Even allowing for data and measurement problems, the evidence suggesting deterioration in performance post-merger still outweighs that going the other way. See, for example, Meeks (1977) and Mueller (1980).

39 Given the nature of the acquisition process figures in the 'total' column must be regarded as estimates.

40 Of course as a percentage of *all* mergers which took place the figure is minute: a fraction of 1 per cent.

41 For a further discussion see Utton (1979).

42 Compare Jensen and Ruback (1983) with Mueller (1977).

43 Case 6/72 *Europemballage and Continental Can* v. *Commission* (1973) European Community Review 215. The Commission's view on article 86 had first been expressed in a memorandum in 1966.

CHAPTER 8 COLLUSION AND REGULATION

1 We will use the terms collusion and cartel interchangeably to mean any horizontal agreement between firms to determine jointly terms and conditions of trading.

2 With modern methods of communication and information transfer, contacts indiscernible to the outsider may, of course, have taken place.

3 For a comprehensive discussion of OPEC see Danielson (1982).

4 As the appendix to chapter 7 shows, it is possible to defend a cartel on a number of grounds before the Restrictive Practices Court, but in practice very few defences have been successful.

5 Excluding the USSR and the Eastern Bloc.

6 The Monopolies and Mergers Commission gave this as a reason for recommending against the merger between Beecham or Boots and Glaxo (MMC, 1972).

7 See the example Richardson (1960).

8 This is what occurred in the important Yarnspinners case where the Court was

convinced that the removal of the restriction was likely to cause serious local unemployment (one of the grounds specified in the 1956 Act) but then decided on balance that the restriction should not continue. See Swann *et al.* (1974).

9   The effective implementation of the latter Act was made easier by several cases brought under the 1956 Act clarifying what constituted an agreement 'to like effect'. Firms that abandoned a registrable agreement but then formed another, ostensibly covering different matters but in fact having the same result, were likely to continue to infringe the Act. In the series of important cases in the early and middle sixties the Court set out clearly which type of arrangements fell into this category. For a fuller discussion of these cases see Swann *et al.* (1974, chapter 2).

10 It was under this section of the 1968 Act that the Minister gave exemption to perhaps the most well-known service agreement of all, involving the so-called 'rule book' of the Stock Exchange. Successive Labour and Conservative ministers had refused exemption and much work had been done preparing the case for Court. Within six months of becoming Minister for Trade and Industry, however, Mr Parkinson granted an exemption, saying that he had received adequate assurances from the Stock Exchange Council that the public interest would be protected. The fundamental changes in the rules that followed this arrangement came into effect in the Autumn of 1986.

11 The opposition aroused over the exemption of the Stock Exchange restrictions may have been sufficient to ensure that in future the discretion will not be used.

12 *Annual Report of the Director General of Fair Trading.*

13 A third issue, parallel pricing or conscious parallelism, is discussed in the next section.

14 It was at this point that the Review recommended that the practice of tie-in sales and full-line forcing should be referred to the MMC with the clear implication that it was likely to find against the practice and lead to its being banned. In the event, as we have seen (chapter 7 above) the MMC considered that in most instances tie-ins were not likely to operate against the public interest.

15 We have already referred to the other review, *The Review of Monopolies and Mergers Policy* (1978), in chapter 7.

16 Although at the time of the Great Depression in the 1930s the Supreme Court did show a more tolerant approach to an attempt by Appalachian coal-mining firms to alleviate their hardships by establishing a joint selling agency; but the decision in favour of the restriction has not been treated as a precedent; see Scherer (1980).

17 Since 1974 when the maximum fines were raised, violations of the Act have also been treated as felonies carrying a maximum prison sentence of three years compared with one year previously.

18 Under section 4 of the Clayton Act which amended the Sherman Act.

19 An influential exception may be the National Economic Development Office which has argued strongly in favour of suspending the Restrictive Practices legislation in cases where this would assist in the 'rationalization' of the industry. See, for example, NEDO (1978).

20 In the sample, 18 were studied in depth (four where the agreement had been

allowed by the Court, six where it had been struck down and eight where it had been abandoned) and 22 in less detail. The period studied ended in 1971.

21 When it became plain that information agreements were to be made registrable (in the 1968 Act) many firms abandoned them rather than register.

22 For a full discussion of the dominant firm case see Scherer (1980) and Markham (1958).

23 As we have noted above, an *agreement* to fix prices would have been *per se* illegal under the Sherman Act.

24 A conclusion that, as we have seen, is not universally accepted.

CHAPTER 9   REGULATING NATURAL MONOPOLY AND DOMINANT ENTERPRISES
IN THE PUBLIC SECTOR

1 Where the efficiency is judged according to the Pareto principle which assumes, of course, that the resulting income distribution is acceptable.

2 Such a case could be represented in the diagram, for example, where demand increased from D_1 but by an amount insufficient to justify an expansion of capacity. The area equivalent to FJH would in this case be smaller than the area equivalent to JGK. Capacity would not be extended beyond Q_2 and the price would be determined by the intersection of FH and the new demand curve.

3 For a detailed discussion see Millward (1971).

4 The major political objection is that they are highly regressive.

5 We appreciate that one school of thought entirely rejects the notion of objective costs and therefore rejects the whole of the analysis on which marginal cost pricing is based. For a critique along these lines see Littlechild (1978, chapter VII) and references cited therein.

6 The Gas Act 1948, s.41.

7 For a detailed discussion see Nelson (1964, chapter 6).

8 Subsequently raised to ten per cent.

9 See for example Nield (1961).

10 More recently ministers have argued that a major reason for privatizing these industries is to prevent their successors from intervening directly in their affairs. The point is taken up again in chapter 10.

11 The point has been highlighted in a consultant's report to the National Economic Development Office and incorporated in their 1976 report on the nationalized industries (NEDO 1967).

12 In some cases, of course, the competition may be intense. The prime examples are the competition from road transport faced by the railways and from oil faced by the electricity and gas industries.

13 See in particular Alchian and Demsetz (1972) and Demsetz (1968).

14 In the general election campaign of 1983 the issue of privatization played a very small part in comparison with unemployment or inflation even though the Conservatives had set out clearly their plans for privatization.

15 In the light of more recent work on this issue, however, the relative importance of technical and allocative efficiency may need to be modified. See, for example, Cowling and Mueller (1978) and Scherer (1980).

16 British European Airways and British Overseas Airways Corporation.

17 He also refers to the generally superior methods of investment appraisal attempted in the public sector compared with the private sector.

18 His second book was published in 1981 but had been completed in 1980.

19 The following comments draw on my contribution to Gretton (1983).

20 Although it has been possible since 1973 to refer restrictive labour practices to the MMC none has been referred.

21 The literature on the nationalized industries abounds with examples of decisions being taken on purely political grounds but being justified on social grounds (e.g. proposed rail closures through marginal constituencies miraculously and expensively saved.)

22 Full details of the studies referred to in the text are given in Millward.

CHAPTER 10 PRIVATIZATION AND DE-REGULATION

1 Thus according to John Moore, Financial Secretary to the Treasury 'even where competition is impractical privatization policies have been developed to such an extent that regulated private ownership of monopolies is preferable to nationalization' (17 July 1985).

2 In particular whether replacement cost or historic cost should be used in the calculations.

3 Long-run marginal cost exceeding short-run marginal cost implies that the ratio of the cost of capital, r, to the marginal product of capital MP_k (long-run marginal cost) is greater than the ratio of the cost of labour, w, to the marginal product of labour, MP_L (short-run marginal cost) i.e. $\dfrac{r}{MP_k} > \dfrac{w}{MP_L}$ or $\dfrac{MP_L}{MP_k} > \dfrac{w}{r}$ which with a normal production function implies that production is too capital intensive.

4 As we noted in the previous chapter, since the 1978 White Paper the nationalized industries have been working to externally imposed rate-of-return targets.

5 The categories included consumer safety and health, job safety and other working conditions, environment and energy, financial reporting and other financial and industry-specific regulation. The first category accounted for well over half of the total in each year.

6 For example Elisabeth Bailey was appointed a member of the Civil Aeronautics Board and Darius Gaskins was appointed chairman of the Inter-state Commerce Commission.

7 Baumol clearly believes the theory is an important contribution but suggests that it amounts to an 'uprising' rather than a 'revolution' (Baumol, 1982).

8 Those most closely associated with the development of the theory have emphasized this point (cf. the quotation from Bailey in chapter 6).

9 The CAA (1984b) gives a list of 44 of the larger US airlines between 1978 and 1983, fourteen of which were not in existence in 1978.

10 The issue is made even more complicated by the attitude of the Labour Party which is opposed to any significant interference at all with the nationalized sector.

11 Indeed not only the Opposition. In a widely reported speech in the House of Lords late in 1985, the former Conservative Prime Minister, Harold

MacMillan, spoke of the policy as equivalent to 'selling off the family silver'.
12　At the time of the privatization of British Telecom in 1984, a correspondent to *The Guardian* newspaper made a similar point: 'To sell British Telecom is a bold step; but to sell it for cash to people who already own it is most imaginative' *The Guardian*, 3 November 1984.
13　For a full list see Brittan (1984, p. 111).
14　Mercury was originally formed as a consortium of Cable and Wireless, BP and Barclays Bank, but subsequently became a subsidiary of Cable and Wireless.
15　The respective importance of the two licensed firms can be gauged from their respective investment plans. Mercury envisages a total investment in its network of £200 millions while BT expects to spend £1800 millions *annually* on capital equipment. Its total assets exceed £10,000 millions (Vickers and Yarrow, 1985).
16　*The Economist*, 20 March 1982.
17　For a detailed assessment of the question see Ashworth and Forsyth (1984).

CHAPTER 11　CONCLUSION

1　The DGFT can refer a dominant firm to the MMC and also report on anti-competitive practices (see appendix 7.1)
2　Harvard University is reported as having spent 60,000 labour hours in the academic year 1974/5 in its attempt to satisfy regulations of the Federal Government (Koch, 1980).

References

Akerloff, G.A. (1970) The market for 'Lemons': quality uncertainty and the market mechanism, *Quarterly Journal of Economics*

Alchian, A.A. and Demsetz, H. (1972) Production, information costs and economic organisation, *American Economic Review*

Allen, G.C. (1968) *Monopoly and Restrictive Practices*, Allen and Unwin

Areeda, P. and Turner, D.F. (1975) Predatory pricing and related practices under section 2 of the Sherman Act, *Harvard Law Review*

Arrow, K.J. (1971) *Essays in the theory of risk bearing*, Markham Press

Arrow, K.J. and Hahn, F.H. (1971) *General Competitive Analysis*, Holden-Day

Ashworth, M. and Forsyth, P. (1984) *Civil Aviation Policy and the Privatisation of British Airways*, Institute of Fiscal Studies

Averch, H. and Johnson, L. (1962) Behaviour of the firm under regulatory constraint, *American Economic Review*

Bailey, E.E. (1981) Contestability and the design of regulatory and antitrust policy, *American Economic Review*

Bain, J.S. (1968) *Industrial Organisation*, Wiley

Baumol, W.J. (1979) Quasi-permanence of price reductions: a policy for prevention of predatory pricing, *Yale Law Journal*

Baumol, W.J. (1982) Contestable markets: an uprising in the theory of industry structure, *American Economic Review*

Baumol, W.J. and Bradford, D.F. (1970) Optimal departures from marginal cost pricing, *American Economic Review*

Baumol, W.J., Panzar J.C. and Willig, R.D. (1982) *Contestable Markets and the Theory of Industry Structure*, Harcourt, Brace, Jovanovich

Baumol, W.J. and Ordover, J.A. (1985) Use of antitrust to subvert competition, *Journal of Law and Economics*

Beales, H., Craswell, R. and Salop, S.C. (1981) The efficient regulation of consumer information, *Journal of Law and Economics*

Benham, L. (1972) The effect of advertising on the price of eyeglasses, *Journal of Law and Economics*

Besen, S.M. and Woodbury, J.R. (1983) Regulation, deregulation and antitrust in the telecommunications industry, *Antitrust Bulletin*

Blair, R. and Kaserman, D.L. (1983) *Law and Economics of Vertical Integration*, Academic Press

Bork, R.H. (1978) *The Antitrust Paradox*, Basic Books

Borrie, G. and Diamond, A.L. (1981) *The Consumer, Society and the Law*, Penguin

Breyer, S. (1978–9) Analysing regulatory failure: mismatches, less restrictive alternatives and reform, *Harvard Law Review*

British Business 13 July 1984

Brittan, S. (1984) The politics and economics of privatisation, *Political Quarterly*

Buchanan, J.S. (1980) Rent seeking and profit seeking *in* Buchanan, J.S., Tollison, R.D. and Tullock, G. (eds) *Toward a Theory of the Rent-seeking Society*, Texas A and M Unviersity Press

Caves, R.E. and Porter, M.E. (1977) From entry barriers to mobility barriers, *Quarterly Journal of Economics*

Census of Production, 1968 (1971) *Summary Volume*, Part 158, HMSO

Chamberlin, E.H. (1958) Product heterogeneity and public policy, in Heflebower, R. and Stocking, G. (eds) *Readings in industrial organisation and public policy*, Irwin

Civil Aviation Authority (1984a) *Airline Competition Policy*, Civil Aviation Authority

Civil Aviation Authority (1984b) *Deregulation of Air Transport*, Civil Aviation Authority

Clapham, J.H. (1938) *An Economic History of Modern Britain*, Cambridge University Press

Clark, J.M. (1940) Towards a concept of workable competition, *American Economic Review*

Clark, J.M. (1955) Competition: static models and dynamic aspects, *American Economic Review*

Coase, R.H. (1970) The theory of public utility pricing and its application, *Bell Journal of Economics and Management Science*

Cowling, K. Cable, J. Kelly, M. McGuinness, T. (1975) *Advertising and Economic Behaviour*, Macmillan

Cowling, K. and Mueller, D.C. (1978) The social costs of monopoly power, *Economic Journal*

Danielson, A.L. (1982) *The Evolution of OPEC*, Harcourt, Brace, Jovanovich

DeFina, R. and Weidenbaum, M. (1978) *The Taxpayer and Government Regulation*, Center for the Study of American Business, Washington University

Demsetz, H. (1968) Why regulate utilities? *Journal of Law and Economics*

Demsetz, H. (1974) Two systems of belief about monopoly, *in* Goldschmid, H.J., Mann, H.M. and Weston, J.F. (eds) *Industrial Concentration: The New Learning*, Little, Brown and Co.

Director General of Fair Trading (1981) *T.I. Raleigh Industries Ltd*, HMSO

Dixit, A. and Norman, V. (1978) Advertising and welfare, *Bell Journal of Economics*

Eads, G.C. (1983) Airline competitive conduct in a less regulated environment: implications for antitrust, *Antitrust Bulletin*

Easterbrook, F.H. (1981) Predatory strategies and counterstrategies, *University of Chicago Law Review*

Elliott, D.C. and Gribbin, J.D. (1977) The abolition of cartels and structural change in the United Kingdom, *in* Jacquemin, A. and deJong, H. (ed) *Welfare Aspects of Industrial Markets*, Martinus Nijhoff

Engineering and Chemical Supplies (Epsom and Gloucester) Ltd v. *AKZO Chemie UK Ltd*, 3 *Common Market Law Reports*, 694, 1983

Federal Trade Commission (1980) *Effects of Restrictions on Advertising and*

Commercial Practice in the Professions: The Case of Optomerics, Federal Trade Commission

Financial and Economic Objectives of the Nationalised Industries. (1961), HMSO

Fisher, F.M. (1979) Diagnosing monopoly, *Quarterly Review of Economics and Business*

Forsyth, P. (1983) Airline deregulation in the United States: the lessons for Europe, *Fiscal Studies*

Fromm, G. (ed.) (1981) *Studies in Public Regulation*, MIT Press

Greer, D.F. (1983) *Business, Government and Society*, Macmillan

Gretton, J. (ed.) (1983) *Monitoring Performance in the Public Sector*, Proceedings of the Third Deloitte, Haskins and Sells Accounting and Auditing Research Symposium

Grossman, S. (1981) The informational role of warranties and private disclosure about product quality, *Journal of Law and Economics*

Hammond, E.M., Helm D.R. and Thompson, D.J. (1985) British Gas: options for privatisation, *Fiscal Studies*

Hart, P.E. and Clarke, R. (1980) *Concentration in British Industry, 1935–75*, Cambridge University Press

Hartley, K. and Tisdell, C. (1981) *Microeconomic Policy*, Wiley

Hayek, F.A. (1948) *Individualism and Economic Order*, University of Chicago Press

Hotelling, H. (1938) The general welfare in relation to problems of taxation and of railway and utility rates, *Econometrica*

Hurwitz, J.D., Kovacic, W.E., Sheehan, T.A. and Lande, R.H. (1981) Current legal standards of predation, *in* Salop, S.C. (ed.) *Strategy, Predation and Antitrust Analysis*, Federal Trade Commission

Jensen, M.C. and Ruback, R.S. (1983) The market for corporate control, *Journal of Financial Economics*

Joskow, P.L. and Klevorick, A.K. (1979) A framework for analysing predatory pricing policy, *Yale Law Journal*

Kahn, A.E. (1968) The graduated fair return: comment, *American Economic Review*

Kay, J.A. and Sharpe, T.A.E. (1982) The anti-competitive practice, *Fiscal Studies*

Kirzner, I. (1974) *Competition and Entrepreneurship*, University of Chicago Press

Koch, J.V. (1980) *Industrial Organisation and Prices*, Prentice-Hall

Koller, R.H. (1971) The myth of predatory pricing, *Antitrust Law and Economics Review*

Lamberton, D.M. (1971) *Economics of Information and Knowledge*, Penguin Books

Leibenstein, H. (1978) X-inefficiency Xists – reply to an Xorcist, *American Economic Review*

Lerner, A. (1934) The concept of monopoly and the measurement of monopoly power, *Review of Economic Studies*

Lipsey, R.G. and Lancaster, K. (1956–7) The general theory of second best, *Review of Economic Studies*

Littlechild, S.C. (1978) *The Fallacy of the Mixed Economy*, Institute of Economic Affairs

Littlechild, S.C. (1981) Misleading calculations of the welfare losses from monopoly, *Economic Journal*

Machlup, F. (1955) Characteristics and types of price discrimination *in Business Concentration and Price Policy*, Princeton University Press

Markham, J.W. (1958) The nature and significance of price leadership, *in*

Heflebower, R.B. and Stocking, G.W. (eds) *Readings in Industrial Organisation and Public Policy*, Irwin

McGee, J.S. (1980) Predatory pricing revisited, *Journal of Law and Economics*

McKie, J.W. (1970) Regulation and the free market, *Bell Journal of Economics and Management Science*

Meeks, G. (1977) *Disappointing Marriage: A Study of the Gains from Merger*, Cambridge University Press

Merkin, R. and Williams, K. (1984) *Competition Law: Antitrust Policy in the UK and the EEC*, Sweet and Maxwell

Milgrom, P. and Roberts, J. (1982) Predation, reputation and entry deterrence, *Journal of Economic Theory*

Millward, R. (1971) *Public Expenditure Economics*, McGraw-Hill

Millward, R. (1982) The comparative performance of public and private enterprise, *in* Roll, E. (ed.) *The Mixed Economy*, Macmillan

Millward, R. and Parker, D.M. (1983) Public and private enterprise: comparative behaviour and relative efficiency, *in* Millward, R., Parker, D.M., Rosenthal, L., Sumner, M.T. and Topham, N. *Public Sector Economics*, Longman

Monopolies and Restrictive Practices Commission (1953) *Report on the supply and export of matches and the supply of match-making machinery*, HMSO

Monopolies and Restrictive Practices Commission (1955) *Collective Discrimination*, HMSO

Monopolies and Restrictive Practices Commission (1956) *Report on the Supply of Certain Industrial and Medical Gases*, HMSO

Monopolies Commission (1963) *Report on the Supply of Electrical Equipment for Mechanically Propelled Land Vehicles*, HMSO

Monopolies Commission (1964) *Wallpaper*, HMSO

Monopolies Commission (1966) *Electrical Wiring Harnesses for Motor Vehicles*, HMSO

Monopolies Commission (1968) *Clutch Mechanisms for Road Vehicles* HMSO

Monopolies Commission (1970a) *Refusal to Supply*, HMSO

Monopolies Commission (1970b) *Professional Services*, HMSO

Monopolies Commission (1972) *Beecham Group Ltd and Glaxo Group Ltd, The Boots Company Ltd and Glaxo Group Ltd: A Report on the Proposed Mergers*, HMSO

Monopolies Commission (1973a) *Parallel Pricing*, HMSO

Monopolies Commission (1973b) *Chloriazepoxide and Diazepam*, HMSO

Monopolies and Mergers Commission (1976) *Indirect Electrostatic Reprographic Equipment*, HMSO

Monopolies and Mergers Commission (1978) *Report on the Supply of Electric Cables*, HMSO

Monopolies and Mergers Commission (1980a) *The Inner London Letter Post*, HMSO

Monopolies and Mergers Commission (1980b) *British Railways Board London and South East Commuter Services*, HMSO

Monopolies and Mergers Commission (1980c) *Domestic Gas Appliances*, HMSO

Monopolies and Mergers Commission (1981a) *Central Electricity Generating Board*, HMSO

Monopolies and Mergers Commission (1981b) *Full-line Forcing and Tie-in Sales*, HMSO

Monopolies and Mergers Commission (1981c) *Bicycles*, HMSO

Monopolies and Mergers Commission (1981d) *Concrete Roofing Tiles*, HMSO
Monopolies and Mergers Commission (1982) *Car Parts*, HMSO
Monopolies and Mergers Commission (1983a) *Civil Aviation Authority*, HMSO
Monopolies and Mergers Commission (1983b) *National Coal Board* (2 volumes), HMSO
Monopolies and Mergers Commission (1985) *Animal Waste*, HMSO
Mueller, D.C. (1977) The effects of conglomerate mergers: a survey of the empirical evidence, *Journal of Banking Finance*
Mueller, D.C. (1980) *The Determinants and Effects of Mergers: An International Comparison*, Oelgeschlager, Gunn and Hain
National Economic Development Office (1976) *A Study of UK Nationalised Industries* (2 vol), HMSO
National Economic Development Office (1978) *Competition policy*, HMSO
Nationalised Industries: A Review of Economic and Financial Objectives (1967), HMSO
Needham, D. (1983) *The Economics and Politics of Regulation*, Little, Brown and Co.
Nelson, J.R. (ed.) (1964) *Marginal Cost Pricing in Practice*, Prentice-Hall
Nelson, P. (1970) Information and consumer behavior, *Journal of Political Economy*
Nield, R.R. (1961) Replacement policy, *National Institute Economic Review*
O'Brien, D.P., Howe, W.S., Wright, D.M. and O'Brien, R.J. (1979) *Competition Policy, Profitability and Growth*, Macmillan
O'Brien, D.P. and Swann, D. (1968) *Information Agreements, Competition and Efficiency*, Macmillan
Organisation for Economic Co-operation and Development (OECD) (1983) *Consumer Policy During the Past Ten Years*, OECD, Paris
Office of Fair Trading (1982) *Opticians and Competition*, HMSO
Olson, M. (1982) *The Rise and Decline of Nations*, Yale University Press
Peltzman, S. (1975) The effects of automobile safety regulation, *Journal of Political Economy*
Peltzman, S. (1976) Toward a more general theory of regulation, *Journal of Law and Economics*
Polanyi, G. and Polanyi, P. (1974) Parallel pricing: a harmful practice? *Moorgate and Wall Street*
Posner, R.A. (1974) Theories of economic regulation, *Bell Journal of Economics*
Posner, R.A. (1975) The social costs of monopoly and regulation, *Journal of Political Economy*
Posner, R.A. (1976) *Antitrust Law*, University of Chicago Press
Prais, S.J. (1976) *The Evolution of Giant Enterprises in Britain*, Cambridge University Press
Price Commission (1976) *Prices of Private Spectacles and Contact Lenses*, HMSO
Price Commission (1979) *Dolland and Aitchison Group — Charges and Margins for Optical Products*, HMSO
Pryke, R. (1971) *Public Enterprise in Practice*, MacGibbon and Kee
Pryke, R. (1981) *The Nationalised Industries*, Martin Robertson
Pryke, R. (1982) The comparative performance of public and private enterprise, *Fiscal Studies*
Review of Monopolies and Mergers Policy (1978), HMSO
Review of Restrictive Trade Practices Policy (1979), HMSO
Richardson, G.B. (1960) *Information and Investment*, Oxford University Press

Salop, S.C. (ed.) (1981) *Strategy, Predation and Antitrust Analysis*, Federal Trade Commission

Schap, D. (1985) X-inefficiency in a rent-seeking society: a graphical analysis, *Quarterly Review of Economics and Business*

Scherer, F.M. (1976) Predatory pricing and the Sherman Act: a comment, *Harvard Law Review*

Scherer, F.M. (1980) *Industrial Market Structure and Economic Performance*, Rand McNally

Scherer, F.M. (1985) On the current state of knowledge in industrial organisation, paper presented at the Conference on *Mainstreams in Industrial Organisation*, University of Amsterdam

Schmalensee, R. (1979) *The Control of Natural Monopolies*, Lexington

Schultze, C.L. (1977) *The Public Use of the Private Interest*, Brookings Institution

Schumpeter, J.A. (1965) *Capitalism, Socialism, and Democracy*, Allen and Unwin

Sharpe, T. (1984) Privatisation, regulation and competition, *Fiscal Studies*

Smith, P. and Swann, D. (1979) *Protecting the Consumer*, Martin Robertson

Spence, A.M. (1973) Job market signalling, *Quarterly Journal of Economics*

Stein, J.L. and Borts, G.H. (1972) Behaviour of the firm under regulatory constraint, *American Economic Review*

Stigler, G.J. (1947) The kinky oligopoly demand curve and rigid prices, *Journal of Political Economy*

Stigler, G.J. (1957) Perfect competition historically contemplated, *Journal of Political Economy*

Stigler, G.J. (1966) *The Theory of Price*, Macmillan

Stigler, G.J. (1968) *The Organisation of Industry*, Irwin

Stigler, G.J. (1975) The theory of economic regulation, *in* Stigler, G.J. *The Citizen and the State*, University of Chicago Press

Stigler, G.J. (1976) The Xistence of X-efficiency, *American Economic Review*

Sutherland, A. (1969) *The Monopolies Commission in Action*, Cambridge University Press

Swann, D. (1979) *Competition and Consumer Protection*, Penguin Books

Swann, D., O'Brien, D.P., Maunder, W.P.J. and Howe, W.S. (1974) *Competition in British Industry*, Allen and Unwin

Telser, L.G. (1960) Why should manufacturers want fair trade?, *Journal of Law and Economics*

The Nationalised Industries (1978), HMSO

Turvey, R. (1969) The second-best case for marginal-cost pricing *in* Margolis, J. and Guitton, H. (eds) *Public Economics*, Macmillan

Tyson, W.J. (1979) Government relations with the public industrial sector *in* Devine, P.J., Lee, N., Jones, R.M. and Tyson, W.J. *Introduction to Industrial Economics*, Allen and Unwin

Utton, M.A. (1979) *Diversification and Competition*, Cambridge University Press

Utton, M.A. (1985) Predatory pricing and the regulation of dominant firms, *Department of Economics, University of Reading*

Utton, M.A. (1986) *The Profits and Stability of Monopoly*, Cambridge University Press

Vickers, J. and Yarrow, G. (1985) *Privatisation and the Natural Monopolies*, Public Policy Centre

Weidenbaum, M.L. (1981) *Business, Government and the Public*, Prentice-Hall

Williamson, O.E. (1966) Peak load pricing and optimal capacity under indivisibility constraints, *American Economic Review*

Williamson, O.E. (1972a) Economies as an antitrust defence: the welfare tradeoffs, *reprinted with amendments in* Rowley, C.K. (ed.) *Readings in Industrial Economics* vol. 2, Macmillan

Williamson, O.E. (1972b) Dominant firms and the monopoly problem: market failure considerations, *Harvard Law Review*

Williamson, O.E. (1975) *Markets and Hierarchies*, Free Press

Williamson, O.E. (1976) Franchise bidding for natural monopolies — in general and with respect to CATV, *Bell Journal of Economics*

Williamson, O.E. (1977) Predatory pricing: a strategic and welfare analysis, *Yale Law Journal*

Wilson, J.Q. (1974) The politics of regulation, *in* McKie, J.W. (ed.) *Social Responsibility and the Business Predicament*, Brookings

Wiseman, J. (1957) The theory of public utility price — an empty box, *Oxford Economic Papers*

Index